HUGO BLACK
The Alabama Years

Hugo Black

VIRGINIA VAN DER VEER HAMILTON

HUGO BLACK

The Alabama Years

LOUISIANA STATE UNIVERSITY PRESS   *Baton Rouge*

ISBN 0–8071–0044–7
Library of Congress Catalog Card Number 75–181566
Copyright © 1972 by Louisiana State University Press
All rights reserved
Manufactured in the United States of America
Printed by Heritage Printers, Inc., Charlotte, North Carolina
Designed by Dwight Agner

Chapter 13 is based on an article, "Hugo Black
and the K.K.K.," originally published in *American
Heritage*, April, 1968

For Larry

Preface

Almost any Alabamian, white or black, unsophisticated or meagerly educated, can name one man who was a justice of the United States Supreme Court. That name may be spoken with praise or, more often, profanity, but Hugo La Fayette Black, who left Alabama for Washington in 1927, remained a presence of major, almost legendary, proportions in his native state. He was an associate justice of the Supreme Court for so many years that most Alabamians were vague as to what he did before and how he got the job. But any gray-haired man of seventy or eighty on Twentieth Street in Birmingham will tell you quickly enough that Hugo Black, beginning in the now-dim era of the Coolidge administration, was once United States senator.

Because Alabama's population is relatively sparse, its people have, among other advantages, an intimacy with their public figures not permitted the masses of more crowded states. Thousands of his fellow Alabamians claimed acquaintance with Justice Black. Many visited him in Washington and talked over old times. Others wrote him, feeling free, if they chose, to excoriate his judicial decisions. I made my own acquaintance with the justice in a prime setting to experience his tenacity and will—across a tennis net. Later, when I became a neophyte reporter for the Associated Press in Washington, I occasionally was assigned a menial chore which took me to a basement room directly below the

Supreme Court chamber. The day's decisions were shot through pneumatic tubes by the regular AP reporter in the courtroom and it was my responsibility to telephone this news to the downtown office. In this proximity and at occasional get-togethers of Alabama exiles in the nation's capital, I renewed my acquaintance with Justice Black. When I strayed into academic life and cast about for the topic of a doctoral dissertation, I recalled the old, half-forgotten story that Hugo Black, early in his political career, had joined the Ku Klux Klan. I was curious about why this had happened and intrigued by the seeming paradox that a onetime Klansman had become an eloquent voice for human rights. Was this another example of Robert Penn Warren's theory that a political figure must taint himself with evil in order to achieve the power to do good?

Always gracious, receptive, and accessible to students of his career, Justice Black like most men, naturally preferred that his triumphs be remembered, his frailties forgotten. He freely gave me access to the small collection of papers he had retained from his Senate files, but I found them routine and disappointing. In the early stages of my work, he consented to two interviews. But aside from his courtesy and cooperation in these matters, Justice Black had no knowledge of nor connivance in the contents of this book.

This study makes no pretense of being a personal biography, delving into innermost thoughts and private matters. It does aspire to be a political biography, probing the labyrinth of Alabama politics in an effort to discover what forces, other than his own, shaped Hugo Black and set him upon the road to the Court.

In my search, which stretched over five years, I became indebted to many a helpful research assistant in libraries and archives of Washington, Hyde Park, Tuscaloosa, and Montgomery, but my greatest debt in this category is to the staff of the Birmingham Public Library, where microfilms of Alabama newspapers and a comprehensive Southern Collection proved invaluable. My colleagues in the field of history, James F. Doster, Thomas B. Alexander, Charles G. Summersell, Evans C. Johnson, and Edward S.

LaMonte, read portions of this study at various stages and contributed many helpful suggestions. Miss Amelia Walston was a pains-
taking typist with uncanny ability to decipher my copy. The long
gestation of this book evoked varied reactions from a husband,
mother, daughter, and son—encouragement, tolerance, bewilder-
ment, and, above all, patient endurance for which I am grateful.

Virginia Van der Veer Hamilton

Birmingham, Alabama
September, 1971

Contents

Illustrations

HUGO BLACK
The Alabama Years

I

Son
of Clay
County

February in northeastern Alabama is harsh and gloomy, the dourest month of the year, filled with a succession of rainy days that chill body and spirit. The land is rarely transformed by snow, and its thin topsoil trickles downhill in red-orange rivulets, born of the rain's constant onslaught. Pines on the hillsides and a few cedars, adorning graveyards and front lawns, cling tenaciously to shreds of green foliage; oaks, sweetgum, beech, poplar, and elm are stripped bare.

On such a February day in 1886, a little procession of buggies and wagons crossed Enitachopco Creek in rural Clay County and wound upward along a rutted chert road to a clearing on a hill. William La Fayette and Martha Ardellah Toland Black were bringing the body of their seventh child, Della, born just two years earlier, to the Toland family burying ground in Mount Ararat Cemetery.[1]

Below this high, remote graveyard lay wooded fastnesses and Appalachian foothills where Muscogees had roamed and hunted until white men, early in the nineteenth century, settled the fertile valleys on all sides of their domain. The creek which rustled below Mount Ararat Cemetery was named for the Aunettechapco village once nestled on its banks, but white interlopers, finding the Indian

---

[1] Hazel Black Davis, *Uncle Hugo: An Intimate Portrait of Mr. Justice Black* (Amarillo, 1965), 33.

lexicon more confusing than musical, called all these tribes simply "Creeks."

Because their mountainous realm was poorly suited for cotton, the Creeks were the last Indians to be evicted from Alabama. Their resistance was also the fiercest, broken finally by the great white warrior Andrew Jackson, who trapped the Creeks in Horseshoe Bend on the Tallapoosa River in March, 1814, and broke their fighting spirit. Twenty years later the Creeks yielded at last to the relentless white settlers, ceded their ancient hunting grounds in March, 1832, and prepared to set forth on the long trail west.[2]

One of the many Scotch-Irish pioneers who hastened from Georgia to claim the newly opened land was George Walker Black, paternal grandfather of the child in the burial box, who had set himself up as a storekeeper and farmer in the hamlet of Crossville. Too poor to own slaves, the Georgians took up axes and attacked the forest, wrestled stumps from virgin fields, and hitched mules to wooden plowstocks to carve furrows for corn, cotton, wheat, oats, and sorghum. Their small clearings could be seen from the cemetery, landmarks in a gently rolling sea of trees which white men, in half a century, had only begun to decimate.

On the windy hilltop, graveside rites for Della Black must have been brief. Her mother, heavy with the weight of another child, should not be out long in such weather. Wagons and buggies wound down the hillside and back toward the little crossroads called Harlan, made up of "Fayette" Black's general store, his house, and two tenant cabins. Harlan lay deep within an Alabama county created in 1866 and named, somewhat wistfully, for the Whig pacificator Henry Clay, who had sought so long to prevent the great holocaust of civil war. Fayette Black had run away at fourteen to join the Confederate forces, and Jud Street, Martha's uncle, had marched into Yankee gunfire at Gettysburg.[3]

[2] Willis Brewer, *Alabama: Her History, Resources, War Record and Public Men from 1540 to 1872* (Tuscaloosa, 1872), 182–83.

[3] Marie Bankhead Owen, *Alabama: A Social and Economic History of the State* (Montgomery, 1938), 412–13; Victor Sholis, "One Young Man, Hugo Black—A Country Boy's Rise," Chicago *Daily Times*, August 18, 1937,; Hugo L. Black, "Reminiscences," *Alabama Law Review*, XVIII (Fall, 1965), 3–4.

As Fayette Black's family grew, he had added four small bed-rooms to his one-room log cabin and also a kitchen, connected to the rest of the house by an uncovered walkway of wooden planks. Clapboards, made from trees cut on his land, concealed the orig-inal log cabin. Supported by rock pillars, the house stood a few feet above ground; underneath, chickens, cats, dogs, and pigs might wander or doze. An outdoor privy and a barn completed the necessities of life for Fayette and Martha Black and their six re-maining children.[4]

Against the rain and raw winds of February, the family de-pended for warmth upon a rock-chimneyed fireplace in the main room. The logs were heaped high on February 27, 1886, when a boy baby was born in the spool bed carved by his maternal grand-father, James Toland, and was placed beside his mother under the coverlet of wool she had spun and woven.

His name, entered in the family Bible following those of Ora, Robert Lee, Orlando, Vernon, Pelham, Daisy, and Della, was imposing, even pretentious, by rural standards: Hugo, for the French novelist Victor Hugo, whose books had found their way into this household in the Alabama wilderness, and La Fayette, for his father and in memory of the storied marquis who had traveled through these Creek lands before Fayette Black was born.[5] But other than his French names, there was no omen to mark the eighth and last child of Fayette and Martha Black as one set upon a future path quite apart from that of his brothers, sisters, and Clay County neighbors.

When March came, the Blacks resumed their rural chores, a placid, monotonous rhythm which had been shattered by birth and death within a single week. Fayette, his sons and tenants turned to the annual rite of preparing the land for spring plowing. They cleared bushes and briers from fence corners and ditch banks and chopped down and burned dry cornstalks from last year's crop. New ground, carved from the forest during winter months,

---

[4] John P. Frank, *Mr. Justice Black: The Man and His Opinions* (New York, 1949), 4.

[5] Davis, *Uncle Hugo*, 61–62; Frank, *Mr. Justice Black*, 4.

was cleared of brush heaps, and perhaps a day was set for log-rolling, with neighbors invited to help pile the heavy logs for burning. In the chill mornings of early March, coves in these Appalachian foothills rang with the high-keyed hallooing of young men and boys, cajoling their reluctant mules: "Ho-hee-hee, ho-hee-hee, ho-hee-ho, he-hee-hee."

By May or early June, seed corn had been carefully placed in the richer bottomlands, cotton seed in the thin soil of eroded hill-sides. When fields were chopped in the heat of July, every able-bodied man and child was summoned to take up a hoe, root out weeds and grass, and thin the young plants. If Fayette Black grew fall wheat and spring oats, both were reaped, bundled, and shocked in June and July. By the end of July, all fall crops had been "laid by" and the community paused to rest for harvest.[6]

August, then, was the month for picnics, revivals, all-day sings, hunting, fishing, courtship, love, and matrimony. To pass the time of day, farmers met at country stores like that of Fayette Black to gossip and talk politics, whittle, chew tobacco and squirt its rich, brown juice onto the dusty soil, and indulge in a game of marbles, croquet, checkers, or horseshoes.

Older children put aside their farm work and made their way along the country roads to some small school, in session early be-cause it would close for six weeks in September and October so that its pupils could help pick the cotton. On Fayette Black's land, the children gathered in one of the small outbuildings to learn such rudiments as they could from their eldest brother, Robert Lee. As a child of three, Hugo paid an occasional brief visit to this family schoolhouse.[7]

Martha Black and her daughters pursued their own rituals, milking, carding cotton thread by hand, spinning, dyeing, and weaving coarse cotton or woolen cloth for trousers, coats, sheets, or dresses, knitting the countless socks needed for eight children.

---

[6] The author is indebted for this and the following descriptions of rural Clay County in the late nineteenth century to the accounts by a contemporary of Hugo L. Black, Mitchell B. Garrett, entitled *Horse and Buggy Days on Hatchet Creek* (Tuscaloosa, 1957).

[7] Frank, *Mr. Justice Black*, 5.

Martha, small and slight of build, arose early to knead biscuit dough, grind coffee beans, fill pitchers with sorghum molasses and buttermilk, and fry the home-processed ham or bacon whose pungent odor would summon her household to breakfast. At noon the family gathered for the day's main repast, often cornpone, buttermilk, fried chicken, boiled garden vegetables seasoned with bacon, sweet potatoes, and deep dish apple or peach pies. Leftovers from midday commonly made up the evening meal.

On Mondays Martha took a huge bundle of family clothing to a cast-iron washpot in the back yard. She smeared the clothes with soap, homemade from lye and waste fats; then boiled them in the washpot, gingerly lifted the smoking pile with a "battling stick" to the "battling block"; pounded, soaped again, rinsed, and hung the clothes in the sun to dry. A small boy was kept busy carrying pails of water from well to tubs and washpot, and tending the fire under the pot.

In Clay County farmhouses, general housecleaning took place spring and fall. To fight bedbugs, called "chinches" in Alabama, feather and straw beds and quilts were brought into the yard to be scalded, dried, and swabbed with stiff feathers drenched with turpentine. Cracks and crevices in the wooden planks of the house were turpentined for the same purpose; then the floors were scoured with warm water, soap, and fine, white sand, and the whole house left open to air and dry.

The center of the Blacks' family life was the kitchen, with its large, wood-burning cookstove, dining table, barrels for flour and meal, and a loom. A few steps from this kitchen was the well, with curb, windlass, cedar bucket, and gourd dipper. In the humid Alabama summertime, kitchen windows and doors were left open in hopes of catching a breeze. Cooking smells drew such hordes of flies that, when the table was set, all plates were turned bottomside upward. After the children were seated and the meal blessed, each protected his food as best he could from the bold flies.

With the coming of fall, flies disappeared, to be followed by the other discomforts of life that were inherent in such a vulnerable structure. On winter evenings the Blacks, like other Clay

County farm people, gathered before their open fireplace, warmly toasted on one side of their bodies and equally chilled on that part turned away from the flames. Drafts of wintry air flowed through chinks in the logs and clapboards. By eight o'clock on a winter evening, the most comfortable refuge was bed, shared with sisters or brothers in one of the small, unheated bedrooms. At dawn it fell to the eldest son to crawl from bedwarmth to toss sticks of resinous "fat pine" and new logs on the ashes of last night's fire, then venture outdoors along the wooden walkway to the kitchen to kindle the cookstove for breakfast.

Unlike most Clay County farm families, Fayette and Martha Black had chores other than those of land and household. While Fayette kept his store accounts, Martha performed the few duties of postmistress of Harlan. Her forebears, Tolands, Langstons, and Streets, were somewhat more prosperous than those of her husband. One grandfather, Hugh Toland, had come to America in 1797 at the age of ten when his parents fled their native Ireland because they sympathized with the United Irishmen, an abortive independence movement patterned upon the principles of the French Revolution. A cousin of the Tolands, Robert Emmet, had been one of the leaders of this unsuccessful rebellion.

Disembarking in Charleston, the Tolands moved inland to the Laurens district of South Carolina, where Hugh married Mary Langston, whose father had fought under Francis Marion, the Swamp Fox, in the American Revolution. Their son James, a cabinetmaker, settled in Alabama and married Mildred Street of Bluff Springs, the daughter of Hezekiah Street, a well-to-do planter and a slaveowner. Martha, daughter of James and Mildred, was educated at an academy, a sign of privilege for a young southern girl, and Thomas Orlando, her brother, became a successful lawyer in faraway California. It was a comedown for the Tolands, so the family story goes, when Martha married Fayette Black, the country storekeeper. Some said that she taught him to read and write, and that Fayette, thereupon, became one of Clay County's few subscribers to the Montgomery *Advertiser*. Undoubtedly it was Martha who brought novels by Victor Hugo and Sir Walter

Scott, along with the Bible and Burpee's seed catalogue, to the Black household.[8]

Martha Toland Black was not likely to limit her children's education to what might be learned from the eldest in a makeshift schoolhouse. In December, 1889, when Hugo was not yet four, Fayette Black moved to the county seat Ashland, named for Henry Clay's Kentucky home, so that his children might have schooling. He paid cash for a modest, five-room frame house and entered into partnership in a general merchandise store. The firm became the largest in town, carrying a ten- to fifteen-thousand-dollar stock of those items which Clay County residents could not produce at home. After the solitude of Harlan, Ashland, with three hundred fifty residents clustered around its courthouse square, must have seemed a metropolis to the young Blacks.[9]

As a leading merchant, Fayette Black inevitably became acquainted with political quarrels and factions in the county seat. Far north of the rich soil of Alabama's Black Belt, Clay County was predominantly a region of white yeoman farmers. In 1890, 14,601 whites and 1,704 Negroes lived in this county, a ratio in direct reversal of the heavy black majorities in more fertile counties.[10] Clay's few blacks usually worked as field hands, hired at a wage fixed for the entire year. Because a landowner had no money until cotton was sold in the fall, the hired man customarily took most of his pay in chewing tobacco, snuff, coffee, and clothing on his employer's credit at the store, or in corn, molasses, or bacon from the farmer's own crib and storehouse.

Most tenants, or sharecroppers, were whites, either sons, sons-in-law, or "po' white" drifters from other areas. They rented a few acres from a landowner who provided tools, land, and draft animals in exchange for half of the major crop, or land only in

[8] Joel C. DuBose (ed.), *Notable Men of Alabama* (Atlanta, 1904), I, 409–10; Dan O. Dowe, "Hugo Black's Childhood in Clay County," Montgomery *Alabama Journal*, July 4, 1960; Frank, *Mr. Justice Black*, 6; interview with Thomas Toland, Ashland, Alabama, October 9, 1969.

[9] Davis, *Uncle Hugo*, 34; Frank, *Mr. Justice Black*, 5.

[10] Thomas McAdory Owen, *History of Alabama and Dictionary of Alabama Biography* (Chicago, 1921), I, 276.

exchange for a third of the grain and a fourth of the cotton. The first arrangement was called renting "on halves"; the second, renting "for a third and a fourth."[11]

When the crops were in, a hired hand was lucky to break even with the account he had charged at the store; tenants would show a small balance or a deficit, and the landowner counted it a good year if he came home from the cotton market with a few silver dollars. In 1870 cotton brought 20¢ a pound; by 1880, it had dropped to 10¢. An acre planted in cotton brought in only $18; an acre of corn, $10.91; wheat, $12.48. Fertilizer alone cost the farmer $40 a ton.[12] In the 1890s, when cotton slipped downward to 6 cents, small landowners and merchants alike felt the pinch. Merchants like Fayette Black, who advanced tools, seeds, provisions, and supplies in early spring at interest rates ranging from 50 to 75 percent, further protected themselves by taking a lien on the forthcoming crop or a mortgage on the land itself.[13] Farmer and merchant, then, were bound together for the season, at the mercy of such vagaries as drought, weevils, railroad rates, prices of finished goods, and the interest rate charged by northern financiers. Some merchants required farmers with whom they dealt to plant the sure money crop, cotton, leaving the merchant to sell meat, corn, and vegetables at a profit. Cotton thus fastened its hold upon hired hand, tenant, landowner, and merchant, leaching their soil, economy, and spirits.[14]

In counties like Clay, small landowners were particularly responsive to the clarion calls of agrarian unrest in the 1890s. The Farmers' Alliance and Populism gave voice to their discontent over two decades of falling farm prices, aggravated by a nationwide industrial and financial depression. In northern and southeastern Alabama, passions were easily aroused in behalf of

[11] These descriptions of the landowner's relationship with his hired hands, tenants, and the merchant are taken from Garrett, *Horse and Buggy Days*, 89–101.

[12] John B. Clark, *Populism in Alabama* (Auburn, 1927), 35–36.

[13] It is estimated that 80 to 90 percent of Alabama cotton growers used the crop lien as their basic credit system in 1890. Allen J. Going, *Bourbon Democracy in Alabama* (Tuscaloosa, 1951), 95.

[14] Clark, *Populism in Alabama*, 35–36.

Populist schemes for an income tax, government ownership of railroads, a ban on land ownership by aliens, antitrust laws, free coinage of silver, and the plan for federal subtreasuries under which a farmer might deposit his crop in government warehouses in return for money or credit and thereby escape financial bondage to his local merchant.

On a mild April evening in 1892, hundreds of farmers, wives, and children gathered in the Ashland square for a rally in support of Reuben F. Kolb, onetime captain in the Confederate Army, scion of a leading plantation family in the Black Belt, but a renegade from the political philosophy of his class. Once a large cotton planter with many black laborers, Kolb had abandoned cotton in favor of "Kolb's Gem," advertised in seed catalogues as America's most famous watermelon. In one season alone, he cut two-hundred thousand melons for seeds to be shipped by the carload to seedhouses. Appointed in 1887 to the newly created post of Alabama's commissioner of agriculture, Kolb had set about with equal initiative to promote the welfare of farmers in an overwhelmingly rural state. His brainchild "Alabama on Wheels," a railroad car loaded with the state's products, toured the Northwest for sixty days in 1888 to stimulate immigration and investment.[15]

When Kolb persuaded the Alabama legislature to support a series of farmers' institutes at which experts and prominent farmers would speak on agricultural topics, there were charges that he was using his post to build a political machine. He headed the Farmers' Alliance in Alabama and came to national attention as president of the Farmers' National Congress, which met in Montgomery in 1889 to voice complaints against banks, railroads, manufacturers, and all others whom the rural man believed to be his oppressors.[16]

Such activities inevitably brought Kolb into conflict with the

---

[15] Jerrell H. Shofner and William Warren Rogers, "Joseph C. Manning: Militant Agrarian, Enduring Populist," *Alabama Historical Quarterly*, XXIX (Spring-Summer, 1967), 7–37; Francis Sheldon Hackney, "From Populism to Progressivism in Alabama, 1890–1910" (Ph.D. dissertation, Yale University, 1966), 18–46.

[16] Clark, *Populism in Alabama*, 77–84.

established hierarchy of Alabama politics, the Democratic machine of Black Belt cotton planters, railroad, industrial, and mineral interests, and hordes of local office holders, which had held undisputed sway since the state was "redeemed" from Reconstruction in 1874. When Kolb sought the Democratic nomination for governor in 1890, "wool hats" for the first time outnumbered "silk hats" on the floor of the party's convention. On the first ballot, Kolb was within a few votes of nomination. But he and his rural supporters were political tyros compared to the experienced machine. When his four opponents pooled their votes to nominate Thomas G. Jones, a compromise candidate, Kolb bowed temporarily to the power of party bosses.[17]

In Clay County Kolb found an audience willing to go even further than he. While he insisted upon remaining within the traditional Democratic fold, calling himself a "Jeffersonian Democrat," a new third party was born. Young Joseph C. Manning founded the People's Party of Alabama in Ashland during the spring of 1892. Boyish and charming at twenty-two, Joe pleaded fervently with his fellow Alabamians to "abandon the Bourbon Democrats." Where he got his passion, not even Joe knew. "It was just in me; I was never a Bourbon Democrat," he said.[18]

Manning's brothers, one a merchant and the other a newspaper editor, were lifelong Democrats and opposed his radical views so strongly that they aroused sympathy for Joe in many a voter. Only once did Fayette Black, a creditor and a man of conservative political leanings, go so far as to support an acknowledged Populist for probate judge. To be Populist in Clay County in the 1890s was to risk social ostracism, loss of credit, even physical attack.[19]

But in the heated election of 1892, Manning's party showed unexpected strength in Clay County, electing the probate judge, sheriff, and tax collector. In one backwoods cove, young Demo-

[17] *Ibid.*, 86–115.
[18] Joseph C. Manning, *From Five to Twenty-Five: His Earlier Life as Recalled by Joseph Columbus Manning* (New York, 1929), 18.
[19] Manning, *From Five to Twenty-Five*, 18; Frank, *Mr. Justice Black*, 6; Hackney, "From Populism to Progressivism," 18.

crats, fortified by hip flasks of "Oh-be-joyful," ringing cow bells, and yelling Indian war whoops, marched two miles by torchlight to serenade Tull Goza, a local leader of the People's Party, shouting their defiance of further Populist victories.

Staunch Democrats took what comfort they could from the news that Grover Cleveland had been elected President and Reuben Kolb again narrowly defeated for governor. Wage earners, miners, and yeoman farmers had voted for Kolb, but thirteen of fourteen Black Belt counties, firmly in the grip of local white machines, returned huge majorities which tipped the election for Jones. If the returns were to be believed, thousands of black sharecroppers and farm hands had cast their ballots against the champion of working-class people.[20]

But the spirit of Populism continued to agitate rural Alabama. Joe Manning, wearing a white hat and billed as "the Clay County Evangel" and "the boy orator," toured the state, haranguing audiences of farmers, miners, and city laborers to overthrow the Bourbons and put their own spokesmen into office. Reuben Kolb, declaring that Negro voters had been intimidated, purchased, and even resurrected from the dead in the Black Belt, called for political and legal rights of the blacks, eliciting from Democrats their ancient battle cry: "Who can look upon the fair and lovely women of this land and endorse this principle and the man who maintains it?" As racial feelings intensified, forty-eight blacks were lynched in Alabama in 1891 and 1892.[21]

In 1894 "Run Forever" Kolb made his third bid for the governorship, supported by Populists and Jeffersonians, a mixture which regular Democrats derisively called "Kolbites, Republicans, Third Partyites, Ex-Greenbackers, Scalawags, Rag-Tails and Bobtails." As in 1892 large Black Belt majorities turned the tide against him. The aroused Populist campaign committee called upon its

[20] Historians believe there is little doubt that Kolb would have won in a fair election in 1892. Hackney, "From Populism to Progressivism," 38; Garrett, *Horse and Buggy Days*, 222–23.

[21] Shofner and Rogers, "Joseph C. Manning," 14; Hackney, "From Populism to Progressivism," 56.

followers to "assert the sovereign power, before which thrones totter, sceptres fall and the outrages of tyrants cease." [22]

"This time I am going to take my seat if they shoot me in my tracks," Kolb vowed. But although he took the oath of office from a justice of the peace in Montgomery, only a few of the eighty-three thousand who had voted for him followed Kolb up Goat Hill to Alabama's capitol. William C. Oates, the Democratic nominee, had already taken his oath on a spot hallowed in southern lore because Jefferson Davis had stood there to assume the presidency of the Confederacy. When state troopers with bayonets barred Kolb from mounting the capitol steps, Joe Manning begged: "Go ahead, Captain. They may kill you, but you will go down in history as a martyr to the Populist cause." Kolb stopped short of martyrdom and turned away. A sprinkling of curious citizens heard him deliver his "inaugural address" from the bed of a wagon, then drifted away. Lacking a martyr and with no crowds of angry citizens to man its barricades, the Populist revolution of 1894 fizzled out. William C. Oates took up the duties of governor without further challenge. [23]

In this same election, Clay County sent Joe Manning to join thirty-four other Populists in the Alabama House of Representatives. He had run for the People's Party against the Democratic nominee Bennett Garrett, a "hardshell" Baptist preacher with a flowing beard. The parties scheduled fifteen debates, with a grand windup in Ashland on the Saturday before election day. Democrats brought in their ablest orators from over the state but Joe Manning, the hometown boy, bested them all. Even his brother admitted: "We thought we had Joe today, but I just tell you it is impossible to beat him in a joint debate. I never heard such oratory in my life; he simply swept that crowd." [24] Certainly Brother Garrett was no match for Joe. In their only face-to-face debate, the preacher urged voters to choose a man, not a beardless boy. If

[22] Hackney, "From Populism to Progressivism," 80–86.
[23] *Ibid.*; Shofner and Rogers, "Joseph C. Manning," 20; Clark, *Populism in Alabama*, 158–59.
[24] Manning, *From Five to Twenty-Five*, 49.

whiskers had anything to do with it, Joe jumped up to reply, both of them should drop out of the race and let Clay County elect a billy goat! The audience howled with delight and Brother Garrett never agreed to another debate.[25]

The decade of Populist tumult in Alabama was the boyhood of Hugo Black. In search of what excitement Ashland had to offer, the storekeeper's small, wiry son attended every rally, torchlight parade, and stump speech. On election nights he hung about the polls until the last vote was counted. He heard Manning passionately denounce Grover Cleveland, Bourbon oligarchs, and Yankee financiers; and he listened enraptured as "Professor" Henry Clay Simmons of Millerville, another renowned local orator, excoriated Judge Hiram Evans and the Democratic courthouse ring of Clay County. Before entering politics Hiram Evans had been Ashland's school principal but, on becoming probate judge, he essayed, in Joe Manning's words, to be "cock-of-the-walk, bell wether, the great I am" of Clay County. After "wild and wooly hill-billy Populists" ousted him from office, Judge Evans and his son Hiram moved west, but young Hiram would be heard from again in Alabama.[26]

When Hugo was ten, Clay County Democrats echoed the silvery words of another youthful orator, William Jennings Bryan of Nebraska: "Thou shalt not press down upon the brow of labor a crown of thorns; thou shalt not crucify mankind upon a cross of gold." Such melodramatic phrases did not sway Fayette Black. Fearing that Bryan, with his free silver fantasies, would lead the country to ruin, Fayette voted in 1896 with seven thousand other Alabamians for the conservative Gold Democrats John M. Palmer and Simon B. Buckner. But the agrarian battle cries of the 1890s aroused in young Hugo an instinctive and enduring sympathy for the underdog.[27]

When national Populism and the Democratic Party fused and

[25] *Ibid.*, 60; Hackney, "From Populism to Progressivism," 90.

[26] Manning, *From Five to Twenty-Five*, 8–9; 16–17; James Saxon Childers, "Hugo Black, Always an Alabamian," Birmingham *News*, January 31, 1937.

[27] Interview with Justice Hugo L. Black, Montgomery *Advertiser*, October 30, 1955.

lost with Bryan in 1896, the People's Party of Alabama was already in decline. Its candidates appeared on the ballot until the century turned, but Populism never seriously threatened Democratic control again. Its leaders drifted into the Republican Party, as Joe Manning did, or slipped, like Reuben Kolb, back into the Democratic fold.[28]

In 1901 regular Democrats rewrote Alabama's 1875 constitution, disfranchising not only its burdensome black population but also many of the poor-white Populists. Pruning the electorate was a matter of convenience for the rising industrialists of North Alabama, who wanted to achieve stricter regulation of railroad rates without having to outvote huge and fraudulent Black Belt majorities; and also for the Black Belt itself, weary of the problems, risks, and political sham of controlling black voters.

To vote in Alabama under the new constitution, a male, twenty-one or older, now had to thread a maze of residence and literacy tests, be a property owner or have been lawfully employed for most of the preceding twelve months, and be innocent of a long list of crimes, including vagrancy. Before casting his ballot, furthermore, he must pay, until he reached the age of forty-five, an annual, cumulative poll tax of $1.50, due the first of February before an election. Registrars, however, would admit to the ballot all soldiers, and their descendants, even if illiterate and without jobs or property, who had fought for the United States or the Confederacy in any war since 1812. Others would be registered who showed evidence of "good character" or an understanding of "the duties and obligations of citizenship under a republican form of government."[29] Asked if Christ and His disciples could register under the good character clause, one delegate replied candidly: "That would depend entirely upon which way He was going to vote."

J. Thomas Heflin, a budding young demagogue, soothed many an uneasy conscience when he explained to fellow delegates that

[28] Hackney, "From Populism to Progressivism," 90.
[29] *Ibid.*, 238–39.

the ballot was a natural right for a white man, but a privilege for the black man. God had ordained the Negro to be the white man's servant, Heflin said, and "as soon as you elevate him, you ruin him." [30]

The poll tax alone disfranchised 23 percent of the total white male population of voting age. While the white vote declined almost a fourth, the black vote practically ceased to exist, but not until the new constitution itself had been ratified in a 1901 referendum, with Negro voters in the Black Belt providing the margin to assure their own disfranchisement. Much praise for this victory was showered upon a young United States congressman from Birmingham, Oscar W. Underwood, who had headed a fourteen-man campaign committee named by the Democratic State Executive Committe to lead the drive for ratification. [31]

In 1902 the Alabama legislature passed its first Jim Crow law, requiring separation of the races in railroad cars and stations. In that same year, the state Democratic convention voted to replace the convention system of electing candidates with an all-white primary, preferring to fight out its differences within a party primary rather than risk again the possibility of a two-party system. [32]

As Joe Manning, by then a small-town Republican postmaster, had predicted, white supremacy had proven a "false mating call," whose true intent was to disfranchise all, both black and white, who threatened the Bourbon Democrats. [33] Controlled by a drastically reduced electorate of propertied, white regulars, Alabama turned its attention to mild Progressivism in the form of railroad reforms and education progress. Not for a quarter of a century would "plain folks," disguised beneath the white hoods of the Ku Klux Klan, successfully sweep their own men into the major citadels of political power in Alabama. When that day came, Hugo Black and Hiram Evans, the younger, whose fathers had been

---

[30] *Ibid.*, 251–53.   [31] *Ibid.*, 255–79.
[32] *Ibid.*, 255.
[33] Shofner and Rogers, "Joseph C. Manning," 18.

Democratic regulars when the People's Party made political hay in Clay County, would loom large.

When crops were laid by each summer, it was court time in Ashland. Through the courthouse windows, checker players outside could hear a hot-tempered local lawyer threaten to "sue out a writ of juris-de-strickum" against the judge, or the dulcet persuasions of city barristers from Birmingham or Montgomery. A frequent spectator at these trials from the age of six, Hugo Black came to know all these lawyers and their tactics. Seated on a courtroom bench, he fancied how he might have asked a shrewder question or more cleverly won the jury's sympathy, and dreamed of the day when he would be a lawyer, as Great-Uncle Jud Street predicted. The dramas enacted in Ashland's suffocating courtrooms intrigued young Hugo far more than such boyish pastimes as pitching silver dollars or horseshoes, playing croquet, or fishing.[34]

Court week, when sweet cider and watermelons were sold in the courthouse square; the closing exercises of school, at which Joe Manning, in his boyhood, played the harmonica; and the two-week revivals held each year by the Baptist and Methodist churches were Ashland's important events. Once a year the Sell Brothers single-ring circus found its way back into these hills, and a country boy would be treated to the marvelous sight of its three, mangy elephants lumbering down the dusty road, or the siren sounds of its five-man brass band. Sometimes a magic lantern and sleight-of-hand show played its one-night stand in Ashland. Or, with a bit of cajoling, Great-Uncle Jud could be persuaded to regale his young descendants with tales of his days as a prisoner of the Yankees.

But for excitement, entertainment, and pure terror, church revivals beat them all. Exhorted by a visiting evangelist to choose between the golden streets of Heaven or the fiery pit of burning Hell, an imaginative boy, upon going to bed on a hot summer

34 Black, "Reminiscences," 3–4.

night, would pull the covers up over his head. Clay County took religion seriously. One of the sights of Ashland was Judge Hiram Evans, a Methodist, standing in the shade of a building, engaged in violent argument with a Baptist as to whether salvation could be achieved merely by being sprinkled or only by total immersion.[35]

To earn pocket money, Hugo worked in his father's store, sold soda pop on the Fourth of July, and occasionally picked cotton. When he was older, he learned the more remunerative trade of setting type for the weekly Clay County *Advance* at thirty cents a column. To set two and a half columns took all day, but it was a far more pleasant occupation than stooping over in the hot sun to separate cotton from its bolls. The *Advance,* edited by a broad-minded South Carolinian, W. R. Whatley, opposed Judge Evans and his courthouse cronies, and its youthful typesetter heard plenty of political talk. Hugo counted it a banner day when, to fill out a column, he was allowed to compose his own news items.[36]

An even more lucrative venture was to drive a wagon twenty-two miles to Goodwater, a small railroad town in Coosa County, and to wander along its crowded main street, marveling at the smoke-belching locomotives, the vehicles and draft animals, and the "city fellers," come to bargain for cotton. At night Hugo slept under a blanket in the wagon. In the chill of morning, he would load the supplies his father had ordered and urge his mules up into the hills toward Ashland.[37]

His passion for court cases and politics set Hugo somewhat apart from other boys, as did his local repute as a dandy, based upon a blue sailor suit, which he favored, and a Lord Fauntleroy outfit, made and foisted firmly upon him by his adoring sister Ora. In school Hugo acquired another distinction. Although he took no IQ tests to prove it, he was obviously a gifted student. At six he read with ease in fourth-grade readers. Schoolmates noted en-

---

[35] Manning, *From Five to Twenty-Five,* 8–9, 62–63.

[36] *Ibid.,* 15–16; Childers, "Hugo Black, Always an Alabamian"; Frank, *Mr. Justice Black,* 7.

[37] Frank, *Mr. Justice Black,* 8; Garrett, *Horse and Buggy Days,* 96.

viously that Hugo's quick mind grasped the lesson on first reading and retained it tenaciously thereafter. In declamatory contests he performed with enthusiasm and without a trace of nervousness.

At nine or ten, Hugo and his friend C. M. Pruet stayed one school term with Ora, who had married C. M.'s brother Alexander and lived in the country six miles from Ashland. The boys walked barefoot to the one-room, two-teacher Spring Hill Academy, housed in a simple frame building near Ora's home. After school Hugo would lie in the Pruets' yard for hours, absorbed in a history book, a Walter Scott novel, or the Bible.[38]

In the days before Hiram Evans entered Clay County politics, he had been an Ashland school teacher. Clad in a long coat and brandishing a cane, "Professor" Evans was famed for his habit of pacing silently in front of his class for what seemed at least half an hour. Finally he would bang his cane on the table and proclaim: "Young gentlemen and young ladies, if you can't say something good about a man, don't say it!" Many a student, Hugo among them, never forgot this phrase.[39]

In the higher grades, Hugo attended Ashland College, a combination of high school and junior college. Like the academies which preceded public education in the South, Ashland College was supported by tuition, paid by patrons such as Fayette Black, and controlled by trustees, elected by the citizens of Ashland. A similar "college" existed at Lineville, six miles away. Both offered courses in literature, logic, Latin, Greek, physics, chemistry, astronomy, higher mathematics, and rhetoric. In rhetoric Hugo gained a measure of local fame when he and Cleveland Allen won a public debate against "Sweet William" Pruet and a challenger from Alexander City. Hugo and Cleve, favoring a canal through the isthmus of Panama, bested Ben Ray and "Sweet William," who

---

[38] Hugo's fabled brilliance in school is attested to by many sources, among them his brother Robert Lee Black, interviewed in the Birmingham *Post*, August 13, 1937; interview with C. M. Pruet, Ashland, October 10, 1969; Dowe, "Hugo Black's Childhood," Montgomery *Alabama Journal*, July 4, 1960; Sholis, "One Young Man"; Frank, *Mr. Justice Black*, 6.

[39] New York *Times*, September 15, 1937.

supported the Nicaraguan route so fervently championed by Alabama's Senator John Tyler Morgan.[40]

Although diplomas from Ashland and Lineville colleges were not as prestigious as those from the University of Alabama or state teachers' colleges, they were sought by boarding students from other parts of the state, as well as by natives. Clay County people took pride in the belief that their county educated more school teachers in proportion to its population than any other in the state.[41]

Hugo was educated not only by Ashland College and the everyday world of politics and law but also by the teachings of his parents. From Martha Black he absorbed a love of gardening as well as of books. Roses, phlox, violets, honeysuckle, and scuppernong grapes flourished around the Blacks' simple house. After the Alabama fashion, the residence contained a central hall, parlor, kitchen, parents' bedroom, girls' bedroom, and boys' bedroom.[42]

Once when an elderly Negro who worked for Fayette Black came to the back door at noon to deliver a parcel, Martha told her youngest son to offer "Uncle Dan" some dinner. Hugo started to take the plate to the back steps, as local custom decreed, but his mother, to his great surprise, bade him bring Uncle Dan into the kitchen to eat. Martha Black's small gesture of independence from the time-worn racial mores made a lasting impression upon her young son.[43]

An ominous racial tragedy shook Ashland during one summer of Hugo's youth. Eli Sims, a friendly young Negro who had occasionally given Hugo rides in his wheelbarrow, went swimming in the same creek where the white boys swam. When one white youth ordered him to leave, Eli "sassed" him. The white boy went

[40] Black, "Reminiscences," 3–4; interview with Ben Ray, Birmingham, February 11, 1967.
[41] Black, "Reminiscences," 4.
[42] Frank, *Mr. Justice Black*, 5–6.
[43] Justice Black recalled this incident of his boyhood to a longtime friend, William Hendrix, a Birmingham reporter, according to the Birmingham *News*, January 14, 1938.

home, got his gun, and shot Eli dead. Because he was the son of a prominent and well-liked citizen, the white youth went free, although everyone in Ashland conceded his guilt. The Sims murder troubled Fayette Black's sense of justice so deeply that, in the next election, he supported the Populist candidate for probate judge rather than the Democratic judge involved in the murder trial.[44]

Although he came to question his father's political creed, Hugo, as a child, was obedient to the strict moral code laid down by Fayette Black. Coffee drinking, smoking, and card playing were forbidden the young Blacks. At the Baptist Church each Sunday, they were cautioned against gambling, dancing, and the demon rum. But to illustrate Christian tolerance for his astounded children, Fayette on one Sunday invited Ashland's leading sinner, known to the whole town as a "worldly man," to share dinner with the Blacks. The other guest was the Baptist preacher.[45]

Fayette, when only fifty-two, died in September, 1900, a respected man in his little community. He left an estate worth $25,000 to be divided, at Martha's death, among the children who survived them. A son, Vernon, had died in 1895 at the age of seventeen, probably from the effects of typhoid fever.[46]

Death took another toll in the Black family early in the new century. Pelham Black, named for a boy artilleryman, John Pelham, whose bravery at Fredericksburg had earned the accolade "Gallant Pelham" from Robert E. Lee, was Hugo's favorite brother. Pelham, who was regarded in the Ashland area as even more gifted than Hugo, had gone into law as his profession. Proudly Hugo had taken his friend C. M. Pruet to the courthouse to watch Pelham try his first cases. Late on a June evening in 1902, Pelham was driving home alone in his buggy through the hills

[44] Interview with C. M. Pruet, Ashland, October 10, 1969; Frank, *Mr. Justice Black*, 8–9.

[45] Frank, *Mr. Justice Black*, 6–7; Sholis, "One Young Man," 14. Justice Black recounted the incident of Sunday dinner to William Hendrix. Birmingham *News*, January 14, 1938.

[46] Davis, *Uncle Hugo*, 34; interview with Thomas Toland, Ashland, October 10, 1969.

between Talladega and Ashland. His tired and thirsty horse wandered into a deep creek, the buggy overturned, and Pelham drowned.

It was whispered around Ashland that Pelham, in violation of his father's teachings, had been on a drinking spree. Hugo, sixteen, was grieved and shocked. It must be true, then, as Fayette and the evangelists had warned, that alcohol was a demon which lured good men to their destruction.[47]

At Fayette's death, Hugo's eldest brother, Robert Lee, took over his father's store. Lee and his wife, Hattie Belle, lived in the family home and, as Hugo grew up, so did an ever-increasing brood of young Blacks. "Every year a new Black," marveled the neighbors, as Lee and Hattie Belle began to fill the modest frame house with children.[48]

With Pelham dead, Hugo faltered briefly in his long-cherished determination to become a lawyer, turning for advice to Orlando, then the most successful of Fayette's sons. Orlando, after graduating from Ashland College, had spent two years at medical school in Birmingham, and had studied further at the highly regarded University of the South in Sewanee, Tennessee. He set up practice in the small town of Wilsonville, Alabama, and married an Episcopalian, a mark of social status, but Orlando remained a staunch Baptist, the faith in which he had been reared. He was only twenty-nine when his photograph and biography appeared in the 1904 edition of *Notable Men of Alabama*, wherein he was described as "a young physician of merit and promise."[49]

Both Orlando and Hugo's mother wanted the youngest Black to follow this pattern of success. Mostly to please them, Hugo enrolled in 1903 at Birmingham Medical College, eighty-six miles from home. Although his career as a medical student lasted only a year, its brevity was not because of Hugo's academic short-

---

[47] Dowe, "Hugo Black's Childhood," Montgomery *Advertiser*, July 4, 1960; interview with C. M. Pruet, Ashland, October 10, 1969.

[48] Hugo Black's experiences in his brother's household are described affectionately and at length in Davis, *Uncle Hugo*.

[49] DuBose, *Notable Men of Alabama*, I, 409–10.

comings. He could master texts in medicine as well as those of any other discipline, and, in nine months, completed two of the three years' work required for graduation. But after Hugo spent a summer as Orlando's assistant at Wilsonville, the doctor, reluctantly, and the student, joyfully, agreed that medicine was not his calling. Hugo, they decided, should go to the university and prepare for the law.[50]

Early one brisk September morning in 1904, as leaves began to redden on the hillsides of Clay County, Hugo Black and Cleveland Allen put their belongings in a one-horse buggy, climbed aboard, and set out for Goodwater. At that dingy little railroad town, they met Benjamin F. Smith, of Alexander City, and John Wesley Vardaman, of Coosa County, and all four boarded the Central of Georgia, bound for whatever opportunities the University of Alabama might offer. They changed trains in Birmingham and, aboard the Alabama Great Southern, arrived in Tuscaloosa late that afternoon. Cleve and Hugo put up for the night at the McLester Hotel, Tuscaloosa's finest.[51]

Ashland and Birmingham resembled western frontier towns rather than genteel settlements of the antebellum South. But Tuscaloosa, named for the fierce "black warrior" who fought DeSoto in 1540, was an older and prouder city, occupying a river site favored for more than a century by Choctaws and Creeks. Settled by white men about 1819, it was Alabama's capital for twenty years during the flush times of the cotton kingdom. Tuscaloosa had also been chosen as the home of the state university, which opened in 1831. When the Creeks of eastern Alabama relinquished their lands and began the long western trek, they passed through Tuscaloosa and camped on this newly-cleared campus. Old citizens vividly remembered the dashing horsemanship of the Indian boys who galloped their ponies through Tuscaloosa's streets. In the closing days of the Civil War, a troop of Yankee cavalry burned the university. But it was rebuilt after the war, and Senator

50 Black, "Reminiscences," 4; Davis, *Uncle Hugo*, 34.
51 Black, "Reminiscences," 4.

John T. Morgan persuaded Congress to compensate Alabama for the raid.[52]

When Hugo Black first saw Tuscaloosa in 1903, it still had an air of graciousness. Its lyrical name, spreading oak trees, and white-columned homes made a pleasing impression upon young men from the back country. Hugo and Cleve rode the electric dummy car out University Avenue and rented a room at the home of a chemistry professor, known affectionately to his students as "Gazoondikes."[53]

Presenting his Ashland College diploma, Hugo applied for entrance to the liberal arts college as a sophomore. Having spent an entire year on his venture into medicine, he was eager to finish in three years instead of four. But the admissions office, to his dismay, refused to accept him into sophomore standing unless he passed an entrance examination. Feeling that it would take time to prepare for an examination, Hugo appealed to the president for special permission to enter as a sophomore. His request received a sympathetic hearing, for the president, Dr. John W. Abercrombie, had once headed Ashland College. But even Dr. Abercrombie insisted that if Hugo's professors, at the end of one semester, felt he was inadequately prepared for sophomore classes, he would have to return to freshman status. He could, however, enter the two-year Law School without examination. In a hurry to finish his formal education, Hugo enrolled in law.[54]

The Law School was a stepchild of the university and occupied its least desirable classrooms. Its students were not even assured of rooms in the barracks or board in the dining room, both privileges readily available to other students for a total fee of $150 a year. But its two-man faculty impressed Hugo Black. Professor William S. Thorington, with handle-bar mustache, had served on Alabama's Supreme Court. Professor Ormond Sommerville, a shy, kindly scholar, had practiced law and had also taught Latin and

[52] Thomas Chalmers McCorvey, *Alabama Historical Sketches* (Charlottesville, Va., 1960), 95–111; Going, *Bourbon Democracy*, 163–64.
[53] Black, "Reminiscences," 6.   [54] *Ibid.*, 6–7.

Greek at the university. Both used Walker's *American Law* and preached the gospel that laws should be made by legislators, not by judges. Their classroom techniques consisted of asking complex legal questions, followed by the challenge: "If so, why so, and if not, why not?"[55]

Hugo was one of seven in a class of twenty-three whose grades for all courses of the two-year law curriculum averaged 95 or above. Whether by his own choice or because, as a country boy without social connections, he was not "rushed," he did not join a fraternity, as did thirteen fellow law students. But his classmates chose Hugo to be class secretary both years.[56]

In his free time, Hugo visited the liberal arts college where his scholastic capabilities had been doubted. Listening to lectures on history, he hungered for the time and opportunity to learn more about ancient Greece or political economy. From an English professor he absorbed the advice that the best writing is also the simplest, and often the shortest.[57]

Hugo occasionally went home to Ashland. On one of these visits, perhaps influenced by the amenities of Tuscaloosa, he persuaded his sister-in-law Hattie to replace the family's forks and knives, made of wood and spring steel, with a set of silver-plated tableware. Another homecoming was poignant. Martha Black died February 17, 1905, at fifty-nine, leaving Hugo, not yet twenty, bereft of both parents. At his mother's death, he came into one-fifth share of Fayette Black's estate and, thereafter, regarded the Lee Blacks as his closest family.[58]

After the fashion of yearbooks, the *Corolla* of Alabama poked fun at university students. Borrowing quotations it labeled one young man, in Alexander Pope's words, as "a wit among dunces and a dunce among wits." Another drew Shakespeare's cutting phrase: "God made him a man and therefore let him pass for a man." Below Hugo's picture in 1905 appeared the charitable words: "I am one of those gentle souls that will use the devil

55 *Ibid.*, 8–10.
56 *Ibid.*, 10; Davis, *Uncle Hugo*, 69.
57 Black, "Reminiscences," 7.
58 Davis, *Uncle Hugo*, 65.

himself with courtesy." But the following year, under the graduation photograph of a solemn young man with a penetrating gaze, the *Corolla* characterized Hugo in sentiments once used by Dr. Samuel Johnson: "This fellow seems to possess but one idea and that is a wrong one." Six members of the law school class of 1906, the *Corolla* predicted optimistically, would become justices of the United States Supreme Court, but it did not specify which six. That May, on the stage of Morgan Hall, the University of Alabama bestowed upon the young man from Clay County, who had been too impatient to seek a liberal arts diploma, the degree of Bachelor of Laws.[59]

To pay for his education, Hugo had spent a sizable portion of his inheritance. Now he invested fifteen hundred dollars more in a handsome set of law books and placed them alongside his diploma in a second-floor office overlooking the Ashland square. From his window he could see the new, yellow-brick courthouse which had replaced the structure where he had spent so many hours of his boyhood. On its dome stood a shining figure, balancing the scales of justice.[60]

Hugo had ample time to gaze upon this scene. Ashland still regarded him as the brightest boy in town, but not as a lawyer. Farmers and businessmen took their legal problems to older men. To while away his time, Hugo strolled to the drugstore and made the frugal purchase of six nickel cigars for a quarter. He had strayed from Fayette's code, but cigars might make a young lawyer seem older and wiser. Those who observed him were amused to see that he took only one cigar, making separate trips to the drugstore to pick up each of the other five.[61]

There was little else to do. Occasionally a businessman asked him to collect a bill, or a company in Atlanta paid him fifty cents apiece to check on those in Clay County who applied for insurance by mail. Hugo made overtures to enter a firm in Birmingham, but its senior partners decided upon another neophyte who

[59] Black, "Reminiscences," 8–10; Davis, *Uncle Hugo*, 69.
[60] Davis, *Uncle Hugo*, 34.   [61] Dowe, "Hugo Black's Childhood."

seemed to show more promise. Fortunately the Lee Blacks, with three children already and a fourth on the way, provided a lively home life, a bed, and ample meals.[62]

In the chilly dawn of February 12, 1907, fire destroyed the building which housed Hugo's office and reduced to ashes his prized new set of law books. He had not been able to afford insurance. The fire and the indifference of townspeople to his shingle cost Ashland one lawyer. With his suitcase, the remainder of his dwindling inheritance, and the optimism of one who has just attained his twenty-first birthday, Hugo Black departed for Birmingham.[63]

[62] Sholis, "One Young Man," 14; Frank, *Mr. Justice Black*, 13.
[63] Davis, *Uncle Hugo*, 34; interview with Robert Lee Black, *Birmingham Post*, August 13, 1937.

II

"Hugo-
to-Hell"
Black

Raw, roistering Birmingham, born in Reconstruction only six years after Appomattox, had been laid out by a handful of postwar entrepreneurs on a site where two railroads, the Alabama and Chattanooga and the South and North Alabama, were to cross. Mindful of the coal, iron, and limestone, basic to steel, buried in these Appalachian foothills, its founders named it hopefully for the great industrial center of the English Midlands. Men who fancied they could raise a city in this wooded valley near the antebellum village of Elyton had mapped out broad, straight streets with their T-squares and scrambled through the wilderness to stake off lots, frightening jack rabbits which crossed their paths.[1]

By 1907, when Hugo Black arrived to make Birmingham his home, many of its founders' dreams had come to pass. A city had actually risen out of the woods and, as its leaders intended, Birmingham's streets were plumb and symmetrical, not crooked avenues evolved from cowpaths or Indian trails. Its population had swelled to more than fifty thousand, attracted by the jobs and by the booming prospects of coal mines, blast furnaces, pig iron foundries, cotton mills, and a flourishing trade in lumber, wholesale groceries, dry goods, and hardware. Birmingham seemed to symbolize the gradual modernizing of the postwar South and to

[1] John C. Henley, Jr., *This is Birmingham* (Birmingham, 1960), 15–28.

promise that the industrial gap between North and South, upon which so many Southerners blamed their defeat, would someday be closed.[2]

The city acquired not only this fledgling lawyer in 1907 but also the mighty United States Steel Corporation which, with President Theodore Roosevelt's blessing, took over the properties of the Tennessee Coal, Iron and Railroad Company. Electric streetcars, buggies, and an occasional automobile hustled along its main streets; 380 electric lights brightened them after dark; and a half-dozen skyscrapers, some as tall as ten stories, had sprung up.

If Twentieth Street was largely unpaved and almost impassable by afternoon because of heavy clouds of dust, and if long freight trains often blocked major intersections or ran down careless pedestrians, these inconveniences were minor. Its promoters fondly labeled Birmingham the "Magic City," but residents of older, seasoned towns like Montgomery, Mobile, and Huntsville regarded it with a mixture of disdain, amazement, and envy.[3]

Such developments may have fulfilled its founders' dreams but other aspects of their creation must have seemed like nightmares. In the 1880s and 1890s, with its rough populace of miners and mill workers, 60 percent white and 40 percent black, their city gained the less flattering nicknames of "Bad Birmingham" and "Murder Capital of the World." On Saturday nights in such notorious districts as Buzzard's Roost, Pigeon Roost, Scratch Ankle, Dry Branch, and Beer Mash, corner saloons lured workers to exchange payroll dollars for liquor and prostitutes. Birmingham's record of murders, gambling, and drunkenness gave it the reputation of the nation's most crime-filled city. Christmas Eves were particularly riotous, celebrated to the echo of pistol shots and by the steady consumption of alcohol.[4]

Fast on the heels of sin came the zealots of righteousness,

[2] *Ibid.*, 108–21; Martha Carolyn Mitchell, "Birmingham: Biography of a City of the New South" (Ph.D. dissertation, University of Chicago, 1946), 177.
[3] Henley, *This is Birmingham*, 108–21; Mitchell, "Birmingham," 63.
[4] Henley, *This is Birmingham*, 97–101; Mitchell, "Birmingham," 100–11.

vowing to protect grimy miners and dusty cotton pickers from the temptation and solace of liquor. The Black Belt, too, wanted to reassure its white minority that their women would be safe from the "liquor-crazed black." Railroad excursion cars filled with temperance leaders, Methodist and Baptist preachers, farmers, and merchants converged on Birmingham in 1904 and organized Alabama's Anti-Saloon League. After B. B. Comer, endorsing county option, was elected governor in 1906, the Alabama legislature passed a local option law. Counties fell like dominoes into the dry column and by November, 1907, forty-five of sixty-seven had banned legal sales of alcoholic beverages.[5]

The prohibition election in Jefferson County, home of Birmingham, was conducted with particular zeal. On election morning, thousands of women and children thronged downtown to sing "Jefferson is Going Dry" to the tune of "Bringing in the Sheaves," wave placards reading "Down with Booze" and "Vote for the Home," and pin white bows on those converted. When the polls closed, the drys had won by 1,750 votes. On New Year's Day, 1908, Birmingham became, to all outward appearances, a dry city.[6]

Hugo Black, having lived in Birmingham as a medical student, had some prior knowledge of the city. He took quarters in a boarding house, which crowded four men to a room, and rented desk space from Bonner Miller, an attorney, for seven dollars a month. To meet people, he affiliated with the Masons and Knights of Pythias, lodges to which he had belonged in Ashland, and, following his father's precepts, attended the First Baptist Church faithfully and became one of its Sunday school teachers.[7]

He had kept his connection with the Atlanta insurance company and continued to check on mail-order applicants, making more acquaintances and earning, in busy months, as much as

---

[5] James Benson Sellers, *The Prohibition Movement in Alabama, 1902–1943* (Chapel Hill, 1943), 101–14.

[6] *Ibid.*, 117–18.

[7] Childers, "Hugo Black, Always an Alabamian"; Frank, *Mr. Justice Black*, 15.

fifty dollars. Bonner Miller threw his young neighbor an occasional minor case, such as a dispute between owners of two pigs over who was entitled to six piglets which had resulted from the mating. Although he searched the law books, Black could find no precedent for his client's claim to all six. A judge in Pratt City, with a touch of Solomon, settled the matter by awarding three piglets to each disputant.[8]

It was not piglets but a Negro convict who brought Hugo Black to the notice of men prominent in Birmingham's establishment. Willie Morton sought a lawyer because he had been forced to serve twenty-two days beyond his prison sentence as a laborer leased to a steel company. Bonner Miller turned over this unpromising claim to his young tenant, and Black prepared extensively to win satisfaction for Willie.[9]

Chain gangs of convicts working on the streets were an everyday sight in Birmingham but, unseen by most citizens, half of the convicts of the state labored underground in the mines of Jefferson County. Black, like most Alabamians, was well acquainted with convict leasing, the system devised after the Civil War to relieve southern penitentiaries and small county jails from a growing burden of prisoners. Most of these inmates were Negroes, whose infractions of the law were no longer punished by plantation owners. Mines, cotton mills, and steel companies leased convicts from the state, taking on the problems of their feeding, housing, and discipline in return for cheap labor.[10]

Unions fought convict leasing bitterly, arguing that it set up a captive labor force which assured low wages for free miners and an ample supply of strikebreakers. A few humanitarians also deplored a system under which contractors often brutally whipped their lessees, underfed and overworked them, and provided the barest housing to keep them alive. Julia Tutwiler, an aristocratic

---

8 Ben Ray recounted this early case to the author in an interview in Birmingham, February 11, 1967.
9 Childers, "Hugo Black, Always an Alabamian."
10 Mitchell, "Birmingham," 121.

maiden lady turned social reformer, described convict leasing in the 1890s as combining "all the evils of slavery without one of its ameliorating features." But the plan proved profitable and convenient for those who ran the state government, and it was in full flower when Willie Morton brought his case to Hugo Black.[11]

As he peered down from his bench in circuit court one morning, Judge A. O. Lane, a former Birmingham mayor, recognized one of the city's leading attorneys, W. I. Grubb, representing the steel company, but the young man representing the plaintiff was a newcomer. When Grubb offered several motions to dismiss the case, the new lawyer proved quick to reply. Reading Black's carefully prepared demurrers, Judge Lane smiled and turned to the company attorney. "Well, they didn't work, did they, Billy?" he asked. "Let's get down to the case." Black won a $150 judgment, half of which he gave to Willie Morton, keeping $75 as a fee to be split with Bonner Miller.[12]

The Willie Morton case was worth far more to Hugo Black than $37.50. He had won his first verdict and his handling of the case had impressed both Grubb and Lane. To test the new lawyer, Judge Lane had fired a round of tricky legal questions at him, but after each one, as the judge was fond of saying later, "he landed on his feet like a cat and came back at me." Upon reentering city politics in 1910, A. O. Lane had reason to recall Hugo Black's brisk, capable appearance in a courtroom.[13]

Others, too, discovered the enterprising young lawyer from Ashland. A carpenters' union employed him, and in 1908 he played a minor legal role in an all-out effort by the United Mine Workers of America to reorganize its badly demoralized Birmingham district. The UMW had formed its first Alabama local during the Populist fervor of the 1890s, but its strike attempt of 1894 was defeated when Governor Thomas G. Jones ordered state troops to protect scabs from strikers' bullets. A second strike

---

[11] Malcolm C. McMillan, *The Land Called Alabama* (Austin, 1968), 296.
[12] Childers, "Hugo Black, Always an Alabamian."
[13] Sholis, "One Young Man."

lasted from 1904 to 1906, cost the UMW more than a million dollars, but also failed to achieve its objectives. Union membership in the Birmingham district fell from eleven thousand to three thousand.[14]

Strengthened by the coming of United States Steel to Birmingham, coal operators announced in 1908 that wages, already lower than those paid to northern miners, would be cut from 57.5 to 47.5 cents a ton. Taking up the challenge, the UMW called on its members, then seven thousand, to "lay down [their] tools" and protest lower wages, their ten-hour day and sixty-hour week, the use of children and convicts in the mines, food prices charged at mine commissaries, and the company practice of estimating, without scales, the daily weight of coal which a miner had pried from the earth.[15]

It was a summer of violence in the dreary mining communities surrounding Birmingham. As one train filled with strikebreakers made its way toward a mine, three hundred angry miners, yelling and shooting into the air, drove it back. When miners fired on another trainload of scabs and set off the biggest battle in the area since the Civil War, the company asked Alabama Adjutant General Bibb Graves for guns to protect its property. Graves and Governor B. B. Comer refused, reminding the company to imagine the state's position "were the union men to ask for a like number of guns." Governor Comer also declined the entreaty of a miner's wife who urged him to come to see for himself how miners and their families had to guess at the real price of food in their commissaries, while the company "guessed" at the weight of coal which "poor men digs [sic] in that dangerous place."[16]

For eight weeks, lurid accounts of shootings, beatings, riots,

[14] Mitchell, "Birmingham," 129–34; Max Lerner, "Hugo Black, a Personal History," Nation, CXLV, October 9, 1937, 367. The 1894 strike is described in detail in Robert David Ward and William Warren Rogers, Labor Revolt in Alabama: The Great Strike of 1894 (Tuscaloosa, 1965).

[15] Nancy Ruth Elmore, "The Birmingham Coal Strike of 1908," (M.A. thesis, University of Alabama, 1966), 1–40.

[16] Ibid., 43–47.

and lynchings filled Birmingham newspapers. Commenting on the lynching of a Negro charged with dynamiting the home of a non-union miner, the *Age-Herald* equivocated: "Lynch law is to be condemned under any and all circumstances, but lynch law is going to be applied whenever and wherever the strong arm of the law does not protect the innocent and defend the helpless." Miners, in turn, protested that troops were being called up to watch over the lives of "thugs," imported from city slums. On August 8, when three persons were killed during an attack upon a train of strikebreakers, public opinion hardened against the miners.[17]

The violence aroused by the strike alarmed those in Birmingham who feared that a reputation for labor trouble would stifle the magical growth of their community. To quell such a threat, they invoked the racial shibboleths which had served so well in the past. Miners, evicted from company-owned houses because they were on strike, had set up a tent encampment in which families, black and white, lived as neighbors. The *Age-Herald* decried such "social equality," and its woman's editor, recalling nostalgically the "fine, old relationship between white women and Negro mammies," deplored the integrated auxiliaries of miners' wives. The dismayed white community held a mass meeting, at which Judge A. O. Lane presided, and offered to form a citizens' posse to help the governor restore peace.[18]

At the end of August, Governor Comer, citing sanitation as his reason, ordered the National Guard to cut down the tents. The UMW, blaming the use of race prejudice for its defeat, bowed again to military force, and its members returned to work at wages which had been reduced by 20 percent. The union was not to renew the struggle until after the first World War.[19]

As he began to attract labor unions and other clients, Hugo

---

[17] Horace R. Cayton and George S. Mitchell, *Black Workers and the New Unions* (Chapel Hill, 1939), 319; Elmore, "The Birmingham Coal Strike of 1908," 55.

[18] Elmore, "The Birmingham Coal Strike of 1908," 53–63.

[19] *Ibid.*; C. Vann Woodward, *Origins of the New South, 1877–1913* (Baton Rouge, 1951), 362–64.

Black moved from Bonner Miller's office and set up his own, in partnership with Barney Whatley, an Ashland schoolmate who had also come to the city. On some weekends the two went home to Ashland, or Hugo took along a Birmingham friend, Albert Lee Smith, to visit the Lee Blacks. "Uncle Hugo" lectured his small nieces and nephews on the virtues of regular toothbrushing and exercise, good marks in school, and the nutritive values of milk, fresh fruits, vegetables, and, above all, raw eggs. Surrounded by a circle of horrified children, Uncle Hugo would accept from Hattie a freshly broken egg and proceed to swallow it in one gulp.[20]

He constantly remonstrated with Lee on the number of his children, eventually six girls and three boys, reminding him that silk stockings alone would cost a small fortune, not to mention nine college educations. "You're going to send them all to college, aren't you?" he frequently needled his older brother. "I will if I can Hugo, I will if I can," Lee would reply wearily.[21]

In March, 1911, Birmingham was excited by a visit from former President Theodore Roosevelt, come to see the wonders of the new industrial South, to sniff its political air, and to bestow his favorite adjective, "bully," upon United States Steel's model suburb of Corey.

Nowhere on Roosevelt's travels was his famous political joke received more uproariously than by those who attended a huge banquet in his honor at the Hillman Hotel. A Northerner and a Southerner were talking politics in a Pullman smoker, Teddy said, when the Northerner asked why all Southerners were Democrats. "Because," replied the Southerner, "my father was a Democrat, my grandfather was a Democrat, and my great-grandfather was a Democrat, so of course I'm a Democrat." "Then," countered the Northerner, "if your father, grandfather, and great-grandfather were all horse thieves, would you be a horse thief?" "No," retorted the Southerner, "I'd be a Republican!"[22]

---

20 Davis, *Uncle Hugo*, 5–6.   21 *Ibid.*, 7.
22 John R. Hornaday, *The Book of Birmingham* (New York, 1921), 26–28; Birmingham *Age-Herald*, March 11, 1911.

Birmingham's spectacular growth since 1900 had attracted Roosevelt's attention. In the census of 1900, its population was listed as 38,415, but within ten years this figure mushroomed 246 percent to 132,685. The increase came about partly when supporters of "Greater Birmingham" won a long battle in 1910 to annex nine neighboring municipalities. They took care, however, to draw the city's boundaries so as to leave the furnaces and mills of its major steel companies outside of Birmingham and therefore free from city taxes. After only thirty-nine years, Birmingham was Alabama's largest city, third biggest in the South, in spirit more northern than southern. Industries of Jefferson County employed 61,000 and made up an annual payroll of fifty million dollars. Its glow of civic pride was only temporarily dampened April 8, 1911, when a great underground explosion at Banner Mine took the lives of 123 miners, mostly Negro convicts.[23]

In the reflective days following this tragedy, Birmingham installed a new, three-man city commission, named by Governor Emmet O'Neal to replace the old mayor-alderman system. The announced goal of this government, which the *Age-Herald* called "avengers of the people," was to bring business principles to City Hall, weed out graft, and deal with a half-million-dollar deficit. As the commissioners began to fire city employees wholesale, one observer wrote, "an awed silence prevailed at City Hall."[24]

Birmingham's new commissioner of public safety was A. O. Lane, who, a few years before, had witnessed from his bench Hugo Black's first legal victory. Judge Lane promptly fired an aging Confederate soldier as judge of municipal court and told the press: "I have talked with a young lawyer for whom I can vouch. He is quick, enterprising, and smart. He can fill the recorder's bench well."[25]

To the astonishment of subscribers in Ashland, the *Age-Herald*

[23] Graham Romelyn Taylor, "Birmingham's Civic Front," *Survey, A Journal of Constructive Philanthropy*, XXVII January 6, 1912), 1464–84.
[24] George M. Cruikshank, *A History of Birmingham and Its Environs* (Chicago, 1920), I, 118; Birmingham *Age-Herald*, April 8, 1911.
[25] Birmingham *Age-Herald*, April 12, 1911.

of April 12, 1911, bore on its front page a picture of Hugo L. Black. The new judge of recorder's court, Ashland people read, had been hired at an annual salary of $1,500 to replace three judges, one clerk, and twenty-five policemen who had cost the city a total of $32,900 a year.[26]

Next morning Judge Black, just turned twenty-five, appeared promptly in his courtroom and, before 10:30 A.M., tried and decided thirty cases. "There shall be no delay in the matter of summoning witnesses or conducting trials," he told admiring spectators. "I shall require absolute punctuality and the best of order." Court would start at 8:30 A.M. daily, and there would be no afternoon sessions because the new judge did not plan to give up his law practice. "The commission has started off right," commented the Birmingham *News*. "The public is delighted."[27]

From his bench each morning, Judge Black viewed a motley collection of drunks, petty thieves, crapshooters, dope peddlers, loafers, prostitutes, and those who the night before had been hot-tempered or careless with fists, razors, or switchblades. Minor offenders were the clientele of police court, where the dregs of a city famed for violence got their reprimands and sentences.

As its population swelled, so had Birmingham's reputation as a capital of crime and murder. By 1903 alarmed citizens read in the *News* that four persons each month were murdered and in 1909 Birmingham recorded a new high of 142 murders, about 12 victims each month. Well-to-do citizens began to move from the valley to the hills on either side, seeking refuge from dirt, smoke, and crime.[28]

This top stratum of citizens, a mixture of adventurous Northerners and ambitious young men from rural Alabama, was composed of captains of coal, iron, and steel, engineers, real estate promoters, railroad and lumber executives, financial investors, lawyers, doctors, and ministers. Successful at making money, they were even more successful, in the opinion of Ethel Armes, an observant local newspaperwoman, at keeping it. The joys of phi-

[26] *Ibid.*
[27] Birmingham *News*, April 12, 1911.
[28] Mitchell, "Birmingham," 104–12.

lanthropy and patronizing the arts had yet to be experienced by this leadership class, many enjoying the first fruits of affluence. "Before God," one man told her, "I will be damned before I will put my hand in my pocket for anything." [29]

Birmingham's small, elite citizenry existed somewhat uneasily atop a volatile mixture of other peoples. English and cantankerous Scotch-Irish predominated overwhelmingly among white workers; most of them were descendants of frontiersmen who had drifted to the southern piedmont, staked out their clearings, and dared to challenge the Indian for his lands. Even in the first decade of the twentieth century, these men almost universally carried weapons and, if serving on juries, were reluctant to convict their own kind. [30]

Germans made up the second largest group. Birmingham held little appeal for those more recent immigrants from southern Europe whose cultures, foods, and tongues leavened East Coast cities. Italians, generally ostracized and referred to as "dagos," set up small stores in Negro districts or worked in the steel mills; some Greeks operated fruit stands; half a dozen Chinese ran laundries; and fewer than a hundred Syrians peddled jewelry. The total number of residents with the easy-going tolerance of Mediterranean culture was small. [31]

Birmingham's industries, however, drew blacks long before they migrated to cities of the East and Midwest. For thousands it was the first stop on their long journey from cotton fields to urban slums. By 1910 of every one hundred Birmingham residents, thirty-nine were Negroes, and they comprised by far the large majority of those who killed one another or were killed. Law officers were quick on the trigger if the offender were black. When a thirteen-year-old Negro girl was shot and killed by a policeman who saw her stealing a few chunks of coal, blacks met in mass protest at Shiloh Baptist Church and passed a resolution imploring

[29] Ethel Armes, "The Spirit of the Founders," *Survey*, XXVII (January 6, 1912), 1461.

[30] Mitchell, "Birmingham," 56–57.

[31] In 1910 recent foreign immigrants accounted for less than 5 percent of Birmingham's population. *Ibid.*

their white majority: "Be it remembered that the strength and character of a people are manifested as much in protecting the weak and helpless as in conquering the mighty. When will justice be crowned King?"[32]

Alex London, a prominent white lawyer and crusader, was moved to deplore the "cruel, brutal, inexcusable murder of Negroes." In a letter to the *Age-Herald*, he wrote: "We have carried our own, the white people's interest, too far." It was an open secret in Alabama, the lawyer said, that any man "provided he has money and influence enough, and be not a Negro may with impunity violate any criminal statute, even to the extent of murdering his neighbors."[33]

The police chief himself, George H. Bodeker, protested when his record books showed fifteen hundred arrests for one month in 1910. He had been born and reared in the South, Chief Bodeker said, but "such treatment has got to stop." The chief told the *Age-Herald*: "Everyday I see old broken down negro men and women brought into police court and fined a dollar for some little minor offense. The old darkey has not got enough clothes on to make a gum wad; he probably has not enough money to buy a crust of bread, and lives in a little shack somewhere in an alley where he is barely capable of making both ends meet. He has to pay his fine and costs from a loan shark who charges him 25 cents on the dollar a week. The whole thing is wrong."[34]

Despite Chief Bodeker's reminder that the police department existed to protect people, not to collect money for the city, Birmingham's 177 policemen made 15,721 arrests in 1911 and its courts recorded $61,585 in fines. By working prisoners on the streets, the city also saved thousands of dollars. Even in residential areas of the well-to-do, a squad of street sweepers, their leg irons clanking, was an everyday sight and sound.[35]

---

[32] *Ibid.*, 105.   [33] *Ibid.*, 106.
[34] Birmingham *Age-Herald*, August 9, 1910.
[35] Birmingham *Age-Herald*, September 23, 1912; Shelby M. Harrison, "A Cash Nexus for Crime," *Survey*, XXVII (January 6, 1912), 1541–56.

Always strapped for money, Birmingham paid its inadequate police force poorly, and required officers to work twelve hours a day at the hard task of patrolling a burgeoning and disorderly population. As Judge Black took over the gavel of recorder's court, Birmingham was reaping the whirlwind of being a boom town, 40 percent black, a dumping ground for convicts who often took up residence after their sentences were over, and a magnet for the sprees of free miners, released from long hours in grimy, dangerous pits.

Charles H. Mandy, police reporter for the *Age-Herald*, was a regular visitor at morning sessions of recorder's court. He specialized in trivial anecdotes about Negroes and took pride, evidently, in the variety of adjectives he applied to the color of their skin. Among his favorites were "exanthic-tinted coon," "ebony-hued Ethiopian," "saffron-colored negro with tufts of spinach on his chin and cheeks," and "chocolate-colored individual." Mandy's disregard for the sensitivities of his black readers was by no means unusual. The terms "darky," "mammy," and "nigger" often appeared in Birmingham newspapers. For Mandy, Judge Black's courtroom was a treasure trove of anecdotes, and he made the name of the young judge, whom he sometimes called "Hugo-as-far-as-you-like" or "Hugo to-hell," known all over town.[36]

Typical of Mandy's style was his account of the case of Algernon Mortimer, "saffron-colored" and charged with vagrancy, who told Judge Black that he had an "incurable disease." The judge asked him to describe his symptoms. "Appendicitis and bruised blood," replied Algernon. "Point to where it hurts," ordered the judge. When Algernon complied, the former medical student informed him that he had missed his appendix vermiformis by "about a mile." Judge Black ruled, "The specific cure for your disease is work, hard work, and the city has such a job as you need."[37]

"Professor Hugo Black on Palmistry" was the headline above another episode. Mandy reported that Judge Black, at his "morn-

[36] Birmingham *Age-Herald*, January 23, 25, February 7, 14, 1912.
[37] *Ibid.*, January 23, 1912.

ing matinee," asked several Negroes to step up to the bench and show him their palms so he could read their character traits. Then Mandy quoted the judge's decision: "Your hands being spotulated and the lines well-defined denote that it is necessary that you be constantly employed, otherwise you are liable to go stale. Two months' steady employment for the city is your dose. Skiddoo."[38]

Not every police court customer was fined or sentenced. Hugo sympathized with a young black accused, in Mandy's words, of slapping the "dusky cheeks of his inamorata" after she tried to "stob" him with her hat pin. Dismissing this case, the judge confided to his deputy that he had recently ridden on the streetcar with a young lady who wore a hat so large that it would keep her feet dry in a shower of rain. It was fastened with several hatpins of such length and sharpness that the judge said he had been forced to dodge all the way to town "to keep from being impaled."[39]

Scolding a white man who arrived late to face charges, Judge Black said that he could keep his docket up to date only by starting all cases promptly. But when the man protested that he had come a long way, and asked for leniency on the grounds that he was the sole support of an aging mother, the judge's expression softened and the fine went down from twenty-five dollars to five dollars.[40]

Besides amusing his readers with such trivia, Mandy made something of a folk hero of his protagonist, calling him "the young disciple of Blackstone." He reported that Judge Black was a skillful questioner and rarely raised his voice in the courtroom, pronouncing sentences with a soft, southern accent. He fined frequent offenders heavily in hopes of discouraging further visits. At times he showed a light touch, such as the day on which he handed down numerous fines for crapshooting while softly humming a popular tune, "Everybody's doin' it, doin' it, doin' it." One Negro was moved to protest: "Everybody's gittin' it, gittin' it, gittin' it."[41]

38 *Ibid.*, January 25, 1912.   39 *Ibid.*, September 25, 1912.
40 *Ibid.*, January 26, 1912.
41 *Ibid.*, August 29, September 7, 16, 1912.

The young judge had an ear for another tuneful melody, "Oh, You Beautiful Doll," played at one of Birmingham's fashionable dances. "It was simply infectious," wrote the ubiquitous Mandy. "No one that had feet could resist the seductive strains, even Hugo —but we promised not to tell." Reading this, Judge Black may well have pondered the price of fame—and the reaction of his Baptist Sunday school class.[42]

Still a personal teetotaler, he dealt sternly with violators of Birmingham's prohibition law who patronized "blind tigers" and locker clubs which sold liquor illegally. Those unfortunate enough to be caught were stunned to receive five-hundred-dollar fines and ninety-day jail sentences. But a few months after Hugo Black became judge, the city reversed itself on prohibition and, led by Commissioner Lane who favored taxpaying, licensed saloons over "blind tigers," voted wet. During the Christmas holidays of 1911, Birmingham streets were described as a "pagan spectacle." The city recorded nine homicides and forty-six more arrests than during the preceding holiday season.[43]

On occasion Judge Black overruled the police officers who functioned as accusers. Releasing twenty-two Negroes charged by police with disorderly conduct at a dance, he told the officers that they had "no more right to break up that dance than any other." One Negro pleaded guilty to shooting craps but not guilty to possessing a gun found at the scene of the game. "I am inclined to believe you, and you can go," Hugo ruled, whereupon Mandy editorialized: "When a nigger succeeds in convincing Judge Black of his innocence despite the testimony of arresting police officers, he is going some."[44]

Returning from vacation one Monday morning in August, 1912, Judge Black entered the "dingy, dark, dank, and dirty back

[42] *Ibid.*, September 29, 1912.
[43] Sellers, *The Prohibition Movement in Alabama*, 174; Daniel M. Berman, "Hugo L. Black: The Early Years," *Catholic University Law Review*, VIII (1959), 108.
[44] Frank, *Mr. Justice Black*, 18–19; Birmingham *Age-Herald*, August 27, 1912.

room in the city hall that is misnamed a courtroom," to find a packed crowd, a docket of one hundred twenty names, and, as Mandy put it, "an odor that was enough to start the bubonic plague." But the judge, Mandy related, shed his coat, rolled up his sleeves, spit on his hands, and got down to the business of handing out twenty-five- and fifty-dollar fines with "his old time ease and grace of manner." Although he took time to lecture one defendant, accused of branding a woman on the leg, that "branding human beings doesn't go in this community," Judge Black dispensed with all the cases by noon and, according to Mandy, "every one got a hearing."[45]

When critics objected to such speed, an *Age-Herald* editorial writer replied that, considering the number of arrests, there were only two courses open to a judge. He could keep those accused in jail for a month before trial and then send them to the mines to work out the costs of their pretrial imprisonment, or he could, as Judge Black did, hear all cases within twenty-four hours. Between these two undesirable alternatives, however, the *Age-Herald* favored that employed by Judge Black.[46]

Those sentenced, if unable to pay their fines or the rates charged by loan sharks, worked out their time, shackled together on the streets, at fifty cents a day. One transgressor was inspired to compose this poignant couplet on the walls of city hall: "Goodbye my dear old police court, I bid you a fond adieu; someday I may emigrate to h——, but never again to you."[47]

Judge Black and the vignettes of police court may have dominated Charles Mandy's column on the inside pages of the *Age-Herald*, but its front pages in 1911 and 1912 featured a more prominent public figure. He was Birmingham's congressman, Oscar W. Underwood, leader of the Democratic Party in the House of Representatives, chairman of the Ways and Means Committee, and possible Democratic nominee for the presidency. The thought

---

[45] Birmingham *Age-Herald*, August 20, 1912.
[46] Frank, *Mr. Justice Black*, 20.
[47] Birmingham *Age-Herald*, September 16, 1912.

that young Birmingham might produce a President particularly entranced its citizens.

However, Judge Black made the front pages in October, 1912, when it was rumored that, despite an increase in his salary to $260 a month, he was about to resign as judge because of "unpleasant relations" with Commissioner Lane. Asked about the rumors, Judge Black denied any breach with his sponsor but confirmed, regretfully, that he was leaving the service of the city to give more time to his private law practice. "It has been valuable experience," he told a reporter for the *News*, "and afforded me a broad insight into human nature." [48]

On his last day in police court, his friends at City Hall surprised the "genial, young judge" with a small ceremony and the gift of a watch. A fellow judge told the honor guest: "We wish you every success and expect to see you someday in a much bigger place than the judgeship of recorder's court." [49]

[48] Birmingham *News*, October 18, 1912.
[49] *Ibid.*, October 22, 1912.

III

Booze,
Blind Tigers,
and Bloody
Beat

His eighteen months in police court gave Hugo Black more than an insight into human nature. In every cranny of Jefferson County, readers of Mandy's column in the *Age-Herald* knew of "Hugo-to-hell" Black. This taste of the spotlight was heady stuff for a young man only five years out of Ashland. Boom-town Birmingham proved a hospitable environment for an aggressive, ambitious, and talented lawyer, who also had the social advantage of being an eligible bachelor. Black belonged to the Birmingham Bar Association, the Newspaper Club, several lodges, and taught a large adult Bible class in the imposing stone edifice that was the First Baptist Church.[1]

He had formed a new partnership with David J. Davis, whom he had met at his first boardinghouse and who shared Black's hunger for learning. Too poor in their early days to afford other diversions, the two young lawyers had taken turns in the evenings reading aloud Gibbon's *Decline and Fall of the Roman Empire*. But now the firm of Black and Davis enjoyed such a busy practice in contracts, torts, labor, and real estate that there was little time for the Roman Empire. Black's income had risen steadily since the day when he had received $37.50 from the Willie Morton case. In 1914 he earned almost $7,500. But if he dallied long in the

[1] Minutes, Birmingham Bar Association, March 1, 1913.

relative obscurity of private practice, the name of Hugo Black would be soon forgotten by a fickle public.[2]

Therefore, shortly after resigning from recorder's court, Black began to think seriously of entering the tangled thicket of Jefferson County politics. As a logical step from police court, the office of county solicitor caught his eye. In 1914 the post was virtually a sinecure for Harrington P. Heflin, who had held it fifteen years and aspired to reelection. Solicitor Heflin, well known in his own right, was a brother of the flamboyant Alabama political figure Representative J. Thomas Heflin. Nonetheless three challengers announced in March that they would oppose Harrington Heflin in the April Democratic primary. Black, piloting a Model T Ford along the rutted, dusty back roads of Jefferson County, had already been campaigning for six months.[3]

In seeking the office of criminal prosecutor, Black was a potential threat to the fee system, which supported a horde of Jefferson County law officers in notorious luxury. Two years earlier, citizens of social conscience throughout the nation had been shocked to read in a national magazine about flagrant miscarriages of justice in Jefferson County. While Judge Black was wielding the gavel of police court, a team of writers for the *Survey, A Journal of Constructive Philanthropy* had come to town, curious about the sociological makeup of "the magic city." Their findings, which filled the entire issue of January 6, 1912, could scarcely have caused rejoicing at Birmingham's chamber of commerce.

Survey, a reform-minded journal, reported that Birmingham was a city of ardent churchgoers, but that most of them regarded religion with "old-fashioned conventionality" rather than as a force for social change. Because of Jim Crowism, the city burdened itself with a double set of schools, parks, toilets, water fountains, and other public services at a cost which *Survey* said would appall

---

[2] Charles A. Madison, *Leaders and Liberals in Twentieth Century America* (New York, 1961), 364; Frank, *Mr. Justice Black*, 23; Sholis, "One Young Man."

[3] Birmingham *Age-Herald*, March 8, 1914; Frank, *Mr. Justice Black*, 22.

northern communities. Although Birmingham professed to follow the "separate but equal" doctrine of *Plessy* v. *Ferguson,* school property for its white children was valued at $1,374,000, while that provided for a slightly smaller number of black children was valued at only $81,650.[4]

Birmingham's most revered political figures also came under *Survey*'s sharp scrutiny. A. J. McKelway, a North Carolina minister who served as southern representative of the National Child Labor Committee, visited former Governor B. B. Comer's cotton mill enclave Avondale, a few miles east of town, and reported it to be a "dreary" and "oppressive" assembly of one hundred thirty company houses on narrow dirt streets, adorned with privies, coal piles, and outdoor hydrants. His account was illustrated with photographs of drab cottages and grimy children, some as young as ten, who worked at the mill.

McKelway reported that Avondale Mills had a reputation for employing children to work long hours amid its lint, heat, and dangerous machinery. Girls, broken by this hard routine, often ended as prostitutes on "Hell's Half Acre," a row of houses near the village. Comer, as governor, had been a fervent advocate of state control of rates charged by railroads to transport Alabama products, including his own cotton goods, and had wrought reforms in tax structure, welfare services, and public education. But where working conditions in mills were concerned, *Survey* concluded that Comer was hardly a progressive.[5]

Representative Oscar W. Underwood was somewhat more flatteringly portrayed. While representing this steel district in 1911, Underwood had led in framing a tariff bill which included steel rails and barbed wire fencing on its free list. United States Steel had tried to pressure Underwood, *Survey* reported, by threatening to shut down construction of a new steel and wire plant in his dis-

---

4 Graham Romelyn Taylor, "Birmingham's Civic Front," *Survey,* XXVII (January 6, 1912), 1482.

5 A. J. McKelway, "Conservation of Childhood," *Survey,* XXVII (January 6, 1912), 1466, 1523–25.

trict and throw three thousand men out of work if steel products were not removed from the free list. Speaking to packed galleries in the House, Underwood created a sensation when he described the pressures United States Steel had attempted to bring on him.[6]

After a brief period of alarm, many in Birmingham rallied to support Underwood in his tariff principles and in his contention that the low cost of labor and raw materials in Birmingham enabled its steel to compete on the world market. Indeed, a high protective tariff might damage Birmingham, Underwood contended, by bringing about a higher cost of living and forcing industries to pay higher wages. He urged that his city would be better served by a diversity of industry than by relying as much upon steel as had the antebellum South upon cotton. Commending Underwood, *Survey* remarked that this was the first time in Birmingham's history that civic spirit had "faced down industrial subserviency."[7]

Survey reserved its harshest indictments, however, for the fee system and convict labor. Many Alabama employers, it reported, frankly preferred convicts over free laborers, knowing that they could count on prisoners to be at work 310 days a year with no absences to attend picnics, excursions, strikes, or funerals of fellow workers. Each convict in the coal mines was given a daily quota of coal, based on his strength, and if he did not dig it, was duly whipped. Many who mined coal under this duress had been convicted of only minor offenses such as vagrancy, gaming, drinking, or carrying concealed weapons. Of the 123 convicts who had died in Banner Mine, the writer reported indignantly, 21 were serving sentences of less than twenty days, and 5 were serving thirty-day sentences.[8]

Many a minor offender was in jail or at forced labor because of

---

[6] Taylor, "Birmingham's Civic Front," 1484; Birmingham *News*, April 21, 1911.

[7] Evans C. Johnson, "Oscar W. Underwood: The Development of a National Statesman, 1894–1915" (Ph.D. dissertation, University of North Carolina, 1953), 42–55. Taylor, "Birmingham's" Civic Front," 1484.

[8] Shelby M. Harrison, "A Cash Nexus for Crime," *Survey*, XXVII (January 6, 1912), 1541–56.

Alabama's custom of paying sheriffs, deputies, constables, justices of the peace, and clerks by fees rather than by salaries. In rural counties, where the office of sheriff might be only a part-time job, the fee system was not flagrantly abused, but in sizable, industrial Jefferson County, it was an incentive to mass arrests. The sheriff of Jefferson County was widely reputed to take home from fifty thousand to eighty thousand dollars a year, stockpiled from fees which ranged from twenty-five cents to ninety dollars.[9]

In his zest to round up law offenders, the sheriff sent decoys to mining camps to arrange Sunday games of cards or dice. After the game was under way, deputy sheriffs pounced on the players and hauled them off to jail. Free miners, faced with fines of ten to twenty dollars, suddenly found themselves convict miners or semi-permanent residents of the jail. The sheriff was only too glad to keep his jails filled to capacity since he was paid thirty to sixty cents a day to feed each prisoner, a service he frugally performed for seven to nine cents apiece. "When a state fee system steals a man's liberty, it steals about all he has," wrote a shocked muckraker for *Survey*, "but when officials go beyond that and take most of his food allowance, they have stripped him bare indeed."[10]

Even a clerk in the criminal or circuit courts of Jefferson County might take in $25,000 a year from fees, a sum considerably higher than the salaries paid judges who presided over these benches. To earn fees, clerks docketed more cases than could possibly be tried in any term of court, redocketed them later, and issued duplicate subpoenas. *Survey* found, however, that some of Birmingham's leading citizens opposed a system which put a premium on arrests, paid sheriffs, clerks, and others more than the presidents of mining and manufacturing companies, and kept large numbers of the county's labor force behind bars.[11]

Perhaps such an unpleasant picture in the national press stung citizens to action. Two months after *Survey*'s issue on Birmingham appeared, a federal grand jury described local administration of justice as "damnable," "highway robbery," and "extortion." Its

[9] *Ibid.*   [10] *Ibid.*   [11] *Ibid.*

foreman was Birmingham's former Mayor George B. Ward, who presented his report to W. I. Grubb, Black's onetime legal opponent in the Willie Morton case, who had been named a federal district judge in 1909 by his Yale classmate President William Howard Taft.[12]

The fee system, reported the grand jury, victimized poor, humble, and ignorant Negroes, forcing them to flee from arrest on trumped-up charges. "Were they not negroes (*sic*), but members of a more resentful race, anarchism would be prevalent," the grand jury declared. Jurors regretted that they could do no more than listen to "pitiful tales" by victims whose number might be greatly increased "were it not for the giant shadow of the U. S. government standing by with far-reaching arms and a grim determination to at least brook no violation of its statutes." The grand jury, however, recommended that Jefferson County's 150 justices of the peace, 150 constables, and large numbers of deputy sheriffs be paid on a salary basis.[13]

It was into this morass that Hugo Black, just turned twenty-eight, plunged. His homemade advertising technique, outwardly simple and direct, was so effective that sophisticated Madison Avenue persuaders would still be using similar methods half a century later. Every day a small "teaser" advertisement appeared in the Birmingham press, containing only a picture of Black, looking young and earnest, accompanied by the words, "This is your next solicitor," or "The gamblers are against this man for solicitor." Later, his name was added and the wording changed to, "Hugo Black will make a good solicitor—ask the judges" or "ask the voters." Citizens were urged to try him as a "crime suppressor" and promised that Black, when elected, would be found at the courthouse earning his salary by prosecuting criminals.[14]

Birmingham's establishment, eager to clean up the city's reputation, backed Z. T. Rudulph with large advertisements signed

---

[12] Birmingham *Age-Herald*, March 17, 1912; Johnson, "Oscar W. Underwood," 110.

[13] Birmingham *Age-Herald*, March 17, 1912.

[14] *Ibid.*, March 15, 16, 17, 18, 19, 23, 1914.

by men of prominence. Had Heflin been an effective prosecutor, the Rudulph Advisory Committee declared, Jefferson County would not be "the most lawless section of Alabama." Two papers, the *Ledger* and *News*, endorsed Rudulph editorially, with the *News* admitting that the county's crime rate was notorious and fearful, averaging one violent death each working day. The *Age-Herald*, which did not endorse a candidate, admitted that Black was "making a fine fight" but regarded Rudulph as a capable lawyer and the best hope to defeat Heflin. Boldly Black sought to turn his lack of newspaper support into an asset by advertising, "I have not sought the indorsement (*sic*) of any newspaper, monied interest or lawless element."[15]

Referring to the large advertisements for Heflin, Rudulph, and a third candidate, F. D. McArthur, Black emphasized that he had no wealthy financial supporters. His friends were just plain folks, he said, not a "few capitalists or a ring of politicians." However, Judge Grubb, A. O. Lane, and a number of other well-known citizens signed an endorsement headed "Is Hugo Black Qualified?" There were reported to be more than two thousand lesser-known names on the rolls of the Hugo Black Club.[16]

As the campaign peaked, Black and his supporters concentrated on Heflin. Birmingham was flooded with thousands of small pieces of paper, the size of theater tickets, asking the question, "Black or Heflin?" The query was repeated in newspaper ads. In contrast to Black's small advertisements and brisk slogans, Heflin and his supporters bought columns of newspaper space and filled them with lengthy messages from Heflin who pledged, in small print, to work for abolition of the fee system. In an advertisement entitled "Hugo Black to his Friends," Black insisted that large displays could not change election results, his only real opponent was Heflin, he was backed by no monied interest, and was confident of nomination.[17]

---

[15] Birmingham *News*, April 2, 3, 5, 1914; Birmingham *Ledger*, April 5, 1914; Birmingham *Age-Herald*, March 16, April 2, 4, 1914.

[16] Birmingham *Age-Herald*, March 22, April 2, 5, 1914.

[17] Interview with Albert Lee Smith, Birmingham, September 10, 1969; Birmingham *Age-Herald*, March 22, 24, 1914.

Only a few newspaper reporters who had known Black as police judge took his campaign seriously in its early stages. But a week before the primary, the *News* admitted that Black had such a lead in county beats that only big city returns could overcome it. Rudulph's advisors spoke of their "clean, bold and gentlemanly campaign" and mocked Black's "pitiable appeals and astounding claims." F. D. McArthur asserted piously that he would not "sling mud" to get the solicitor's job. Harrington Heflin complained that he had been attacked in a "bitter and unfair fight" but insisted that his opponents would fail to unseat him. Joseph R. Tate, the candidate for circuit solicitor, advertised that he would cooperate with whoever was chosen county solicitor.[18]

As primary day dawned, Boy Scouts began to remove campaign posters from trees. Later the *Age-Herald* would rejoice that every candidate who put posters on trees had been defeated. Alabama's male Democrats arose early, perhaps swallowed a hearty dose of "grandmother's remedy for purifying the blood and renovating the system in the Springtime," and repaired to the polls.[19]

While candidates for solicitor vied in the ads, Birmingham newspapers had given front-page space freely to the bigger political plums at stake in the Democratic primary in 1914. In hotly contested races for governor and United States senator, prohibitionists and progressives squared off against local optionists and conservatives. Former Governor B. B. Comer, staunch friend of the Anti-Saloon League and darling of the Women's Christian Temperance Union, tried to win back the statehouse for "Comerism," a blend of prohibition, railroad regulation, and state welfare programs, which the anti-Comer press stigmatized as radical. Old Reuben Kolb, still smarting from memories of the irregular elections of the 1890s, made a last appeal for retribution. But the governorship went to Charles Henderson, taunted by Comer as the candidate of liquor and railroad interests, who promised prosperity and restoration of conservative business practices. In Bir-

[18] Birmingham *Age-Herald*, April 2, 5, 6; Birmingham *News*, April 7, 1914; March 14, 1938.
[19] Birmingham *Age-Herald*, April 9, 1914.

mingham organized labor, remembering how Comer had struck its tents in the mine dispute of 1908, avenged itself by voting against him.[20]

Conservatives and local optionists also captured the Senate seat. The Seventeenth Amendment had wrought no revolutionary changes in Alabama because, since 1906, Democrats, in their primaries, had instructed the legislature as to their choices for United States senator. In 1914 Underwood, risking his seniority and leadership position in the House for the post of a freshman senator, sought his party's nomination.[21]

Although Underwood was a national figure whose name was on the Democratic tariff of 1913 and who had been a serious contender for his party's presidential nomination in 1912, he was by no means a shoo-in for the Senate. He favored local option over statewide prohibition and represented the state's most populous county, already resented by rural voters as "imperial Jefferson." Unfortunately for Underwood, he could not even claim Confederate ancestry. His father, who sympathized with the cause of the South, had been briefly imprisoned in Louisville for his views, but, upon being released, had taken his family to Minnesota and waited out the war.[22]

As befitted the offspring of Kentucky Blue Grass patricians, Underwood attended the University of Virginia before coming to the young city of Birmingham in 1884. Elected ten years later to represent the Ninth Congressional District, the handsome, affable lawyer rose unspectacularly but steadily in Congress by virtue of his talents as parliamentarian and political manipulator and because he followed George M. Cohan's advice, "Always leave 'em happy when you say goodbye."[23]

Underwood had come to statewide attention when he led the Democratic campaign committee in its successful drive to ratify

---

[20] A. B. Moore, *History of Alabama* (Tuscaloosa, 1951), 753–55.
[21] *Ibid.*, 660.
[22] Johnson, "Oscar W. Underwood," iii–v, 418.
[23] *Ibid.*, iii–v.

the 1901 constitution, disfranchising most blacks and many poor whites. He believed sincerely that Negro participation in politics had been a disastrous experiment, fraught with graft. Several times between 1900 and 1907, he proposed repeal of the Fifteenth Amendment.[24]

As chairman of the powerful Ways and Means Committee and majority leader in the Democratic-controlled Congress of 1910, Underwood came into national prominence. Except in the area of tariff, his political views had grown steadily more conservative, perhaps influenced by his connections with major financial interests in Birmingham. His wife, Bertha Woodward, was the daughter of Joseph H. Woodward, a multimillionaire iron magnate and one of Birmingham's leading industrialists.

Although Underwood had espoused free silver in the 1890s and once favored inheritance taxes, he later spoke of financing the government by a revenue tax on necessities. As he became more closely allied with railroad interests, he grew less zealous about strengthening the power of the Interstate Commerce Commission to regulate safety standards and rebates. An early antagonist of trusts, Underwood gradually lost his zest for antitrust legislation as well.[25]

Such views brought Underwood and William Jennings Bryan into bitter conflict over tariff, trusts, and personal ambitions. The "Great Commoner" even charged in 1911 that Underwood was "tainted with protectionism." Infuriated, Underwood arose before cheering colleagues in the House to denounce Bryan's "absolute falsehood." Underwood had not favored Bryan to be Democratic nominee in 1904. Bryan, in turn, worked for Woodrow Wilson rather than Underwood during the 1912 Democratic convention, where Underwood forces were closely linked with such financial supporters as Thomas Fortune Ryan. A loyal Democrat, Underwood backed many planks in Wilson's "New Freedom" but, except for leading a moderate tariff reform, he was not in the vanguard of Wilsonian reformers.[26]

[24] *Ibid.*, 21–104.   [25] *Ibid.*, 85–86.   [26] *Ibid.*, 343–58.

Underwood's opponent in the Senate race was one of Alabama's folk heroes, Richmond Pearson Hobson of Greensboro, who, as a young naval officer in the Spanish-American war, had deliberately sunk the collier *Merrimac*, in the channel of Santiago Bay in a vain attempt to bottle up the Spanish fleet. This exploit launched Hobson on a political career which took him to Washington in 1906 as a representative. Doubtless with his Senate ambitions in mind, Hobson, in 1913, offered a prohibition amendment to the federal constitution. An orator of charm and ability, he attacked Underwood as a tool of the National Wholesale Liquor Dealers Association of America. Knowing that he was no oratorical match for the persuasive Hobson, Underwood prudently remained in Washington, leaving most of the campaign to his lieutenants. In answer to Hobson's ardent calls for national prohibition, Underwood men deplored "concentration of power in Washington" and raised the ancient cry of states' rights.[27]

When Underwood won by 34,732 votes, the Birmingham *News*, his fervent advocate, predicted that he would be "a worthy successor to those grand, old Romans," Senators John Tyler Morgan and Edmund W. Pettus, both ex-Confederate generals from Selma. Morgan, an able legislator with a passion for an isthmian canal, had represented Alabama in the Senate from 1877 until his death in 1907. Pettus, a conservative lawyer who had served as senator since 1897, died less than two months after Morgan. Prudently anticipating the death of the old Romans, Democrats in their 1906 primary had named Congressman John H. Bankhead and former Governor Joseph F. Johnston as alternate senators, or, as some wags put it, "Senatorial pallbearers." Upon Johnston's death in 1913, one Senate seat became vacant. Now Underwood, having surrendered his House perquisites for freshman status in the Senate, began another careful climb to national attention.[28]

---

[27] Moore, *History of Alabama*, 755–56; Sellers, *The Prohibition Movement in Alabama*, 179–80.

[28] Moore, *History of Alabama*, 660; Johnson, "Oscar W. Underwood," 382–85.

In the spring of 1914, then, while war clouds hovered over Europe and President Wilson engaged in a dangerous tiff with Mexico, Alabamians had been obsessed with the issue of prohibition. Although "prohis" lost both the Senate seat and the governorship, they did establish themselves in two bastions. The new Alabama legislature would be controlled by drys and the lieutenant governor was to be Thomas E. Kilby, dry candidate and wealthy Anniston industrialist.[29]

With such large-scale maneuvers on the statewide stage, the victory of Hugo L. Black in the contest for Jefferson County solicitor attracted little but local interest. However, men who noted political trends were surprised to see how easily this young upstart had outpolled his three opponents. Black received 6,843 votes; the veteran Heflin, 4,572; Rudulph, the establishment candidate, 3,286; and McArthur, 1,875.[30]

Black had fashioned a pattern which would serve him well twelve years later. In advertising he had relied largely upon a plenteous supply of cheap, printed flyers, buying only small newspaper advertisements and implying that his opponents, with their many columns of space, were being financed by sinister interests. Correctly, he had staked his hopes on face-to-face acquaintance with average voters and on learning their opinions and frustrations. On Model-T excursions into remote nooks of Jefferson County, Black found that citizens opposed professional gambling and bootlegging, and were tired of having their jails crowded with hundreds of Negroes who had been arrested, in the cause of enriching their persecutors, for shooting craps on payday.[31]

On election day, November 3, 1914, the *Age-Herald* commented laconically that Democrats, as usual, would sweep the field. The new county solicitor was duly swept into office in an election which attracted only a small turnout of voters. The *News* now spoke of Solicitor Black with regard, describing him as a "competent attorney" with a substantial practice. The *News* re-

---

[29] Moore, *History of Alabama*, 756.
[30] Birmingham *Age-Herald*, April 13, 1914.
[31] Childers, "Hugo Black, Always an Alabamian."

called his performance in the primary with these words: "He went into the solicitor's race confident of victory from the start. When the result of the election was announced, there was great surprise at the big vote he received. Personally, the new solicitor stands high." [32]

At some cost to his pride, Harrington Heflin formally presented his youthful successor on November 30 to Judge William E. Fort of the first division of criminal court. The courtroom was crowded because it was capital week in Judge Fort's division. In retiring Heflin could not resist praising his own record. He declared that he had always tried to temper justice with mercy, to prosecute serious and trifling violators alike, and to keep on good terms with everyone. He insisted that he had nothing but the friendliest feelings for the man who had toppled him from office. But Heflin was not to be long absent from the Jefferson County courthouse. In early January Governor Henderson would name him a judge of criminal court. [33]

Black, in turn, presented the assistants he had selected. Walter S. Brower, William S. Welsh, and Hugo Black, the *Age-Herald* noted, would be "the youngest trio ever to be placed in charge of the county's criminal prosecutions." The paper predicted they would "make a record for themselves." Ironically, in view of the acrimony to come, the *News* reported that Joseph Tate, who had been reelected circuit solicitor, was doing all he could to help initiate the new county team and had pledged to assist the members as much as possible. [34]

When Hugo Black became public prosecutor, Jefferson County's jails were jammed with 374 prisoners whose food alone cost the county three thousand dollars a month. There were 3,268 cases awaiting trial, 35 of them charges of murder. With the com-

[32] Birmingham *News*, November 30, 1914; Birmingham *Age-Herald*, November 3, 1914.

[33] Birmingham *Age-Herald*, December 1, 1914; January 2, 1915.

[34] Birmingham *Age-Herald*, November 30, 1914; Birmingham *News*, November 30, 1914.

plaints of the voters fresh in his mind, Black decided to begin by *nol prossing* the cases of some 500 petty offenders who, he said, were not law violators but hapless victims of the fee system.[35]

Critics were quick to protest. Black, who had pledged to prosecute criminals, was emptying the jail, they said, and turning dangerous men loose upon a helpless community. Leading the outcry were beneficiaries of the fee system, wardens, clerks, and deputies, who saw thousands of dollars in fees vanish with release of their prisoners.[36]

But most citizens of Jefferson County were disgusted with the tainted fee system. In September, 1915, the Alabama legislature passed an act providing that the sheriff, clerks, and certain other officials in Jefferson County be paid annual salaries "in lieu of all other compensation, fees, or emoluments." In the future any fees or commissions were to be deposited in the county treasury. Members of the courthouse ring, accustomed to lavish living, must have suffered financial shock. The sheriff henceforth was to be paid $6,000 a year, and clerks, $3,600.[37]

During the thirty months he served as prosecutor in the onetime "murder capital of the world," Black was to try more murder cases than he could later recall. In his first days in office, he tried one such case which had been on the docket ten years. With the help of his two assistants, eleven other capital cases were tried that first week.[38]

The new solicitor set about also to discourage casual murder in his bailiwick. Almost every Saturday night, some unfortunate celebrant was stabbed, mutilated, or murdered, many in the so-called "bloody beat," a notoriously violent coal mining settlement near Lewisburg. Solicitor Black warned sternly that such behavior

[35] Childers, "Hugo Black, Always an Alabamian"; Birmingham *Age-Herald*, July 15, 1917; Birmingham *News*, July 14, 1917.
[36] Childers, "Hugo Black, Always an Alabamian."
[37] *Acts of the Legislature of Alabama of Local, Private and Special Character Passed at the Session of 1915* (Montgomery, 1915), 374–75.
[38] Sholis, "One Young Man"; Frank, *Mr. Justice Black*, 24; Birmingham *News*, July 14, 1917.

was to be punished to the fullest extent of the law. As if to test the new solicitor, two brothers promptly killed a Negro in the "bloody beat" and burned his body on a pyre. But when the brothers were convicted and sentenced to be hanged, residents of the area got the solicitor's message.[39]

Occasionally a well-to-do citizen felt the sting of the law as administered by Solicitor Black. In the face of pleas from prominent men to "lay off," Black prosecuted Louis Walton, a wealthy merchant of "birth and breeding," on a charge that he had murdered his young partner to collect a thirty-thousand-dollar insurance policy, made out to the firm in which they were shareholders. Walton's friends in Birmingham's business community found it hard to believe that one of their own would kill for money. The first trial ended in a hung jury and, before a second could begin, Walton blew himself and several other passengers to death by exploding dynamite in the washroom of a train.[40]

Talented though he was at swaying a jury, Black did not always win the penalty he sought. He and Walter Brower moved jurymen to tears by their description of the shooting of Gus Goolsby, a seventeen-year-old Negro boy, in the little community of Pinckney City. Goolsby had been convicted of violating a minor municipal ordinance and sentenced to twenty days at cleaning the streets. As he was being escorted to jail by Policeman Albert F. Box, he twisted loose and escaped. When Box fired a shot toward the fleeing boy, Gus stopped and "made a face" at the officer, whereupon Box deliberately lifted his gun and killed him with one shot to the head. This was cold-blooded murder, Black declared, but jurors could not bring themselves to order capital punishment for a white policeman who shot a black youth. Box was convicted of second-degree murder and given a twenty-five year sentence.[41]

By prosecuting the professional gamblers and bootleggers who infested Jefferson County, Black alienated another element of substantial size and influence. One gambler pulled strings and

---

[39] Sholis, "One Young Man."   [40] *Ibid.*
[41] Birmingham *Age-Herald*, October 21–23, 1915.

won a pardon, only to be greeted as he emerged from jail by the solicitor, bearing fresh charges against him. Convicted a second time, the gambler wangled a second pardon. The tenacious Black convicted him a third time, whereupon the gambler served his sentence.[42]

Turning to more powerful forces in the community, the solicitor challenged coal and insurance companies. He prosecuted a coal company for engaging in the common custom, so long protested by the UMW, of shortweighing the coal which a miner dug so as to cheat him of full pay.

Insurance companies asked the new solicitor to put a stop to ambulance chasing. He would do so, Black retorted, as soon as the companies supported a law permitting courts to set aside "quickie" insurance settlements, which were obtained before a worker realized the full extent of his injuries. Insurance men hastily dropped negotiations with the county solicitor.[43]

Birmingham newspapers, too, had reason to regard Solicitor Black with cautious respect. Over the veto of Alabama's wet governor, drys in control of the legislature had triumphantly enacted statewide prohibition into law. To further remove temptation, they passed a second law forbidding liquor advertising in any form within Alabama. When local option ended and prohibition began on July 1, 1915, legal liquor stores closed, but bootleggers and operators of "blind tigers" cheerfully prepared for another bonanza season.[44]

"Liquor domination in Alabama is a thing of the past, thanks be to God," the *Alabama Christian Advocate* rejoiced. But newspapers which favored local option complained at the loss of their lucrative ads, pointing out that they were being forced into a role of virtue which they had neither the constitutional right nor the desire to assume. They contended also that Alabama papers had been placed in an unfair position because out-of-state papers, con-

[42] Sholis, "One Young Man."
[43] Frank, *Mr. Justice Black*, 23–24.
[44] Sellers, *The Prohibition Movement in Alabama*, 184–85.

taining the forbidden ads, entered the state freely under protection of the commerce clause of the federal constitution.[45]

Hugo had not forgotten the morals he had learned at Fayette Black's table nor the bitter lesson of Pelham's death. Furthermore he knew that drys were riding the crest of a political tidal wave. When the operator of a Birmingham newsstand continued to sell publications which advertised liquor, Black sought an injunction. The Birmingham city court refused, expressing its opinion that the antiadvertising law violated the First Amendment.[46]

On appeal to the Alabama Supreme Court, Black won. Granting the injunction, the high court unanimously declared that the antiadvertising law did not contravene either the Alabama or federal constitution and was a proper exercise of state police power. The offending out-of-state papers were banished, but Alabama papers, which had hoped the antiadvertising law would be thrown out, were still bereft of their liquor linage.[47]

During his campaign Black had often told the voters that, as prosecutor, he would protect the innocent as well as convict the guilty. When he noticed an abnormal number of confessions being recorded in the steel-making community of Bessemer, he honored this pledge. At his instigation, a special grand jury investigated the conduct of Bessemer police. Its scorching report made front page news in Alabama and over the nation.[48]

Bessemer police, the grand jury found, obtained confessions from suspects by using third-degree methods "so cruel that . . . [they] would bring discredit and shame upon the most uncivilized and barbarous community." Helpless black prisoners, many arrested on only a vague suspicion of law breaking, were taken from their cells in the middle of the night, the jury reported, tied to a door knob, and beaten with a special leather strap, a buckle at one end and a large flap at the other. Finally, their bodies covered

---

[45] *Ibid.*   [46] *Ibid.*

[47] The case, decided May 13, 1915, is *State* v. *Delaye, Southern Reporter,* LXVIII, 883–99.

[48] Birmingham *News*, September 18, 1915.

with blood, they would confess. The jury said this practice had been going on for many years.[49]

Although the grand jury had no authority to recommend impeachment of municipal officials, it urged nonetheless that three members of the Bessemer police force be removed, two for third-degree practices and the other for habitual drunkenness. In stirring phrases, perhaps written by Black and destined to echo half a century later from the United States Supreme Court, the jury concluded:

A man does not forfeit his right to be treated as a human being by reason of the fact that he is charged with, or an officer suspects that he is guilty of a crime. Instead of being ready and waiting to strike a prisoner in his custody, an officer should protect him. . . . Such practices are dishonorable, tyrannical, and despotic, and such rights must not be surrendered to any officer or set of officers, so long as human life is held sacred, and human liberty and human safety of paramount importance.[50]

Bessemer, aroused and shamed by the national impression that it was a city "where the power of the policeman is supreme," named a citizens' committee to look into the grand jury's charges. After a month of hearings, the committee reported at a sensational meeting of the Bessemer City Council. It recommended the resignations of the president of the council, whose brother was the police officer accused of drunkenness, and of the chairman of the police committee. The chairman complied, but the council president, declaring that it was a political attack, refused to resign. The citizens' group also reiterated the grand jury recommendation that three police officers be dismissed.[51]

After this explosive meeting, the Bessemer scandal died down. Glossing it over, the *Age-Herald* expressed the belief that "matters have been exaggerated." Doubtless, there was some amelioration

[49] *Ibid.*; Birmingham *Age-Herald*, September 18, 1915.
[50] *Ibid.*
[51] Birmingham *News*, October 20, 1915; Birmingham *Age-Herald*, October 20, 1915.

in the treatment of prisoners. But brutal police interrogation would not be forbidden in the United States for another quarter of a century. When that time came, the onetime Jefferson solicitor, who had brought to light police brutality in Bessemer, would speak for the Supreme Court in overturning the murder convictions of four Florida Negroes, from whom "sunrise confessions" had been extracted by police.[52]

At the end of his first year as solicitor, Black had made some progress and many enemies. In October, 1915, the Jefferson County coroner reported the remarkable news that there had been only three homicides in September. The Alabama Supreme Court assigned four extra circuit court judges to help clear up Jefferson's congested docket. Judge Heflin, however, did not always appear eager to speed the course of justice. While Black was busy trying the Box case, Heflin, in a nearby courtroom, postponed for several months the trials of eight capital cases. He and Circuit Solicitor Joseph Tate explained the costly delay by pointing out that there was a clerical error in the initial of one member of the jury venire.[53]

Heflin appeared to have forgotten that he had once claimed only friendly feelings for his successor. In the Democratic primary of 1916, David J. Davis, once Black's partner, sought Heflin's judgeship. "Do you want two former law partners . . . in the criminal court?" Heflin asked frequently in his ads. "Vote for Heflin and prevent it." Heflin won easily.[54]

The 1916 primary was the first test of a new Alabama law passed by the prohibition-dominated legislature. If there were more than two candidates in a race, voters were to indicate both their first and second choices for the office. If no candidate received a majority of first-choice votes, election officials were to add each man's first- and second-choice votes. The candidate who

[52] Birmingham *Age-Herald*, October 21, 1915. The Supreme Court case is *Chambers* v. *Florida*, 309 U. S. 227 (1940).

[53] Birmingham *News*, October 19, December 5, 1915; Birmingham *Age-Herald*, October 21, 1915.

[54] Heflin's advertisements appeared in the Birmingham *News* during March and April, 1916.

then had the largest number won. Adapted from western states, this system eliminated the need of a costly runoff primary. It later proved to have other advantages of vital importance to the future career of Hugo Black.[55]

One of Black's most unusual cases developed in 1916 out of the activities of a new fraternal order, founded a few months earlier by another Alabama country boy, William J. Simmons. Burning a cross before a little band of awed and chilled followers on top of Stone Mountain in Georgia, Simmons proclaimed the rebirth of the Ku Klux Klan. Patterned in costume and rigamarole after the night-riding terrorists of Reconstruction, the twentieth century Klan began as a harmless fraternal band like Elks, Masons, or Odd Fellows. Its creed stressed the natural supremacy of Americans, Protestants, and Caucasians. But as the United States edged nervously toward war, the Klan proclaimed itself defender of the nation against Catholics, Jews, Negroes, aliens, strikers, bootleggers, immoral women, and miscellaneous sinners.[56]

Its earliest successes were in the South where Reconstruction was neither forgotten nor forgiven. Latter-day southern Populists had come to realize that racism, nativism, and anti-Catholicism might add the political equivalent of sex appeal to their reform program. Shortly after he revived the Invisible Empire, Emperor Simmons organized Alabama's first klavern in Birmingham, bestowing upon it the honored name of Robert E. Lee Klan No. 1. Other klaverns sprang up in Bessemer, Montgomery, and Mobile. In 1916, soon after the Robert E. Lee Klan was formed, night riders burned a Catholic church and school in Pratt City, near Birmingham.[57]

To solicit memberships in the fertile territory of Alabama, Simmons dispatched a trusted assistant, Jonathan Frost, to a reunion of Confederate veterans in Birmingham. Frost succeeded

[55] Moore, *History of Alabama*, 758.

[56] David M. Chalmers, *Hooded Americanism: The First Century of the Ku Klux Klan, 1865 to the Present* (Garden City, 1965), 30–33.

[57] William Robert Snell, "The Ku Klux Klan in Jefferson County, Alabama, 1916–1930," (M.A. thesis, Samford University, 1967), 13.

so well that he absconded with the membership fees he had collected. Seeking satisfaction for the old warriors, Black prosecuted Frost. He also made his first acquaintance with an organization which later would be crucial to his career.[58]

Political antennae in Montgomery noted the vigorous, young prosecutor in Jefferson County. Needing a zealous special assistant to prosecute a major whiskey ring, the state attorney general borrowed Hugo Black. Alabama officials, acting on a tip, had swooped into the small town of Girard, across the Chattahoochee River from Columbus, Georgia, and found buildings honeycombed with trap doors and false walls, hiding thousands of gallons of illegal liquor. Barrels were even discovered in the waters of the Chattahoochee, attached by ropes to the Alabama shoreline.[59]

Six Girard citizens, indicted as ringleaders, failed to appear for trial, whereupon Special State Attorney Black dramatically ordered immediate destruction of more than $600,000 in confiscated liquor. The state contended that the defendants forfeited their legal rights and could not enjoin destruction of their property because they failed to appear for trial. Over the angry protests of defense attorneys, barrels of whiskey and beer were emptied into the gutters of Girard and flowed, reeking, to the Chattahoochee.[60]

"Booze Runs in Gutters," proclaimed the Birmingham News above a front-page photograph of Solicitor Black, "the man of the hour in all these events." In shirtsleeves and hard straw hat, Black presided triumphantly over the pungent stream. When a prankish bystander threw a lighted match into a gutter, tall blue flames sprang up, threatening nearby buildings.[61]

Long after their illegal beverages had merged with the muddy waters of the Chattahoochee, the Girard defendants continued to protest seizure and destruction of their property. One case reached the Alabama Supreme Court, which decided that the state had been justified in the seizure, although its officials had not possessed

---

58 Chalmers, *Hooded Americanism*, 78; Charles C. Alexander, *The Ku Klux Klan in the Southwest* (Lexington, Ky., 1965), 5.

59 Birmingham *Age-Herald*, May 17, 1916.

60 Birmingham *News*, August 10, 11, 1916.

61 *Ibid.*, August 12, 13, 1916.

specific search warrants. This "defect," the court majority ruled, had been "cured" by the discovery of illegal goods; however, the judges cautioned that general search could not be condoned in cases involving lawful property.[62]

By early 1917 the courthouse was divided into two camps, with Black and Fort leading one group and Heflin and Tate, the other. Under Alabama law, the authority of county and circuit solicitors overlapped in Jefferson County. Opponents of Black's vigorous prosecutions found in this legal confusion an ideal means to attack him. The showdown began at the opening of a trial in Judge Fort's courtroom, when Black declared that the state was ready and Joe Tate arose to say that the state was not ready. Fort decided in favor of Black as the proper solicitor, whereupon the Tate faction took its case to court. Before Alabama's high court, Tate asserted that he had the right to name all deputy solicitors, including Black's assistants.[63] Drawn into the controversy, the county treasurer sought advice as to which deputy solicitors should be paid from county funds. His counsel was Forney Johnston, a prominent Birmingham lawyer, campaign manager for Underwood in 1914, and the son of Joseph F. Johnston, who had served as governor and United States senator. In two cases before the high court, Johnston argued that the treasurer had acted within the law in declining to pay the salaries of Black's assistants, William Welsh and Ben Ray. The court decided in favor of Tate, declaring that under an act passed in September, 1915, the circuit solicitor had the right to appoint all deputy solicitors.[64]

[62] This case is *E. Hemmel Weil* v. *State ex rel. Dodge, Alabama Reports* (St. Paul, 1920), 203. Black's former law professor, Judge Ormond Sommerville, dissented.

[63] Conversation with Ben Ray, Birmingham, February, 1967; Frank, *Mr. Justice Black*, 30.

[64] The court decided on February 15, 1917 that "the circuit solicitor is a constitutional officer, and his office cannot be destroyed nor an incumbent legislated out of it except as the constitution may authorize, but to require part of his duties shall be performed by the county solicitor, a statutory officer, does not destroy his office." However, the court ruled that, although the county solicitor was the chief prosecutor within Jefferson County, the circuit solicitor alone had the right to appoint deputy solicitors. The county solicitor might appoint

After what the Birmingham *News* called "months of stormy controversy," Black resigned as solicitor, effective August 1, 1917. Although his term would not expire for another year, he wrote Governor Henderson: "I do not feel that I can perform satisfactorily to the people and in accord with my own conscience with these assistants." Assistants named by Tate "are not acceptable to me," Black told the press, adding that he was now solicitor in name only.[65]

Reviewing their term of office, Black and his aides reported that as of June 30, 1917, only ninety-seven prisoners were in the county jail, the food bill was down to a thousand dollars a month, and the docket now contained 608 cases. Even those who opposed Black politically had to admit that conditions had improved. Walker Percy, Birmingham civic leader and chairman of a committee to investigate the salaries of public officials, was asked to comment on how much the county solicitor should be paid. Percy did not favor Black's political and economic ideas but he replied: "It depends upon what solicitor you have in mind. Our present one [Black] would be cheap at $25,000 a year."[66]

His courthouse feud had focused public attention on the embattled solicitor. After his resignation, rumors circulated that Hugo Black was planning to run for "every office in the state from constable to governor." But he announced that he had applied for officers' training and had taken his physical examination. Black was exempt from the draft because he was thirty-one, but, still a bachelor, he decided to volunteer. Earlier he had supported the neutrality views of Secretary of State William Jennings Bryan, but in the spring of 1917, with his country at war and his career at a turning point, Black went into the army.[67]

---

assistants under local laws of Jefferson County, but these were not to be considered officers of the state of Alabama. The cases are: *State, ex rel. Gaston* v. *Black*; *In Re Tate*; *State, ex rel. Tate* v. *Fort. Alabama Reports* (Montgomery, 1920), CXCIX, 321.

[65] Birmingham *Age-Herald*, July 12, 1917; Birmingham *News*, July 12, 1917.
[66] Birmingham *Age-Herald*, July 15, 1917; Sholis, "One Young Man."
[67] Birmingham *News*, July 14, 1917.

Although he preferred the infantry, he and Ben Ray, who also had volunteered, were sent to Fort Oglethorpe to be trained as artillery officers. Overnight, they were rudely transformed from important local officials to the humblest members of a training squad, assigned to KP and other demeaning duties. After three months of initiation, Black was graduated as an officer in the Eighty-First Field Artillery. Eventually he became a captain and served at training fields in California and at Ft. Sill, Oklahoma. He was eager for overseas duty but, although two regiments in which he served were sent to Europe, he was kept at training camp because the army valued his ability as an instructor.[68]

On furlough he went home to Ashland where his sister Daisy gathered the Lee Blacks and other relatives to honor Captain Black at a family dinner. Uncle Hugo, wearing his uniform, posed for pictures with his proud nieces and amused his young nephews by leading them in army exercises.[69]

On December 15, 1919, Black received his honorable discharge and headed for Birmingham. The *Age-Herald* noted briefly: "Captain Black has resumed practice and has opened his office on the ninth floor of the First National Bank building."[70]

Black's experience in the first World War had been tame compared to the battles he had fought at the Jefferson County courthouse. Thirty years later, after winning two campaigns for the Senate and after crossing swords with lobbyists, public utilities, airlines, merchant shippers, and William Randolph Hearst, Black, scarred by the uproar over his nomination to the Supreme Court, would still say that the hottest political battles he ever fought were those as county prosecutor.[71]

---

[68] Daniel M. Berman, "The Political Philosophy of Hugo L. Black" (Ph.D. dissertation, Rutgers University, 1957), 12.

[69] Davis, *Uncle Hugo*, 9.

[70] Frank, *Mr. Justice Black*, 32.

[71] *Ibid.*

IV

⊓⊔⊓⊔⊓⊔⊓⊔⊓⊔⊓⊔⊓⊔⊓⊔⊓⊔⊓⊔⊓⊔⊓⊔⊓⊔⊓⊔⊓⊔

White Robes
and Black
Cassocks

Postwar Birmingham, when Captain Black returned, was approaching the maturity of its fiftieth birthday. But its aspiration to become the major urban center of the South, displacing such older cities as New Orleans and Atlanta, had eluded the metropolis. Its promoters boasted of the tallest office building in the South and of wide, straight streets, but, privately, they grumbled that the city's growth was being stunted by pricing policies of the giant United States Steel Corporation.[1]

Through its subsidiary, the Tennessee Coal and Iron Company, United States Steel dominated coal and ore fields of North Alabama, carefully controlling expansion and pricing so as not to imperil its primary enclave, Pittsburgh, by competition from a sister plant with lower labor costs. "Pittsburgh Plus," a term of opprobrium in Birmingham, referred to United States Steel's policy of fixing steel prices on the basis of the Pittsburgh price plus the freight charge from Pittsburgh to the consumer.

Pittsburgh could sell its steel at competitive prices even in the Birmingham market area. Fabricators clustered around Pittsburgh purchased their raw material at lower costs than those within the shadow of Birmingham plants. There was unconscious irony,

---

[1] George B. Tindall, *The Emergence of the New South, 1913–1945* (Baton Rouge, 1967), 80–82.

therefore, in the boast of its civic leaders that Birmingham was "the Pittsburgh of the South."[2]

Had United States Steel permitted, Birmingham's output could have undersold that of Pittsburgh and other northern steel centers primarily because of the impotence of organized labor in Alabama. Hugo Black, who early in his law career formed connections with labor, had resumed these affiliations and was a sympathetic observer and sometimes participant in the postwar labor-management battles.[3]

Absent from Alabama since its disastrous defeat of 1908, the United Mine Workers returned in 1917 to press during wartime for higher wages, union recognition, and the northern custom of checkweighmen at the scales. This time, with the aid of federal intervention, the UMW won some of its goals. Wages rose 10 to 15 percent, the right to checkweighmen was conceded, but union recognition was withheld.[4]

When the UMW pressed again in 1918 for a wage raise, its effort was thwarted with the enthusiastic assistance of the Ku Klux Klan, which had added "idlers and slackers" to its list of enemies of America. When a union leader appeared at Birmingham's mills to urge a big walkout, the KKK acted. "Suddenly," the New York *Times* reported, "the arm of the Invisible Empire was put forth in the darkness. There was no strike. The man has not been heard of since." Buoyed by this success, the growing Klan chastised others who annoyed it, including "immoral women," who were warned to stay away from soldiers encamped near Montgomery.[5]

Birmingham played little part in the national steel strike of 1919 because union representatives had failed to organize the Alabama steel industry. But the aggressive UMW persuaded Alabama miners to join the national bituminous coal strike that year

---

[2] *Ibid.*
[3] Frank, *Mr. Justice Black*, 34.
[4] Cayton and Mitchell, *Black Workers and the New Unions*, 318; Tindall, *The Emergence of the New South*, 336–37.
[5] Snell, "The Ku Klux Klan in Jefferson County," 14–15.

and won a 14 percent wage increase from a presidential arbitration board.[6]

Heartened, the UMW called a statewide walkout in September, 1920, to compel coal operators to recognize the union. Some fifteen thousand of its twenty-seven thousand members, more than 75 percent of them Negroes, took part in a strike marked by violence reminiscent of 1908. Strikers killed one company official and ambushed men who attempted to return to work. Operators, in turn, ordered strikers evicted from company-owned houses. Thomas E. Kilby, who had risen with the prohibition tide from lieutenant governor to governor in 1919, said the strike was "illegal and immoral." Calling out the militia, he compelled arbitration. Union recognition would not be required, Governor Kilby decreed, nor operators obliged to reemploy men who had struck.[7]

The victorious companies felt the governor's terms were just retribution for a union "with a history of associating the black man on terms of perfect equality with the white man." A committee of Birmingham citizens investigated the strike and reported that "a band of northern Negroes and northern whites . . . went from camp to camp throughout the mining districts, Negro organizers and white organizers speaking from the same platform, arousing passions, inflaming feelings, and for the first time bringing to the Alabama miners, of whom more than 70 per cent are Negroes, the news that they were underpaid and ill-treated." Those in Alabama who opposed labor organization had found anew that racism was a potent weapon with which to fight unionism.[8]

The UMW, which spent three million dollars in its futile postwar effort to organize Alabama, dwindled until its membership represented less than 2 percent of the state's miners. Hundreds of Negro miners migrated to the union fields of West Virginia, Ohio, and Pennsylvania. During the national coal strike of 1922, Alabama's

[6] Tindall, *The Emergence of the New South*, 337.
[7] Sterling D. Spero and Abram L. Harris, *The Black Worker: The Negro and the Labor Movement* (New York, 1931), 360–62.
[8] *Ibid.*, 362.

nonunion mines, operating full time, shipped coal to markets crippled by the strike. The UMW was not to reappear on the Alabama scene for more than a decade.[9]

Labor's postwar unrest also alarmed Senator Oscar W. Underwood, who shared the fears of his close friend Attorney General A. Mitchell Palmer that unions were becoming agents of class government. As Birmingham's congressional representative, Underwood had been careful to keep a prolabor record but, in the Senate now with a large rural constituency, he moved closer to industry's view. In 1919 he even proposed, though unsuccessfully, a drastic, no-strike proviso to what became the Esch-Cummins Transportation Act, thereby alienating labor in his home city. Facing a campaign for renomination, Underwood, speaking in Birmingham, attempted to explain his action but labor was not appeased. As the May, 1920, primary approached, unions lined up to oppose him.[10]

Sensing the postwar mood of the country, the Alabama senator decided, astutely, that this was no time for a Southerner and a wet to seek the presidency. Even to retain his Senate seat, Underwood had political battles to fight at home. Almost a year earlier, a colorful, vigorous opponent, Lycurgus Breckenridge Musgrove of Jasper, had announced against him.

"Breck" Musgrove had the political flair which delighted southern voters. Wealthy because of his coal, banking, and newspaper interests in Walker County, he was famed as a raconteur and genial host. Taking his Alabama cook and ten possums to New York, Musgrove once presided at an elaborate dinner for northern friends, before whom he spread such southern delicacies as Birmingham toddy, persimmon beer, Billy Possum à la Taft, Musgrove candied yams, persimmon and alligator pear salad, spoon bread with Virginia white drips, Alabama black beans, fried hominy, and Kentucky hoecake.[11]

[9] Ibid.
[10] Johnson, "Oscar W. Underwood," 151–74.
[11] Winfred G. Sandlin, "Lycurgus Breckenridge Musgrove," Alabama Review, XX (July, 1967), 205–15.

With Musgrove as host, his guests could expect nothing stronger than persimmon beer. A staunch prohibitionist, he had fought for the dry cause in 1915 when he managed Richmond Pearson Hobson's fierce campaign against Underwood. His dedication to prohibition won Musgrove the post of national chairman of the Anti-Saloon League of America and from this bastion he contributed generously of his time and money to the cause of the Eighteenth Amendment.[12]

In Underwood, who had voted against the Volstead Act and had spoken against Alabama's ratification of the Eighteenth Amendment, Musgrove found a vulnerable target. Two aging political titans, William Jennings Bryan and Thomas E. Watson, came to Alabama to help the anti-Underwood cause. Fighting back, Underwood reminded Alabamians that he had just been chosen minority leader of the Senate, the first man since Henry Clay to lead his party in both House and Senate. He defended his local option stand in the hallowed name of states' rights and attacked labor by evoking fears of Bolshevism.[13]

In turn Musgrove raised the Catholic bugaboo, taunting Underwood, an Episcopalian and a 33rd degree Mason, by calling him "Pope Leo Oscar" and charging him with Catholic sympathies. Musgrove appealed as well to Alabama suffragettes, reminding them that Underwood, Victorian in his concept of the role of women, had also opposed the Nineteenth Amendment. Defending his stand Underwood said this amendment would take control of the suffrage, including Negro votes, out of state hands, possibly resulting in Republican victories in border states and imperiling a Democratic presidential victory in 1924.[14]

Lining up labor, women, and drys, Musgrove urged them to throw out "the fossiliferous old asses of reaction." For good measure he waved the tattered, bloody shirt. While his own father had lost a leg fighting for the Confederacy, Musgrove said, Under-

12 *Ibid.*
13 Evans C. Johnson, "Oscar W. Underwood and the Senatorial Campaign of 1920," *Alabama Review*, XXI (January, 1968), 3–20.
14 *Ibid.*

wood's family had "deserted the Southland." With such an array of charges and disenchanted followers, Underwood's renomination was in serious peril. Only the entrance of a third candidate, Judge Samuel D. Weakley, who split the dry vote with Musgrove, ensured Underwood's narrow victory for a second Senate term. The folksy Lycurgus Breckenridge Musgrove, attuned to the prejudices of his region, had come within eight thousand votes of unseating "Democracy's peerless leader."[15]

Musgrove was not the only candidate to play the clever role of rube in the 1920 Democratic primary. With four years remaining in his Senate term, John H. Bankhead, who founded a political dynasty that would serve Alabama in Congress for sixty-three years, died March 1, 1920. To fill Bankhead's seat, Alabama Democrats chose Representative J. Thomas Heflin, a prohibition convert, over three candidates, all of whom were local optionists and men of prominence, former Governor Emmet O'Neal, one-time Senator Frank S. White, and Ray Rushton.[16]

"Cotton Tom Heflin," billed as "the South's most eloquent orator," won on personality and platform appeal. The prototype of southern political buffoonery, in frock coat and flowing tie, he entertained his audiences with stories which often began, "Once there was a nigger and an old mule . . ." or tales of "Uncle Rastus," "Aunt Mandy," and "dat nigger." A member of the House of Representatives since 1904, Heflin inspired Speaker Joseph G. "Uncle Joe" Cannon to describe him as "an Albanian sunset, a string of big, red firecrackers all going off at the same time." Heflin's only legislative achievement of any note had been to introduce the House resolution creating Mother's Day.[17]

If, as early as 1920, Hugo Black entertained dreams of further

[15] *Ibid.* The vote was Underwood: first choice 66, 916; second choice 2,129; total, 69,045; Musgrove: first choice, 56, 257; second choice, 5,172; total, 61,429; Weakley: first choice, 9,776; second choice, 21,199; total, 30,975. *Alabama Official and Statistical Register* (1919–20), 406–407.

[16] Candidates polled the following totals of first- and second-choice votes: Heflin, 60,616; O'Neal, 36,865; Rushton, 20,548; White, 47,553. *Alabama Official and Statistical Register* (1919–20), 408–409.

[17] Papers of J. Thomas Heflin, Samford University, Birmingham, Alabama; Allan A. Michie and Frank Ryhlick, *Dixie Demagogues* (New York, 1939), 142.

political success, he observed some significant trends in the Democratic primary. It was obvious that the political strength of the great Underwood was waning. It was noted also that, under the new system of totaling first- and second-choice votes in order to decide the winner among three or more candidates, a candidate might win the coveted nomination on one ballot, as had Underwood and Heflin, although polling less than a majority of the total votes cast. In Heflin's victory and Musgrove's strong showing, a political aspirant might sense that plain folk, if united and aroused, could put their choices in office over candidates of social prestige, wealth, and established connections.

Thirteen years after an unknown, untried young lawyer from Ashland had arrived in Birmingham, lacking both high connections and socially prominent relatives, Hugo Black had forced the city to take notice of him. In anticipation of Birmingham's fiftieth birthday, a two-volume listing of outstanding citizens was published. Joseph H. Woodward and his son-in-law, Oscar W. Underwood, led them all, but the name of Hugo L. Black was included in a list of "leading lawyers of today." [18]

His practice, carried on for a time alone and then with a series of partners, had indeed flourished. On the profits of his first three postwar months, Black bought an automobile. Refusing corporate clients and retainers, he chose to specialize instead in damage suits for workmen injured in the line of duty, basing his fee upon a percentage of the judgment he won for his client. In police court, the solicitorship, and county politics, Hugo had learned to understand and persuade typical Alabamians, and he put this talent to good use in influencing juries. The verdicts he won in tort cases during the 1920s became legendary among those who practiced law in Alabama: ten thousand dollars for a girl with a sprained arm and dubious internal injuries, three thousand dollars for a hernia victim, ten thousand dollars for a fireman with an injured leg, fifty thousand dollars for a man falsely accused by the Standard Oil Company of embezzlement.[19]

[18] Cruickshank, *A History of Birmingham*, I, 218; II, 1–3.
[19] Frank, *Mr. Justice Black*. 34–35; Birmingham *Post*, August 13, 1937.

These verdicts stood the test of appeal, but sometimes the Alabama Supreme Court expressed concern that the jury "had been rather too liberal with the money of a defendant." John Millonas, injured at work, was fired when he refused to drop his suit against an insurance company which provided liability insurance for his employer. Pleading for his client's rights, Black convinced the jury to render a twenty-five-thousand-dollar verdict. When the case reached the state's highest court, the award was reduced to six thousand dollars, but the justices commented upon Attorney Black's "strong and passionate appeal to the jury in behalf of the preservation of human rights and the condemnation of oppression." From 1919 to 1925, Black's firm handled one hundred eight cases in the appellate courts of Alabama, fifty-three of them tort cases, mostly injuries.[20]

To keep his name before the community, Black became an incorrigible joiner. In 1915 the Birmingham Chamber of Commerce held a large smoker at the Tutwiler Hotel to welcome him and other new members. A veteran, he joined the American Legion. In 1920 the Birmingham Bar Association elected Black to its executive committee and to a committee to promote registration and payment of poll taxes.[21]

Every Sunday the energetic young attorney got up at dawn to prepare the day's lesson for his Bible class at the First Baptist Church. Church members proudly distributed leaflets urging young men to attend "the greatest men's class in Birmingham" and hear teacher Black's "worthwhile" lessons. Baptists listened spellbound when their Sunday school teacher delivered his best-known lecture: "The Dramatic Life of Moses, Dramatic in Birth, Dramatic in Life, Dramatic in Death." Collecting fraternal memberships with the zeal of a politician, Black belonged to the Masons, Civitans, Odd Fellows, Moose, Pretorians, and Knights of Pythias.[22]

[20] Sholis, "One Young Man"; Frank, *Mr. Justice Black*, 35.

[21] Birmingham *News*, December 7, 1915; Minutes of the Birmingham Bar Association, January, 1920.

[22] The circular is reproduced in Davis, *Uncle Hugo*. Berman, "The Political Philosophy of Hugo L. Black," 14; interview with Charles Harrison.

Lodges such as these and the Ku Klux Klan, observed a visiting reporter for the *Nation* magazine, spread virulent anti-Catholic prejudice in Birmingham. But the major machine of this cause was a secret society calling itself "True Americans," dedicated to the extermination of Catholicism. City officials of Birmingham, elected in 1920 with the support of "TA's," were reported to have dismissed all Catholic employees of the city except two policemen. Owners of private businesses were visited by vigilance committees, who threatened them with boycotts if they did not fire Catholic employees. Readers of the *Nation* were also told that Birmingham abounded in anti-Catholic literature and that "it has become a matter of almost routine necessity in Alabama for candidates for public office to make announcements of their stand against Catholicism." [23]

The "True Americans" may have run Birmingham in 1920 but the Klan was moving rapidly to replace them. In the summer of 1920, it enlisted the promotional talents of James Esdale, an attorney who had studied engineering at Alabama Polytechnic Institute and law at Columbia University. Fabulously successful at building up membership for the Elks, Esdale was asked to promote the Klan. Within six months he was Cyclops, and membership was booming. [24]

On a cold, wet January night in 1921, robed Klansmen paraded in cars through downtown Birmingham and wound their way to the state fairgrounds to display their growing strength by publicly initiating five hundred new members into their "Mystic Cave" at the largest ceremony held thus far by the twentieth century Klan. Ostensibly the occasion marked the fifty-fourth anniversary of the installation of General Nathan Bedford Forrest as Imperial Wizard of the Reconstruction Klan. Actually the initiation was staged to impress Alabama with the potential political power of the Klan. [25]

[23] Charles P. Sweeney, "Bigotry in the South," *Nation*, CXIII (November 24, 1920), 585–86.

[24] Interview with James Esdale, Birmingham, January 10, 1967; Snell, "The Ku Klux Klan in Jefferson County," 10.

[25] *Ibid.*, 17.

Twenty-one horsemen guarded the fairgrounds gate, through which members and initiates were admitted. In the center of the race track, searchlights played on a living cross formed by a thousand white-robed men, each holding a lighted cross with white shaft and red cross bar. Imperial Wizard Simmons, robed in purple, occupied the throne. Initiates, referred to as "aliens," seemed at first nervously amused by the spectacle, but fell silent as the moment came to march to the throne, four abreast, often through water knee-deep on the field, to the beat of a weird refrain. Men from the steel plants, stores, and offices of Birmingham then took an oath, an *Age-Herald* reporter wrote, "to consecrate their lives to the protection of the supremacy of the white race in the South." From their expressions, he added, "it could be seen that the Ku Klux Klan meant business." As evidence that Klan members were "the best class of citizens," the newspaper noted that three hundred of the fifteen hundred owned automobiles, which at all times were at the Klan's disposal.[26]

Crowds of spectators, permitted for the first time to watch the Klan perform its rites, stood on a ridge a short distance away, shivering in the cold rain. Newspapermen clustered on the roof of a nearby house. Explaining why they had parted the traditional curtain of secrecy, Klan officials told the *Age-Herald* that it was done "not for any glory that the klan might have received from it, but to let the public know that they are here, that they were here yesterday, and that they will be here forever."[27]

At Sunday night socials of the First Baptist Church or soirees in the elegant Southern Club, many a Birmingham belle hoped to attract the fancy of the courtly and eligible Hugo Black. But as the years slid by, it appeared that the successful attorney would be a perennial bachelor. He occasionally went to church parties at which unmarried members of the First Baptist congregation were

[26] Birmingham *Age-Herald*, January 28, 1921; New York *Times*, January 28, 1921.
[27] Birmingham *Age-Herald*, January 28, 1921.

invited to meet unattached young men and women of another appropriate faith, usually Methodist or Presbyterian. Sometimes on a Sunday afternoon, he and other young blades rode the dummy line to call on young ladies of good family who lived in the imposing homes along Highland Avenue. Girls admired Hugo's wit. "Never did see anybody so silly," one teased him, whereupon the loyal Albert Lee Smith retorted: "Hugo adjusts his conversation to those he's with!" [28]

Although he was nearing his middle thirties, Hugo might be taken for a man ten years younger. Handball kept him trim and wiry. On a visit to his former partner Barney Whatley, in Glenwood Springs, Colorado, he tried golf but found it dull. Years later Albert Smith remembered what an impatient golfer Black was, and how eager to be finished with the round. But sometime during his young manhood, Black mastered the fashionable sport of tennis, virtually unknown in Ashland, and its fast, competitive pace suited him much better than golf.[29]

With other young men on their way up in the world, Black lived in a rooming house pleasantly located within walking distance of Highland Avenue and near the homes of many attractive and socially prominent girls. But although he lived within a block of the Sterling J. Foster family, he did not meet Josephine Foster until after the war. The difference in their ages was undoubtedly a factor. Thirteen years younger than Hugo, Josephine had been in Virginia at Sweet Briar College, a school considered highly suitable by many southern parents for the education of well-bred, young ladies.

However, Josephine had ideas of her own. In the summer of 1918, she had planned to study journalism at Columbia University, but her attention was diverted by a Broadway poster which urged patriotic women to serve in the Navy's new feminine branch, the Yeomanettes. Caught up in the fervor of Wilsonian idealism, Josephine, eighteen, impulsively volunteered. With fellow Yeomanettes, attired in summer uniforms of white duck or winter blue

[28] Interview with Albert Lee Smith, Birmingham, September 10, 1969.
[29] *Ibid.*

serge with brass buttons, Josephine worked for five months in the file room of a naval intelligence office in New York. When she came home to Birmingham, then, Josephine was a war veteran and, to impress her less adventurous friends, she sometimes wore the blue serge uniform with its flowing cape and stiff-brimmed sailor hat.[30]

This newcomer to the social scene immediately caught Hugo's eye. When Josephine, a girl of striking good looks, appeared at a formal dance at the Southern Club, Hugo was one of the first to manage an introduction. Josephine's escort remembered later that he scarcely saw her the rest of the evening "because Hugo had her behind a palm."[31]

Hugo became a frequent caller at the Fosters' large home on Niazuma Avenue. Although not wealthy nor leaders of Birmingham society, the Fosters had good southern credentials and moved in the best circles. Sterling Foster, who had left the Presbyterian ministry for the more lucrative life insurance business, was the son of a doctor and planter in the Alabama Black Belt. Anne Patterson Foster, Josephine's mother, had come from Memphis where her father, Josiah A. Patterson, was prominent as a lawyer, judge, and member of Congress. She was also related to a former Tennessee governor, Malcolm Patterson.[32]

Like Martha Toland's family a generation earlier, the Fosters may have had some hesitancy about their daughter marrying a man of humbler origins. Not entirely jokingly, they sometimes called Hugo "that young Bolshevik." There was also the difference in age to be considered. But Hugo, at last, was ready for married life. For years he had lived in rooming houses or apartments. With the death of the successful Orlando, only Ora, Robert Lee, and Daisy, all preoccupied with their own families, remained of his seven brothers and sisters. When Hugo developed double

[30] Josephine Foster Black, "I was a Yeomanette," undated clipping from the *Junior League Magazine*, Southern Collection, Birmingham Public Library.

[31] Interview with George Bentley, who escorted Josephine to the Southern Club dance.

[32] Memorial pamphlet for Josephine Foster Black in Hugo L. Black Papers, United States Supreme Court, Washington, D.C.

pneumonia after the war, he had to fight back to health alone. With the same determination which had won him the solicitorship and many a law case, Hugo set out to win Josephine Foster.[33]

Josephine took time to meet other young men, considered by her parents to be nearer her age and social station. Evidently she had no lack of suitors, for Birmingham society columnists spoke of Josephine as "an acknowledged belle of beauty and winsome personality" and "one of Birmingham's most popular society girls."[34]

On February 23, 1921, Hugo Black, soon to be thirty-five, and Josephine Foster, nearing her twenty-second birthday, were married in a simple family ceremony at the Foster home. The newspapers described Josephine's patriotism and the bridegroom's success and spoke of the wedding as "an event of conspicuous social interest in Birmingham and throughout the state." Former Governor Patterson and Mrs. Patterson attended, as did other Foster and Patterson relatives, but Hugo's brother Robert Lee and his two sisters were not reported among those present. The only representative of the bridegroom's family, according to the social columns, was his sister-in-law, Mrs. Orlando Black of Wilsonville.[35]

The bride wore a blue suit, with gray hat and accessories, and was attended by her sister Virginia, as maid of honor. Her brother Sterling Foster, Jr., served as best man. Although Albert Lee Smith and Hugh Locke, two of Hugo's closest friends, had not been formally invited, they attended anyway. Albert Smith recalled later that one of the reasons why Hugo had wanted a small wedding was that, during his long bachelorhood, he had threatened to play many a practical joke on wedding couples and was afraid that jokesters would try to get even with him.[36]

---

[33] Interview with Virginia Foster Durr, sister of Josephine Foster Black, Montgomery, June 30, 1967.

[34] Birmingham *Age-Herald*, February 23, 1921; Birmingham *News*, February 23, 1921.

[35] *Ibid.*

[36] Birmingham *Age-Herald*, February 23, 1921; interview with Albert Lee Smith, Birmingham, September 10, 1969.

For their wedding trip, Hugo took his bride to Glenwood Springs. When Smith put the newlywed couple on the train at Calera, a small town south of Birmingham, he recalled, they sat "like two sticks until I got a piece of mistletoe, held it over Josephine and said, 'Now Hugo, kiss your bride.' " [37]

As Hugo Black began married life, new Republican leaders undertook to restore the nation to "normalcy." President-elect Warren G. Harding, choosing his first cabinet members, nominated Charles Evans Hughes for state and Herbert Hoover for commerce. In Alabama there was general relief that twelve thousand coal miners, on strike almost six months, had agreed to accept arbitration by Governor Thomas E. Kilby. Many readers of the Birmingham *News* regularly consulted a column, "Your Health," written by New York City's Commissioner of Health Royal S. Copeland. In the decade to come, an aggressive young lawyer, virtually unknown outside of Birmingham in 1921, would emerge from obscurity to join most of these men on the state and national scene.

His marriage completed the transformation of Hugo Black into a citizen of substance. As judge, solicitor, World War veteran, successful attorney, Jefferson County political figure, and now a relative of a prominent family, he had come far from his Clay County origins. But it was the influences of his youth, rather than the achievements of his maturity, which particularly fitted Black to succeed in Alabama politics in the 1920s.

A labor lawyer and the victor in many suits by private citizens against large corporations, he was unlikely to appeal to the traditional Alabama leadership. But Black was a sincere prohibitionist and personal abstainer at a time when the majority of Alabamians favored bone-dry enforcement of the Eighteenth Amendment. He was a devout Baptist and Sunday school teacher in an era of fundamentalist and anti-Catholic ferment, and in a state peopled in large measure by Baptist and Methodist voters. Despite his auspicious marriage and financial success, Black, in manner and sym-

[37] Interview with Albert Lee Smith, Birmingham, September 10, 1969.

pathies, still retained an aura of Clay County at a time when rural farmer and city laborer were finding in the Ku Klux Klan a means by which they might share in political power.

In the spring of 1921, bands of restless Klansmen, whips in hand, set out on the warpath in Alabama. One mild April evening, a band of twenty masked men in Sylacauga seized Pearce H. DeBardeleben, a wealthy, Catholic druggist, took him to a lonely spot, stripped and beat him, fractured his jawbone, knocked out most of his teeth, and warned him to sell his drugstore to the first prospective buyer so that he could leave town in ninety days. They accused the druggist of being a threat to community morals and of having said that, with a box of candy, he could take out any man's wife. But DeBardeleben's attorney, Horace Wilkinson of Birmingham, said the Klan's real purpose was to run all Catholics and Jews out of Sylacauga.[38]

Wilkinson appealed for assistance to the Department of Justice on the ground that DeBardeleben had been licensed by the United States to sell narcotics and alcohol. But Attorney General Daugherty's office replied that such matters fell entirely within state police power. DeBardeleben named as his assailants a group of prominent citizens of Goodwater, the railroad crossroads near Ashland, and sued them, unsuccessfully, for $250,000 damages.[39]

On Flag Day in June, 1921, Birmingham Klansmen, forming a line of sixty to seventy-five cars, paraded from downtown to the steel centers of Ensley and Bessemer, waving their slogans of white supremacy, protection of womanhood, and dominance of the American flag. Pausing to address the crowds who gathered, leaders solicited new members who could meet Klan qualifications by being white, Christian, gentile, native-born, and having no foreign allegiance.[40]

In July Birmingham citizens were startled by a sample of the

[38] Hubert Work, Postmaster General, to Attorney General Harry M. Daugherty, April 19, 1921; Horace Wilkinson to Earl Pettus, September 19, 1921, in Ku Klux Klan File, United States Department of Justice, National Archives, Washington, D.C.

[39] *Ibid.*; Snell, "The Ku Klux Klan in Jefferson County," 19–20.

[40] Snell, "The Ku Klux Klan in Jefferson County," 21–22.

Klan at work in their own community. A white man and woman, strangers to one another, were seized by masked men, accused of separate acts of miscegenation, and flogged. The man described his attackers as "educated and refined," but asked that the incident not be investigated, because he would soon be leaving Birmingham. Police were assigned to protect the woman, although the Junior Chamber of Commerce complained that authorities were "apathetic" about identifying the floggers. Judge Heflin ordered an investigation, but the grand jury failed to return a single indictment. Mob violence was bad for the city's reputation, the Birmingham *News* cautioned, but the *Age-Herald* said that Klan leaders stood for law and order and should not be blamed. Imperial Wizard Simmons warned that he would revoke the charter of any klavern whose members took part in such lawless acts.[41]

Floggings, however, seemed like childish pranks compared to the sensational murder which climaxed the hot summer of 1921 in Birmingham. On August 11 Father James E. Coyle, pastor of St. Paul's Cathedral and leader of Birmingham Catholics since 1905, was fatally shot while on the front porch of his rectory in downtown Birmingham, less than a block from the courthouse. His gun still smoking, Edwin R. Stephenson, known as "the marrying parson" because he performed courthouse wedding ceremonies, walked to the office of Police Chief T. J. Shirley and confessed to having fired the shots.[42]

In his jail cell, Stephenson told the *Age-Herald*'s Charles Mandy that he had gone to the rectory in search of his only child Ruth, eighteen, who earlier that same day had married a middle-aged Puerto Rican paperhanger in a ceremony performed by Father Coyle. Stephenson told Mandy that he had called Father Coyle "a dirty dog," whereupon the priest had struck him and Stephenson had fired in self-defense.[43]

The murder of Father Coyle occurred in a city already rent by

---

41 *Ibid.*, 23–24.
42 Birmingham *News*, August 11, 1921; Birmingham *Age-Herald*, August 12, 1921.
43 Birmingham *Age-Herald*, August 12, 1921.

religious animosities. "A deplorable tragedy," the *Age-Herald* commented mildly, but a reporter for the *Nation* was more outspoken. Charles Sweeney, who had described the "True American" movement, returned to cover the Stephenson case and labeled Birmingham "the American hot bed of anti-Catholic fanaticism." The city, he said, was reaping "seeds of hatred," sown by the old Populist Tom Watson. Sweeney reported that Father Coyle had been threatened many times, but the local citizenry and the press had done little to fight threats and bigotry.[44]

By 1920 Birmingham's population had grown to two hundred thousand, but still an overwhelming majority of its citizens were working-class whites or blacks, rivals for industrial jobs. White workers, with their limited education, fundamentalist religion, and economic insecurity, were particularly vulnerable to the siren calls of religious and racial prejudice. Birmingham had twelve Catholic churches, more even than the old French-Spanish citadel of Mobile, and fifteen priests ministered to Catholic parishioners. Catholics supported parochial schools, St. Vincent's Hospital, and an orphan's home. The twin spires of St. Paul's, one of the city's largest churches, had been a familiar part of the downtown skyline since 1890.[45]

If Birmingham newspapers had been lax in fighting religious bigotry, they made no effort to conceal a topic of such obsessive interest to their readers as the Stephenson case. For weeks before the trial opened, the *News* and *Age-Herald* were filled with descriptions of the main characters in the dramatic murder. Leaders of two branches of the Methodist church, popularly known as Northern and Southern, disagreed as to whether Stephenson was a minister in good standing, but both admitted that the defendant had no regular pastorate at the time of the shooting.

Ruth Stephenson Gussman, the eighteen-year-old daughter, provided several pretrial sensations. At a preliminary hearing,

---

44 *Ibid.*; Charles P. Sweeney, "Bigotry Turns to Murder," *Nation*, CXIII (August 31, 1921), 232–33.
45 Cruickshank, *A History of Birmingham*, I, 285.

she was the star witness against her father, describing years of bitter family dissension over her wish to become a Catholic. She had joined the Catholic church on her own, she testified, and not because of the urging of Father Coyle or any other Catholics. Her father, she said, had warned her that if she did not stop attending the Catholic church she would bring about the death of Father Coyle.[46]

In early September a grand jury indicted Stephenson on a charge of murder in the second degree. Ruth made headlines again with the startling announcement that she had left her husband because he had been "bought out" by the True Americans to be a witness in behalf of her father. "He has given his honor as a man for money and betrayed me to my enemies," she wrote in a letter to the *Age-Herald*. Ruth also charged that the True Americans were attempting to have her committed to a mental institution and asked for an injunction to protect herself from being committed "on fictitious examination."[47]

Despite rumors that the trial would be postponed until religious feelings cooled, the Stephenson case opened October 17, 1921. The *News* called it "the biggest criminal trial from many angles ever held in Alabama." The *Post* said there was a little of the atmosphere of the guillotine in revolutionary France. Reporters from wire associations and many newspapers, including the New York *World* and the New York *Times*, were in the courtroom. However, the Birmingham *News* boasted that its reporter J. Fisher Rothermel, using a new noiseless typewriter, could take down the proceedings almost verbatim and would therefore be more reliable than his out-of-town competitors.[48]

Hundreds of "murder fans," unable to get into the jammed courtroom, milled in the courthouse corridors. The legal cast was familiar, except that one member was playing a different role. Judge William E. Fort presided, Circuit Solicitor Joseph Tate

[46] Birmingham *Age-Herald*, August 25, 1921.
[47] *Ibid.*, September 8, 1921; New York *Times*, September 4, 1921.
[48] Birmingham *News*, October 17, 1921.

represented the state, and the former county prosecutor Hugo L. Black headed a team of defense lawyers, including his partner Crampton Harris, and Fred Fite, T. E. McCullough, and John C. Arnold.[49]

Although Solicitor Tate had told reporters that Ruth's testimony was not particularly wanted, the crowd in the courtroom was curious to see whether she would again testify against her father. When her name was called, an expectant hush fell over the courtroom, but there was no answer. Pedro Gussman, however, reported present. For his client, "Judge" Black, as the newspapers still referred to him, entered pleas of "not guilty" and "not guilty by reason of temporary insanity."[50]

The state had summoned dozens of witnesses, but Solicitor Tate startled the press and spectators by resting his case after only one day of testimony by five witnesses. Father Coyle's sister testified that she had heard no commotion on the porch prior to the shooting. Two witnesses told of seeing Stephenson on the porch but said that they did not see the actual shooting. Cross-examining these men, Defense Attorney Black elicited the information that both were Catholics. When the prosecution rested so abruptly, several newspaper reporters surmised that Tate was holding back to make his principal fight on rebuttal.[51]

Seeking to establish "temporary insanity" and self-defense, the defense called Police Chief Shirley who testified to Stephenson's "excitable state" when he surrendered. Chief Deputy Fred McDuff described a knot on Stephenson's head, which might have resulted from a blow. A city policeman and the county physician also testified to having seen the knot and to the defendant's "nervousness." Asked by Solicitor Tate if they were prejudiced against Catholics, all four made denials. The defense thereupon protested that the state was continually injecting religious prejudice into the trial.

[49] Ibid., August 1, October 16, 17, 1921.
[50] Ibid., October 17, 1921; Birmingham Age-Herald, October 18, 1921.
[51] Birmingham News, October 18, 1921; Birmingham Age-Herald, October 18, 1921; New York Times, October 18, 19, 1921.

However, when these officials hesitated to describe Stephenson as "insane," Judge Fort announced that he could see no difference between an abnormal and an unsound mind and continued to admit evidence that Stephenson was not behaving normally on the day of the shooting. This ruling, the *News* said, was a distinct victory for the defense.[52]

On the stand, Stephenson, chewing gum and in clerical garb, again recounted the events leading to the shooting. This time he testified that he had told Father Coyle that "he had treated him like a dirty dog by marrying his daughter to a negro [*sic*]." He claimed that the priest knocked him down, kicked him, and made a move toward his pocket. "I could not see whether he had a pistol or not," the defendant said. "When he did this, I fired."[53]

However, the climax of the defense was not Stephenson's testimony but the appearance of Pedro Gussman. Black brought Gussman to stand silently before the jury. "I just wanted the jury to see this man," the defense attorney said. Reporter Rothermel, of the *News*, wrote at the time that "lights were arranged in the courtroom so that the darkness of Gussman's complexion would be accentuated."[54]

Cross-examining Stephenson, state solicitors asked him if Pedro were a Negro, to which Stephenson replied: "I look upon him as a negro [*sic*]." On rebuttal, Pedro testified that his father and mother had been born in Spain. Black then showed the jury a newspaper picture of Pedro. "I just wanted the jury to see this picture taken before the witness had his hair worked on," Black said. Turning to Gussman, he declared: "You've had the curls rubbed from your hair since you had that picture taken." Denying it, Gussman replied that he had merely had a haircut.[55]

Those who expected the prosecution to present new sensations

[52] Birmingham *News*, October 19, 1921.
[53] New York *Times*, October 20, 1921; Birmingham *News*, October 19, 1921.
[54] Birmingham *Age-Herald*, October 20, 1921; Birmingham *News*, October 20, 1921.
[55] Birmingham *Age-Herald*, October 21, 1921; Birmingham *News*, October 20, 1921.

on rebuttal were disappointed. Solicitor Tate offered to present a new witness to the shooting, but Black objected that new evidence could not properly be introduced on rebuttal. At the end of a week, both sides had completed their presentations. In his summation, Assistant Solicitor John Morrow insisted that the position of the bullet hole proved that Father Coyle had been seated when he was shot. The prosecutor said no testimony had shown that Father Coyle had interested himself in converting Ruth. Urging the jury to decide the case on the facts rather than on prejudice, Morrow concluded: "The eyes of the entire country are turned upon this Birmingham jury. They want to see whether a southern jury will free a murderer because of prejudice." [56]

Tate, in his turn, remarked that it was "peculiar" that both city and county officials had testified on the side of the defendant. If the jury should return a verdict of not guilty, he said, "you will have all the narrow-minded, fuzzy-necked people come and pat you on the back, but the remainder of your lives you will have your consciences to prick and sting you." [57]

Except for the whirring of electric fans, there was absolute quiet in the courtroom when Hugo Black arose to sum up for the defense. As recorded by reporter Rothermel on his noiseless typewriter, Black said that he had tried to be fair in conducting the trial and that the state had been responsible for introducing prejudice. He went on to speak of "glaring inaccuracies" in the testimony of the two Catholic eyewitnesses, who, he told the jury, were "brothers in falsehood as well as faith." Dwelling on Pedro's ancestry, he said that there were twenty mulattoes to every Negro in Puerto Rico. If, as the state contended, Pedro were of "proud Castilian descent," Black said "he has descended a long way." [58]

Reminding the jury members that if they had a reasonable doubt of Stephenson's guilt they must acquit him, Black urged them to return a "fair verdict" without fearing that it would give

[56] Birmingham *News*, October 21, 22, 1921.
[57] *Ibid.*
[58] Birmingham *News*, October 21, 1921; Birmingham *Age-Herald*, October 22, 1921.

Birmingham "a black eye." The *Age-Herald*'s reporter, George A. Cornish, later to become an editor of the New York *Herald-Tribune*, quoted Black as saying in summation:

> Because a man becomes a priest does not mean he is divine. He has no more right to protection than a Protestant minister. Who believes Ruth Stephenson has not been proselited [*sic*]? A child of a Methodist does not suddenly depart from her religion unless someone has planted in her mind the seeds of influence. . . . If the eyes of the world are upon the verdict of this jury, I would write that verdict in words that cannot be misunderstood, that the homes of Birmingham cannot be touched. If that brings disgrace, God hasten the disgrace.[59]

Within four hours the jury reported. In one ballot twelve men arrived at a unanimous verdict of "not guilty." Dismissing them, Judge Fort said: "I believe you have done your best. There will be many opinions, but no one can properly criticize the honest verdict of twelve honest men." Black and fellow defense lawyers shook hands with their client. Just in time to allow Birmingham to turn its full attention to the celebration of its fiftieth birthday, the Stephenson case had ended.[60]

As Judge Fort had predicted, there were many reactions to the verdict. Few voiced criticism openly, however, and local newspapers maintained a prudent editorial silence. But former Alabama governor Emmet O'Neal, a staunch Presbyterian, spoke out bluntly against "odious religious bigotry" in Jefferson County. "No thoughtful citizen could but feel that human life has become cheaper and less secure in Alabama," O'Neal told a meeting of University of Alabama alumni. "We have not advanced far from barbarism if murder is to be justified on account of the religious creed of the victim. Whatever may be our wealth and resources, they will be but dross in the balance if Alabama is a state where murder is justified and where religious hate and intolerance sway the administration of the law."[61]

[59] Birmingham *Age-Herald*, October 22, 1921.
[60] Birmingham *News*, October 22, 1921; New York *Times*, October 22, 1921.
[61] Birmingham *Age-Herald*, October 23, 1921.

Although O'Neal did not refer to Judge Fort by name, it was obvious whom he had in mind when he said that Alabama needed "stronger, abler, and more courageous judges to enforce our criminal law." Quoting Rufus Choate, the former governor declared: "If a man is guilty, and his release demanded by a majority of the people, and the evidence establishes his guilt, and the judge yields to public sentiment, he is unworthy of the office he holds." [62]

Ruth Stephenson Gussman also expressed her opinion. In a letter to the *Age-Herald*, she gave the testimony that she might have given on the witness stand. The state, she claimed, had refused to call her to the stand. She said that she had appeared briefly in the courtroom and kissed her mother and father in order to show the defense that she was in the city and that she had not lost all love for her parents. But Ruth denied that she was reconciled with her parents and again bitterly accused the Stephensons of having punished, humiliated, and beaten her. She insisted that she had often heard her parents express a desire for the death of Father Coyle and the destruction of St. Paul's Cathedral. [63]

The shooting of Father Coyle and the trial of Edwin R. Stephenson would be remembered for many years by Alabamians and by the nation's Catholics. Objecting to the nomination of Black to the Supreme Court sixteen years later, the *Catholic World* mentioned his defense of Stephenson. After almost half a century, J. F. Rothermel, who had covered the case for the *News*, recalled many details of the trial. He still remembered that the courtroom blinds had been drawn in what he considered an attempt to make Gussman's skin appear darker. "I thought then, and I still think, that it was a rather obvious appeal to prejudice," Rothermel said. "Black's conduct of the trial, as a whole, I think, was beyond criticism, with this one possible exception." [64]

It was not Judge Fort but the prosecution which Rothermel

[62] *Ibid.*   [63] *Ibid.*

[64] J. Fisher Rothermel to the author, January 23, 1937. Rothermel was an editorial writer for the Birmingham *News* for many years.

blamed for the outcome of the trial. From the viewpoint of a regular reporter, Rothermel got the impression that Tate and his staff "did not really want to convict Stephenson." The eyewitness, Rothermel suspected, had been deliberately held back until rebuttal, when new testimony would not be admissible.[65]

The Invisible Empire, at work behind the scenes of the Stephenson case, had done its job well. Rothermel recalled that it was common knowledge in Birmingham that the Klan and organizations with similar ideas had raised a handsome sum to pay legal fees for Stephenson's defense. The jury foreman was a Klansman, according to the recollection of James Esdale, who was Cyclops of Robert E. Lee Klan at the time of the trial. As the Klan grew in strength in the 1920s, it was openly acknowledged in Birmingham that Police Chief Shirley, who had testified for the defense, was a leading member and national officer. Defense Attorneys Hugo Black and Crampton Harris became members, and Harris served Robert E. Lee Klan as Cyclops. When Senator Royal S. Copeland of New York fought Black's nomination to the Supreme Court, he offered to bring former Judge William E. Fort to testify to the Senate that he and Hugo Black had been fellow Klansmen. Reminiscing about the Stephenson trial many years later, Esdale said: "Hugo didn't have much trouble winning that verdict."[66]

[65] *Ibid.*
[66] Interview with James Esdale, Birmingham, January 10, 1967.

V

∏∏∏∏∏∏∏∏∏∏∏∏∏∏∏∏∏∏∏∏∏∏∏∏∏∏

Oscar
Won't
Demagogue

The murder of a Catholic priest and the freeing of his killer made an unpleasant prelude to Birmingham's semicentennial celebration. As the city turned to more agreeable topics, the Stephenson case disappeared abruptly from front pages to make room for accounts of a presidential visit. Warren Gamaliel Harding and Oscar W. Underwood had been friends in the Senate and, at Underwood's urging, President and Mrs. Harding came to Birmingham on October 26, less than a week after the close of the trial.[1]

The President's visit was the high point of anniversary festivities. Governor Kilby was at Terminal Station to welcome the presidential party and ride in a motorcade to Capitol Park. Addressing a segregated audience there, the Republican President urged equal educational and economic opportunities for Negroes. Perhaps sensing the hostility of the whites who received his advice in stony silence, Harding added a concept and used a terminology which were to attract numerous followers half a century later. "The black man," said the President about whom whispers of some Negro ancestry still circulated "should be encouraged to be the best possible black man, and not the best possible imitation of a white man." Harding laid the cornerstone of a new Masonic Temple,

---

[1] Evans C. Johnson, "Underwood and Harding: A Bipartisan Friendship," *Alabama Historical Quarterly*, XXX (Spring, 1968), 65–78.

paid a call on Underwood's ninety-one-year-old mother, and predicted to civic leaders at the Tutwiler Hotel that his good Democratic friend Oscar would also be President someday.[2]

But the organization which would thwart Underwood's long dream of the presidency was gathering strength. On the day of Harding's visit to Birmingham, Imperial Wizard Simmons, in an open letter to Americans, pleaded for the right of the Klan "to live and be let alone, because it stands unfalteringly for true Americanism . . . and because it stands first, last, and all the time for maintenance of law." In that same fall, Simmons urged Cyclops Esdale to intensify recruiting efforts in Birmingham, aiming not only at white workers but at the city's leadership class. Organizers were cautioned "to avoid enrolling in the early stages men in politics or men holding office by vote of the people."[3]

In 1922 the Klan laid in Jefferson County the base of a statewide political machine which would dominate the politics of Alabama four years hence. Peacefully or violently, Klansmen made their presence felt. Hooded knights occasionally appeared at funerals to place a red and white floral cross on the casket. Robed Klansmen attended a Methodist revival and put fifty dollars on the collection plate. But masked men also abducted and whipped a Birmingham attorney, threatening to kill him if he did not remarry his former wife. A Negro hotel porter, accused of familiarity with a white woman and of arranging dates for women, was whipped by eight masked men. A flogging victim claimed that he recognized one of his assailants, by his voice, as a police officer.[4]

But Birmingham leaders became aroused only after a well-known and respected physician, Dr. J. D. Dowling, became a

[2] *Ibid.*; Official Souvenir Program, Birmingham Semi-Centennial, October 24–29, 1921, Southern Collection, Birmingham Public Library; Birmingham *News*, October 26, 1921; Birmingham *Post*, October 26, 1921.

[3] Birmingham *Age-Herald*, January 27, 1921; Snell, "The Ku Klux Klan in Jefferson County," 10, 29; Berman, "The Political Philosophy of Hugo L. Black," 52.

[4] Snell, "The Ku Klux Klan in Jefferson County," 31–34.

victim of the whip. On a May evening in 1922, Dr. Dowling, a city and county health officer, was summoned from his home in Roebuck Springs on the pretext that an injured man needed medical attention. Masked men flogged the doctor mercilessly, warned him that he would be killed if he told the newspapers of the affair, and ordered him to leave the city in thirty days. People were tired of his "Kaiser-like acts," Dr. Dowling was told. Four days later newspapers learned of the new flogging. "Help unearth the guilty mob," urged the *Age-Herald*.[5]

Declaring there had been no floggings in the city until the coming of the Klan, the Birmingham Bar Association, split 64–46, voted to "wage unrelenting war on the local mystic organization," which it accused of dealing in religious prejudice. The association proposed that the city adopt ordinances forbidding parades of masked persons and making abduction a criminal offense. The Junior Chamber of Commerce and League of Women Voters joined the bar association in proposing that candidates for public office be questioned as to whether they were Klan members or sympathizers.[6]

When the antimasking ordinance came before the City Commission, so did a large delegation of Klansmen, led by a representative of the Imperial Palace in Atlanta, who argued that removal of masks would hamper the Klan by making its members known to bootleggers. After a stormy, three-hour session, the antimasking law was defeated, but Klansmen and the commission agreed to a mild ordinance making it a misdemeanor to lure a person from his home or business for unlawful purposes. When a political hopeful, Horace Wilkinson, sought to impeach city commissioners on charges that they had failed to indict any floggers, commissioners retained Hugo Black, who successfully argued that the circuit court lacked jurisdiction in such impeachment cases.[7]

As other anti-Klan efforts met defeat, it became obvious that

[5] *Ibid.*, 33–34.
[6] Minutes of the Birmingham Bar Association, May 25, 29, 1922, quoted in Snell, "The Ku Klux Klan in Jefferson County," 37–38.
[7] *Ibid.*, 40–41; Birmingham *Age-Herald*, June 17–22, 1922.

Cyclops Esdale had placed the white hood over the head of many a Birmingham politician. At least two circuit judges and a score of city and county officials were reputed to be members. Edward W. Barrett, editor of the *Age-Herald*, frankly admitted that the Klan "draws support from sources that would cause surprise if they were known." But after all, the editor noted, the Klan had never been proven guilty of lawless acts. Few candidates dared to voice public reproof. T. J. Shirley, running for sheriff, refused to tell the League of Women Voters whether or not he was a Klansman, but said he was heartily in sympathy with Klan ideas.[8]

Halted briefly by public protests, floggings resumed in August and September when six men were whipped, apparently because of involvement in labor unrest. The Junior Chamber of Commerce, declaring it sought to protect the Negro as a valuable labor source "who is more or less helpless and dependent on the white man," sponsored a mass meeting on law enforcement. But in the fall of 1922, seven hundred new Klansmen took their oaths in a ceremony conducted by two thousand members. An excited *Age-Herald* reporter described the induction in these words: "Within the inner circle of crimson tapers and under the glow of the fiery cross, newspapermen last night looked on at the most gigantic naturalization of Klansmen into the invisible empire ever witnessed in the state of Alabama." The main speaker of the evening castigated Catholics, Jews, and, curiously for an Alabama event, Japanese.[9]

In Atlanta, meantime, an important change took place in Klan leadership early in 1923. Hiram Evans, whose father had moved from Ashland to Texas during the Populist uprising of the 1890s, toppled William J. Simmons from the high office of Imperial Wizard. A graduate of Vanderbilt University and a successful dentist, the outwardly respectable Evans would now place his organizational talents at the service of the Klan.[10]

[8] Snell, "The Ku Klux Klan in Jefferson County," 39–43; New York *Times*, November 19, 1923.
[9] Snell, "The Klu Klux Klan in Jefferson County," 44–46.
[10] *Ibid.*, 47–48.

Another son of Ashland, who would also come to national attention under the aegis of the Klan, joined in 1923. As the membership drive of Robert E. Lee Klan No. 1 neared its zenith, Hugo Black agreed to become a member. Apparently the decision was not an easy one, for he let it be known later that he considered the move for almost a year. The Klan's increasing addiction to violence and prejudice must have alarmed him. In 1923 there were additional floggings. Opposing an industrial high school for black students of Birmingham, knights burned a huge cross, visible for miles, on the crest of Red Mountain. On Independence Day more than a thousand Klansmen in Tuskegee demonstrated against President Harding's plan to place Negroes in charge of a rehabilitation hospital.[11]

Robed Klansmen made frequent visits to Baptist and Methodist churches in Jefferson County to present fifty-dollar donations and commend the pastors' Americanism. Citizens were urged to buy only from those stores whose proprietors were entitled to display the initials, "T.W.K." (Trade with Klansmen), and the *T.W.K. Monthly* began to appear in 1923, plump with ads from Birmingham business firms. The Kamelias, a ladies' auxiliary, claimed a membership of three hundred to four hundred women. When a charter member of the Kamelias was buried with the full ritual of her order, it was reported that the white-robed women "made a solemn and beautiful as well as impressive sight."[12]

There were no official membership figures, but a Klan leader at the Tuskegee demonstration claimed to represent fifty thousand Alabama men. By far the largest concentration of Klansmen, however, was in Jefferson County, where fifteen thousand of thirty-two thousand registered voters were rumored to be under Klan control.[13] Although many of the city's political and business leaders had taken the Klan oath, workingmen and middle-class people made up the bulk of its membership.

[11] *Ibid.*, 54–55; *Frank*, Mr. Justice Black, 38.
[12] Snell, "The Ku Klux Klan in Jefferson County," 55–57.
[13] *Ibid.*; New York *Times*, November 16, 1923.

Flaming crosses, parades, and mystic ceremonies provided relief from the drudgery of mining coal and forging steel. White
robes, exotic titles, and the mission of preserving the supposed
superiority of white, Anglo-Saxon Protestants eased feelings of
insecurity and inferiority which had plagued these workingmen
since they had moved from rural independence to impersonal industrial payrolls.[14]

Black, whose sympathies and legal associations lay with the
very people who composed the rank and file of Klandom, might
have convinced himself that, in joining, he could help curb their
baser passions. Politically ambitious and without any machinery
of support, he might encourage this large and well-disciplined bloc
of voters to elect him to high office, easing whatever qualms he
had by the belief that, once in a position of political power, he
could do much to improve their lives.

At a "naturalization ceremony" on September 11, 1923, 1,750
"aliens," Black among them, became Klansmen in full view of
some 25,000 awestruck spectators. Visiting Klan delegations
from Georgia, Mississippi, Florida, Tennessee, Louisiana, and
Texas came for the occasion and, without objection from city
fathers, paraded from downtown to the initiation site, creating
such a gigantic traffic jam that 400 prospective new members
were unable to get to the ceremony on time.[15]

Spectators at Edgewood Park were entertained by a giant barbecue, dancing, swimming, and the daring stunts of aviator Glenn
Messer, who balanced on the wing of his plane and climaxed his
act with a parachute jump. The orderly crowd included many
children. As darkness fell, candidates, eight abreast, formed a
large circle in a dry lake bed at the park. Flaming crosses, a reporter wrote, "added a peculiar, awe-inspiring atmosphere to the
entire surroundings."[16] Moving slowly clockwise, initiates paused

---

[14] Tindall, *The Emergence of the New South*, 191.
[15] Birmingham *Age-Herald*, September 12, 1923; Birmingham *News*, September 12, 1923.
[16] *Ibid.*

at each of three stations to repeat portions of the oath. At one station they intoned: "I swear that I will most zealously and valiantly shield and preserve by any and all justifiable means and methods . . . white supremacy." [17]

At another, they pledged: "I most solemnly vow and most positively swear that I will never yield to bribe, flattery, passion, punishment, persecution, persuasion, nor any enticements whatever coming or offered to me from any person or persons, male or female, for the purpose of obtaining from me a secret or secret information of the Ku Klux Klan. I will die rather than divulge same, so help me God." [18]

From his throne Imperial Wizard Hiram Evans told the giant assemblage they were "Americans, one and all." According to the Birmingham *News*, the presence of other leaders, including the Imperial Kligrapp, Imperial Lecturer, and Imperial Klabee, was "a treat to local Klansmen and their addresses were met with enthusiasm." As the ceremony closed, fireworks lighted the night skies over Birmingham and the famous Klan band of Chattanooga struck up "America." [19]

If Black joined the Klan for political expediency, he timed his move well, for the locus of power in Alabama was about to shift. Fatally attracted to the presidency, Oscar W. Underwood had declined his friend Harding's proposal to nominate him for the secure post of a Supreme Court justice and was campaigning for the 1924 Democratic nomination. But things had not gone well for Underwood since 1920, when the narrowness of his victory had betrayed an ebbing political strength. He was no longer floor leader of Senate Democrats, having resigned in March, 1923, with the excuse of conserving his health. Actually the resignation

[17] New York *Times*, September 13, 1937.

[18] Wizard Simmons quoted this portion of the oath at the *Hearings on the Ku Klux Klan*, Committee on Rules, House of Representatives, 67th Cong., 1st Sess., 1921. The hearings are contained in Microfilm 22463, Library of Congress, Washington, D.C.

[19] Birmingham *Age-Herald*, September 12, 1923; Birmingham *News*, September 12, 1923.

stemmed from dissatisfaction with Underwood's leadership. Democrats criticized him for accepting, while he was Senate leader of the opposing party, Harding's invitation to serve as a delegate to the Washington Naval Conference of 1922. Lacking a Senate majority and unable to exert discipline in a forum of unlimited debate, Underwood was not as effective a floor leader in the Senate as he had been in the House.[20]

Furthermore many of his fellow Democrats, including Woodrow Wilson during his presidency, considered Underwood essentially conservative and out of step with progressive ideas except moderate tariff reform. His old enemy William Jennings Bryan was fond of calling Underwood "a tool of Wall Street." Increasingly Hamiltonian in his economic views, Underwood had shifted on most issues from prolabor to promanagement in response to his ties with the new industrial South. His closest friends were railroad attorneys, and his campaign manager Forney Johnston was a corporation lawyer who represented, among other clients, the Frisco Railway. In 1922 Underwood, who had originally favored government development of the Muscle Shoals region of the Tennessee River, urged that Congress accept the private enterprise approach of Henry Ford. He also differed with the Democratic majority by favoring a cut in the maximum surtax.[21]

In his home state, however, Underwood still had the support of major newspapers, the Alabama Bar Association, the Alabama Manufacturers Association, the Alabama Democratic Executive Committee, Governor William W. "Plain Bill" Brandon, and all former living governors. In January, 1923, the Alabama legislature formally requested him to become a presidential candidate, even enacting a law to provide that the man who won Alabama's presidential primary might personally name the state's delegation to the Democratic convention. After an interval of feigned inde-

[20] Johnson, "Underwood and Harding," 65–78.

[21] Johnson, "Oscar W. Underwood," 147–48, 172–74, 414; Martin Torodah, "Underwood and the Tariff," *Alabama Review*, XX (April, 1967), 115–30; Birmingham *Age-Herald*, July 10, 1924.

cision, Underwood told the legislature on July 31 that he would make the race. The first avowed candidate for the 1924 Democratic nomination, he staked his hopes and Senate career on a denunciation of the Ku Klux Klan, injecting into the campaign an issue which would rend the Democratic Party. In October, 1923, speaking in Houston, a Klan stronghold, Underwood strongly attacked a secret organization of "class and clan."[22]

In challenging the Klan, Underwood was engaged in a deliberate maneuver to block the nomination of his rival, William Gibbs McAdoo, by placing McAdoo in the awkward position of collaborating with the Klan. Happily for Underwood, this strategy coincided with his personal convictions. The Klan, he sincerely believed, was a threat to America because it set itself above law and Constitution by taking the power of punishment into its own hands. Campaigning in faraway Maine he pictured Alabama as terrorized by Klan activities. In Birmingham a grand jury, charged with investigating Underwood's contention, reported it could find no evidence of such a situation.[23]

With Underwood openly defying the Klan, the senator's Alabama opponents stirred restlessly. "Breck" Musgrove, who had come so close to defeating Underwood in 1920, sought to rally his old allies, drys, women, and labor, and add to them the senator's newer enemies, war veterans alienated by Underwood's opposition to a soldiers' bonus, and the Klan. But Klan leaders, fearing possible defeat in a preconvention contest with Underwood, failed to align their following in behalf of Musgrove and gave lukewarm support to a third candidate, Marvin A. Dinsmore.[24]

The Alabama primary campaign was enlivened by mudslinging and by the reappearance of Underwood's old enemy William Jen-

[22] Lee N. Allen, "The 1924 Underwood Campaign in Alabama," *Alabama Review*, IX (July, 1956), 176–79; Tindall, *The Emergence of the New South*, 242–43.

[23] Lee N. Allen, "The McAdoo Campaign for the Presidential Nomination in 1924," *Journal of Southern History*, XXIX (1963), 217–18. Oscar W. Underwood to C. A. Beasley, October 18, 1923, in Oscar W. Underwood Papers, Alabama Department of Archives, Montgomery; Snell, "The Ku Klux Klan in Jefferson County," 75–76.

[24] Allen, "The 1924 Underwood Campaign in Alabama," 181.

nings Bryan, who was campaigning for Musgrove. His rivals spread rumors that Underwood had been born in the North, that his ancestors had fought for the Union, and that he had renounced his Masonic affiliations and joined the Catholic church. Drys, in particular, were fearful that Underwood might endorse a wet plank in the Democratic platform and, if unsuccessful himself, might support Alfred E. Smith for the nomination. To allay these fears, Underwood let it be known that former Governor Comer, leader of the drys, would be allowed to name half of Alabama's convention delegates.[25]

Confident therefore of victory, Underwood's friends on the Alabama Democratic Executive Committee set an early date, March 11, 1924, for their primary. When he won overwhelmingly, Underwood became the first Democratic candidate to control delegates, representing the twenty-four votes of Alabama and soon to be legendary for their loyalty to him. But when Underwood met McAdoo, who had straddled the Klan issue, in five southern primaries, McAdoo won them all. Then McAdoo gained three more southern delegations, leaving Underwood with only Alabama, a handful of scattered delegates, and a forlorn hope of nomination.[26]

In a final effort to fasten the stigma of the Klan on McAdoo, Underwood sought to force the Democratic national convention to censure the Klan by name, hoping thereby to inherit a bloc of eastern votes loyal to New York's Alfred E. Smith. But when Forney Johnston, preparing to nominate Underwood, condemned the Klan, he touched off fistfights, parades, and demonstrations by its supporters and opponents. After the tumult died down, Underwood's resolution lost, and a moderate plank, deploring racial and religious prejudice but calling no names, was adopted. Smith supporters, including Franklin D. Roosevelt, had sided with Underwood, while McAdoo delegates favored the milder rebuke. But the vote was close enough to make it clear that McAdoo lacked sufficient strength to win the nomination. At the end of 103 ballots,

---

[25] *Ibid.*, 183–84.
[26] *Ibid*; Tindall, *The Emergence of the New South*, 243.

weary Democrats compromised on the "Wall Street lawyer," John W. Davis of West Virginia.[27]

His Alabama delegation had stood loyally by Underwood. On each of the 103 ballots, diminutive "Plain Bill" Brandon stood up on his chair to immortalize in Democratic annals the phrase, "Alabama casts twenty-fo' votes for Oscar W. Underwood!" With its delegates split but voting under the unit rule, Alabama was the only southern state to cast its entire vote in favor of censuring the Klan by name.[28]

As Democrats quarreled over the Klan in Madison Square Garden, five thousand Birmingham Klansmen, riding in a thousand cars with license plates covered, paraded from the steel mills of Fairfield to East Lake Park, a distance of some fifteen miles. For their convenience city police stopped other traffic along the route and saw to it that traffic lights remained green. The East Lake rally surpassed even that at which Hugo Black had become a member. More than forty thousand gathered to watch the initiation of four thousand new candidates. Senator Underwood told the New York *World* that the parade was an effort to intimidate him, Alabama delegates, and the Democratic Party.

"It will not succeed," Underwood said. "I am not afraid either in a political or a personal sense of the Ku Klux Klan. I maintain that organization is a national menace. . . . It is either the Ku Klux Klan or the United States of America. Both cannot survive. Between the two, I choose my country." [29]

Underwood's anti-Klan strategy probably assured his defeat. It cost him all the southern delegates except those of Alabama. Al Smith was reported to have told Underwood that he would support him if Underwood could get two more southern delegations, but when Underwood called to his neighbors in Georgia, Tennessee,

[27] Tindall, *The Emergence of the New South*, 242–44; Allen, "The McAdoo Campaign," 225; New York *Times*, September 17, 1937; Hugh Dorsey Reagan, "The Presidential Election of 1928 in Alabama" (Ph.D. dissertation, University of Texas, 1961), 19–21.

[28] Allen, "The Underwood Campaign," 186.

[29] Snell, "The Ku Klux Klan in Jefferson County," 71–75.

Mississippi, and other southern states, "he called in vain." Most
delegates probably were neither Klansmen nor sympathizers but
they were unlikely to nominate a conservative Southerner, a wet,
and an intransigent foe of the powerful hooded order.[30]

The Klan hastened to dramatize its victory and Underwood's
defeat. Wizard Evans later boasted that he would have made Underwood the Democratic nominee had it not been for the Houston
speech. "Oscar would have been nominated instead of John W.
Davis," he told Birmingham Klansmen, "had he just simply 'set.' "
But it was not Underwood's temperament to "set." Deploring this
trait, an Underwood supporter at the convention commented sadly: "Oscar won't demagogue, not even a little." As the convention
ended, rumors circulated that Underwood would not stand in
1926 for reelection to the Senate.[31]

At a Kansas City Klonvocation in September, 1924, delegates
from the "realm" of Alabama vowed to retire Underwood in 1926.
Meeting in October to initiate seven thousand new Birmingham
Knights, Klansmen cheered wildly as a coffin, containing an effigy of Underwood, was "laid to rest" through a trap door in the
speakers' platform. Underwood felt his once-secure Senate base
shifting like quicksand beneath his feet. A friend, University of
Alabama President George H. Denny, in a letter to Underwood,
described the situation with old-fashioned courtesy: "In Alabama,
at the present time, fame is not burning its incense at the ancient
shrines."[32]

There are two things that count more than almost everything else
in this life. Those things are work and endurance. . . . Remember that
diplomacy mixed with persistence and work gets results. . . . It is right
for you to study people as well as books. You never make a friend in

[30] Torodah, "Underwood and the Tariff," 130; Microfilm scrapbook in Papers
of J. Thomas Heflin; Allen, "The 1924 Underwood Campaign," 186–87.

[31] New York Times, September 17, 1937; E. D. Renna to Oscar W. Underwood, Jr., March 20, 1939, in Oscar W. Underwood Papers.

[32] Virginia V. Hamilton, "The Senate Career of Hugo L. Black" (Ph.D. dissertation, University of Alabama, 1968), 31; George H. Denny to Oscar W.
Underwood, July 4, 1925, in Oscar W. Underwood Papers.

vain. Also I want to remind you of the benefit of exercise, swimming, tennis or any other things that give you both pleasure and benefit. . . . There is a predisposition on the part of many of our family to become moody, despondent, cynical, unduly critical of others, and pessimistic. That is an excellent thing to avoid. Optimism brings more happiness and makes more friends and gets more of anything it goes after.[33]

Hugo Black, in 1922, was writing to hearten his eighteen-year-old niece Hazel upon the news that she was runner-up, but not winner, in a college scholarship competition. The third of Lee Black's nine children, bright, aspiring Hazel, valedictorian of her high school senior class, must have reminded Hugo of himself, the smartest youngster in Ashland, eager to learn about the world beyond the mountains. But Lee had not prospered after the fashion of his storekeeper father or his brothers, Orlando and Hugo, and he had invested calamitously in cotton futures. Only with the assistance of a successful brother in Birmingham was there any chance of financing nine college educations.[34]

Hugo helped pay the college expenses of Lee's four oldest children, Grace, Hollis, Hazel, and Mildred, and they, in turn, helped their younger brothers and sisters. Hazel became a special protégé, admiring her uncle so unreservedly that her father said: "If Hugo told her to jump into the fire, she'd jump." Visiting Birmingham for the first time, Hazel rode her first elevator, was admonished by her uncle never to wear silk stockings which had been darned ("Save somewhere else but wear perfect hose"), and was reminded not to be over-generous with the "Yes, ma'ams" and "Yes, sirs" expected of young people in Ashland. "Yes, ma'am" and "Yes, sir," Uncle Hugo told Hazel, were hangovers from Civil War days, denoting a feeling of servitude or embarrassment. "Yes" would be sufficient, he suggested, or "Yes, Mr. Smith" and "Yes, Mrs. Jones." He urged his niece, "Practice the cultured, refined speech you would use in any social circles." Grateful though she was for advice, Hazel found her uncle no easy taskmaster. When she pre-

---

[33] Davis, *Uncle Hugo*, 47–48.   [34] *Ibid.*, 7–10.

sented him with her first college grades, 5 A's, 3 B's, and 2 C's, he wrote her: "Don't you think they should all have been A's?"[35]

Observing Hazel's wide-eyed reactions to his style of living, Hugo could reflect how far he had come from Ashland. Josephine, born to southern gentility, had created in their two-story French provincial home on Altamont Road, overlooking Birmingham, an appropriate setting for a successful lawyer, his wife, and two sons, Hugo La Fayette, Jr., and Sterling Foster. It was Josephine who arranged tasteful bouquets of flowers and taught Lou, the Negro cook, to serve mint jelly with lamb. Like other young Birmingham matrons of proper background, Josephine was a member of the Junior League, but she was doubtless the only Junior Leaguer who also belonged to the American Legion. Young, impressionable Hazel, visiting her uncle, tried as best she could to emulate Josephine's flair for sewing, choosing table linens, playing Chopin preludes, and selecting clothes free from "doodads." At his wife's suggestion, Hugo gave Hazel twenty-five dollars for one of the new permanent waves. "Looks certainly count in this world," he advised his niece.[36]

With Hugo well established in his profession, the Blacks experienced none of the typical deprivations of newlywed young couples. Black's income, rising toward the forty thousand dollars he would make in 1925, would soon match that of any lawyer in Alabama. Members of the Birmingham Country Club, a few blocks down Red Mountain, Hugo and Josephine played on its tennis courts and golf course. There was a large, attractive library in the house on Altamont Road, its shelves stocked with books Hugo had always wanted to read. In the living room was a baby grand piano for Josephine's Chopin preludes, and for Hugo to play, by ear, Negro spirituals, folk songs, and light classics.[37]

Altogether, life was pleasant. As "Judge" Black told members

[35] *Ibid.*, 11–13, 58.
[36] *Ibid.*, 15–22; Berman, "The Political Philosophy of Hugo Black," 14.
[37] Davis, *Uncle Hugo*, 21; Montgomery *Advertiser*, October 30, 1955; interview with Justice Hugo L. Black, Washington, D.C., September, 1966.

of the Ensley Kiwanis Club, dozing over remnants of peas and fried chicken: "In order to be a good citizen, one is compelled to observe the Golden Rule, to first of all protect his body which is the temple of his spirit, and to protect and maintain one's home."[38] But his own restless drive, Underwood's quagmire, the booming Klan, and Alabama's militant drys combined to propel Black from the comforts of private life back into the political limelight.

In 1923 Alabama had been legally dry seven years, and Judge Elbert H. Gary, chairman of the board of United States Steel, saw nothing but good in the results. Judge Gary told the New York *Times* that, thanks to prohibition, Birmingham, once a frontier mining town where crime and immorality flourished, was virtually a model city. But prohibition, like liberty, demanded eternal vigilance. In Birmingham the Klan was only too eager to help, bribing bellhops to act as informers and disguising Klansmen as telephone repairmen so they might enter homes to search for illegal liquor. Household and hotel bootleggers seemed petty game, however, compared to the huge whiskey ring uncovered in November, 1923, in Mobile, Alabama's seaport.[39]

Dependent on shipping for its prosperity and steeped in the Latin traditions of Spain and France, old, moss-hung Mobile had a more permissive attitude toward alcoholic beverages than its devil-haunted neighbors in North Alabama. Deprived of liquor to sweeten their shore leaves, sailors preferred almost any port to Mobile. Knowing this, Mobile leaders had long urged local option, and, when this was defeated, some of the more enterprising undertook to provide for their city's needs.[40]

In two days federal agents seized ten thousand quarts of illegal liquor, valued at more than $100,000. Unable to store such a heavy cargo on the weak floors of the Federal Building, agents placed it in an alley, surrounded by electrically charged barbed

---

[38] Birmingham *News*, March 28, 1924.
[39] New York *Times*, July 31, 1923; Snell, "The Ku Klux Klan in Jefferson County," 67.
[40] Sellers, *The Prohibition Movement in Alabama*, 120.

wire and guarded by a patrol armed with sawed-off shotguns. Flashing red lights played over the forbidden fruit. District Attorney Aubrey Broyles announced that the campaign to dry up Mobile would be the most thorough since the advent of national prohibition.[41]

Shortly before Christmas, a federal grand jury indicted 117 prominent Mobilians, including Chief of Police P. J. O'Shaughnessy, County Commissioner Dr. A. G. Ward, and Frank W. Boykin, a wealthy businessman whom Mobile would later honor with long tenure in Congress. All were charged with conspiracy to bribe District Attorney Broyles. In retaliation they contended that the district attorney had attempted to bribe them. When Broyles, at his own request, was temporarily relieved of duty, the Department of Justice announced that a special assistant attorney would be assigned to the case.[42]

Unable to find an aggressive Republican prosecutor in overwhelmingly Democratic Alabama, Attorney General Harlan Fiske Stone and his assistant, Mabel Walker Willebrandt, asked Hugo Black, who had so vigorously prosecuted prohibition violators in the Girard cases, and as solicitor of Jefferson County, to handle the government's case. Twenty-one attorneys represented the defendants in what the Birmingham *News* described as "one of the bitterest legal conflicts in Alabama history."[43]

"The only real soldier, in times of peace, is the man who walks in obedience to the law," Prosecutor Black told the court. The government, he said, expected to show that the defendants, who claimed to be engaged in "bona fide grocery business, bona fide palace market, bona fide restaurants, were in reality engaged in bona fide bootlegging." The trials, enlivened by occasional dramatic moments, consumed most of April and May, 1924. Black charged that Boykin had been a close associate of Mal Daugherty,

---

41 New York *Times*, November 19, 26, 1923; Mobile *Register*, November 23, 1923.
42 Mobile *Register*, December 19, 1923.
43 Frank, *Mr. Justice Black*, 36–37; Birmingham *News*, April 2, 14, 1924.

brother of the disgraced former Attorney General Harry M. Daugherty. A man who once served as secretary to Police Chief O'Shaughnessy admitted that he had been a "fixer" between the chief and bootleggers. Feelings in the courtroom became so tense that two defendants engaged in what newspapers described as a "fistic encounter," and spectators were searched for concealed weapons.[44]

Midway through the trials, Black dropped conspiracy charges against some defendants, including Boykin and Ward, on grounds of insufficient evidence. Hugh Sparrow, a reporter who daily covered the trials for the Birmingham *News*, called the move "a clever maneuver" to strengthen the government's case against the remaining defendants. On May 22, in what Sparrow described as a "holiday-like atmosphere," convictions were handed down for eleven men, including O'Shaughnessy, and the biggest case ever heard in Mobile federal court was over. The "rum trials" or "booze trials," as headline writers nicknamed them, had occupied front-page space for months in the newspapers of Mobile, Montgomery, and Birmingham; and the name of Special Prosecutor Black, resolute avenger of law and the drys, was known in all corners of Alabama.[45]

To coal miners and the rank and file of laboring men, also, Hugo Black was a dogged fighter on whom they could depend if their rights were threatened. Since 1919, when Governor Kilby described convict leasing as "a relic of barbarism . . . a form of human slavery," sentiment had grown in Alabama to abolish the practice. The Kilby legislature approved a plan for the state itself to operate certain coal mines where convicts would be used as miners, but costs had proven prohibitive. However, in 1923 the proposal was revived. Black, serving as president of the Alabama Prison Reform Association, protested that Alabama should not go into the business of mining coal. By selling convict-mined coal to the identical operators from whom the mines had been leased,

[44] Birmingham *News*, April 29, May 2, 8, 1924.
[45] *Ibid.*, May 10, 22, 1924.

Alabama would be giving some operators a decided advantage over others and "striking at the wage scale of the free miner," Black wrote Governor Brandon. Furthermore, he pointed out, convicts would lose their right to sue in state courts in cases of injury or death due to negligence. "Taking away from an injured convict his right of recovery is so cruel and inhuman that I do not believe you, as their representative, will tolerate it," Black wrote.[46]

Willie Morton, the convict kept at work in the mines twenty-two days beyond his prison sentence, had been Black's first legal client in Birmingham. In January, 1925, when Black was a successful and well-known damage suit lawyer, he pleaded the cause of another Negro convict before the United States Supreme Court. Henry Lewis, while working in the mines, had been seriously injured in an accident which he claimed had been caused by negligence on the part of the company. Black persuaded Justice Edward T. Sanford, responsible for the Fifth Judicial Circuit, to place the case of *Lewis* v. *Roberts* on the high court's docket *in forma pauperis*, offering to argue it without compensation if the court would assume incidental costs.[47]

Lewis v. *Roberts* involved a minor statute rather than a constitutional issue, but Black believed that Henry Lewis, though poor and disabled, was entitled to a hearing before the nation's highest court if he were the victim of injustice. A lower court had awarded Lewis four thousand dollars damages, but the company, before paying him, declared bankruptcy. When Black filed a claim against the company's estate, a federal district court ruled that, under the Bankruptcy Act, the company was liable only for debts owed to those with whom it had contracts. Henry Lewis, a convict, had no written contract. Black presented Lewis' claim to Chief Justice William Howard Taft and Associate Justices Joseph McKenna, Oliver Wendell Holmes, James C. McReynolds,

---

[46] Birmingham *Age-Herald*, December 28, 1923; Moore, *History of Alabama*, 816; Tindall, *The Emergence of the New South*, 213.

[47] Stephen Parks Strickland, (ed.), *Hugo Black and The Supreme Court* (Indianapolis, 1967), xxiii-xxv.

George Sutherland, Pierce Butler, Louis D. Brandeis, Edward T. Sanford, and Willis Van Devanter.[48]

Evidently the sharp, enterprising, but little-known Birmingham lawyer could convince the high court as well as Alabama juries, because the justices returned a unanimous verdict in favor of Henry Lewis. Twelve years later, when Black succeeded to Van Devanter's seat, he would find Justices McReynolds, Sutherland, Butler, and Brandeis, all of whom had heard the Lewis case, still on the high court. Except for Brandeis, the older justices would seldom again be so readily won by the arguments of Hugo Black.[49]

While Black was in Washington, Birmingham newspapers were filled with accounts of Klan activities and rumors about the future plans of Senator Underwood. Casting about for more sinners to punish, Klansmen took it upon themselves to burn crosses before three houses of prostitution and to close down a dance hall, with the Chief Klavalier announcing from the bandstand: "There will be no more dances in this hall on account of immorality—that's final." E. Y. Leech, editor of a new Birmingham newspaper, the *Post*, was bold enough to protest that masked men should not be doing the work of police. "Of course," wrote Leech, tongue in cheek, "we presume that all this raiding is done by those who have never tasted a drink, never carried a gun, and never broken any law."[50]

When Public Safety Commissioner W. B. Cloe said he welcomed outside aid "of whatever nature" to help rid the city of immorality, it began to dawn on Birmingham how deeply the Klan had infiltrated its police force. Members of Robert E. Lee Klan ardently endorsed higher pay for Birmingham policemen, most of them Klansmen. "Law and order," the Klan proclaimed piously, "can be maintained in the community only by . . . an adequate and well-paid police department." Masons, too, had close ties with the Invisible Empire. At a Birmingham Klan initiation in 1924, the speaker estimated that 1,125,000 Masons were Klan members because they realized that "the Klan's ideals were iden-

[48] *Ibid.*   [49] *Ibid.*
[50] Snell, "The Ku Klux Klan in Jefferson County," 80–83.

tical with their own." Hundreds of Birmingham citizens had observed Christmas Day, 1923, by attending a special showing in the Masonic auditorium of D. W. Griffith's spectacle, "The Birth of a Nation."[51]

Sporadic floggings in 1924 caused little excitement, but an epidemic of whippings in March of the next year aroused a furor in Birmingham. A railroad oiler, who dug a tunnel under the lavatory of a grammar school so he could peep at the girls, was briefly arrested and released. When he returned to work, a band of two hundred unmasked men abducted him. The oiler was still missing five days later and rumors circulated that he had been castrated. An Italian grocer, accused of selling whiskey and keeping his store open on Sundays, was severely beaten by masked men. Another Italian, bound over to a grand jury on charges involving a young boy, was abducted and whipped. Masked men, using pine saplings or leather straps, whipped a Negro grocer, a sixty-year-old white doctor, and another white man, whom they accused of letting his wife support him.[52]

Why, demanded the *Post*, had no floggers been arrested? Even if some of the flogging victims were guilty of serious and unpleasant offenses, "haven't we police officers and prosecutors and courts to handle them?" Mob violence, the editor warned, was bad for business and a threat to lawful government. Agreeing that floggers had injured "the good name" of Jefferson County, the *News* declared: "Either we have a civilized community, or we haven't . . . and it is time we found out." But the pastor of South Highlands Methodist Church consoled his flock with the thought that "you don't hear of the 200,000 good people who were not flogged and didn't flog anybody."[53]

Other clergymen, encouraged by the press, spoke more boldly. Methodist ministers resolved formally to condemn "these outrages as repugnant to every sense of decency and justice." The pastor of the First Christian Church said "a city where floggings prevail will carry forever the mask of disgrace." A Baptist preacher admitted

[51] *Ibid.*, 66–69, 73–74.   [52] *Ibid.*, 85–88.
[53] *Ibid.*, 88–90.

that he had a high regard for the Klan, "but if this is their method of doing business, I am ready to change my opinion." Sheriff Shirley, whose Klan affiliation was open knowledge, felt compelled to call on citizens to help apprehend floggers. Although neither grand nor petit juries had responded to calls for punishment of floggers, Judge Fort again charged a grand jury to look into twelve cases. The *Post* implored jurymen to "prove that law is still supreme in Jefferson County." [54]

The grand jury, meeting in this highly volatile atmosphere, heard testimony from several flogging victims, and actually indicted seven men, charging them with violation of Alabama's statute against "white-capping," or assaults by masked bands. But the first accused flogger to come to trial was found "not guilty." Gradually charges against the others were dropped, the public lapsed back into apathy, and there were no more flogging indictments in 1925. [55]

With Birmingham agitated over floggings, the Klan pursued other causes, peaceful but no less threatening. The *T.W.K. Monthly* advertised for boys, aged twelve to eighteen, "white, Protestant, Gentile, native-born Americans and of good, moral, Christian character" to become junior Klansmen. The order also displayed an interest in schools, making an abortive effort in 1925 to gain control of the Birmingham Board of Education. To do so, it sought to replace with its own candidate a board member who had voted against allowing the Klan to hold meetings in Phillips High School. The Klan was reported to be behind a campaign to remove the principal of Woodlawn High School, a widely respected educator and a Jew. When the school board voted 3–2 against the Klan, pandemonium broke out in a council chamber packed with Klansmen and sympathizers. The attempt to control public education and oust the Jewish principal had failed. In 1925 there were limits to Klan power in Birmingham. [56]

---

[54] *Ibid.*, 89–91.   [55] *Ibid.*, 92–94.

[56] *T.W.K. Monthly*, II (February, 1925), 25; Snell, "The Ku Klux Klan in Jefferson County," 94–97.

Police Commissioner Cloe, a member of the school board who voted for the Klan's candidate, felt moved to comment: "I say the Klansmen are a good bunch of men, or they wouldn't be knocked so much. Take that raid on the Brookside dance hall. I say God bless them. It may be your sons or your daughters who are going to hell. . . . They say Ku Kluxers don't want Jews to teach. I never heard that, but I will say that if we want Christ and the Bible in our schools, then we must have Christ-like people to teach." [57]

In mid-May, 1925, two significant real estate transactions attracted interest in Birmingham. The Klan announced its purchase of the Birmingham Athletic Club, which it planned to renovate into "one of the largest and most comfortable assembly places for klansmen in the South." In Washington Senator Underwood let it be known that he and his wealthy wife had bought Woodlawn, a Virginia showplace overlooking the Potomac within sight of Mount Vernon. The historic Georgian mansion had been built at the turn of the nineteenth century on land originally belonging to George Washington. His purchase of Woodlawn intensified rumors that Underwood was about to announce his retirement. [58]

Before making his decision irrevocably, Underwood came home in a forlorn hope that political winds might shift in his favor. He and Republican Vice-President Charles G. Dawes spoke in Birmingham's municipal auditorium against the Senate's cherished rule of unlimited debate, which Underwood said gave a few men, or one man, the power to block majority will. In Montgomery, Underwood told an audience that he favored a cut of 15 percent in the maximum surtax, a figure even below that proposed by Treasury Secretary Andrew W. Mellon. Commented the New York *Times*: "Always independent, Senator Underwood has now linked himself with Senator [Carter] Glass, of Virginia, in a program of tax reduction diametrically opposed to the plan of Democratic leaders." If Underwood sought renomination, the *Times* predicted that he would meet with formidable opposition from organized

[57] *Ibid.*
[58] Birmingham *News*, May 15, 1925; New York *Times*, May 16, 1925.

labor and "radical elements." From a friend in South Alabama, Underwood heard the disheartening news that the Klan had added many members in that area. J. Miller Donner wrote, "I look for them to oppose you actively. They are already opposing you."[59]

More than a year before the primary and without waiting to hear the senator's decision, candidates began to announce for Underwood's seat. The best-known entrant was Thomas E. Kilby of Anniston, elected lieutenant governor in 1914 and governor in 1918 with the ardent support of dry and anti-Catholic voters. At the end of his term in 1923, Kilby, by improving schools, prisons, highways, and welfare services, reducing indebtedness and equalizing taxes, had forged a record of business progressivism. Commending him, the Birmingham *News* said Kilby's greatest contribution as governor had been his determination to "uphold the majesty of the law," an obvious reference to Kilby's action in calling out the state militia to compel arbitration in the coal strike of 1920–1921. When the former governor announced his Senate candidacy, the *Age-Herald* thought that "the Alabamian who goes to the Senate will have to defeat Kilby." Another early aspirant was James J. Mayfield, a former state supreme court justice and ardent Underwood supporter, whose entry set off fresh rumors of the senator's withdrawal.[60]

To the surprise of many political observers, Hugo L. Black, whose only previous elective office had been that of county solicitor, also announced his ambition to succeed the storied Underwood, who had served almost thirty years in House and Senate. Black's supporters told the press that he would have a "progressive platform that will appeal to the forward-thinking citizens of Alabama, and will be in line with the ideals exemplified by his private and public life." The *News* admitted that the new candidate had

[59] Birmingham *Age-Herald*, May 29, 1925; New York *Times*, June 14, 1925; J. M. Bonner to Oscar W. Underwood, June 23, 1925, in Oscar W. Underwood Papers.
[60] Birmingham *News*, June 7, 1925; New York *Times*, June 14, 1925. For a study of Kilby's governorship, see Emily Owen, "The Career of Thomas E. Kilby in Local and State Politics" (M.A. thesis, University of Alabama, 1942).

built up a large statewide following in recent months by prosecuting the Mobile rum trials.[61]

"I've got an idea I'd like to run for the Senate," Black had confided to his former partner David J. Davis. When Davis cautioned
that a senator's ten-thousand-dollar salary would be far less than
his current earnings, Black unconcerned, brushed aside the subject
of money. Dr. Sterling J. Foster, his father-in-law, reminded Hugo
that he was still unknown in many parts of Alabama. In seeking
to replace Underwood, he would be ignoring the usual political
stepladder of state office and boldly aiming to capture one of the
three top elective jobs that Alabama had to offer. Josephine Black,
who had little inclination for political life, did not press her objections because she was sure that her husband could not win.
Even devoted Hazel wondered if Uncle Hugo could possibly be
elected. Only the Ashland *Progress*, destined to be Black's one
supporting newspaper, was foolhardy enough to predict, in a burst
of local pride, that the "gifted and distinguished native son" of
Clay County would be an easy winner.[62]

On July 1, 1925, Underwood bowed out. In his own handwriting, he informed Victor H. Hanson, publisher of the Birmingham *News* and Underwood's close acquaintance and advisor for
twenty-five years, "When my present term expires, I shall retire
from politics." After more than a quarter of a century in public
life, his economic conservatism had estranged Underwood from
other national leaders of his party, and the vagaries of the 1920s
had alienated him from rude, new political forces in Alabama.
At sixty-three he was a casualty of his presidential ambitions,
which had led him to open defiance of the Klan, and likewise the
victim of a streak of stubborn liberality which had prompted him
to oppose prohibition and organized intolerance. The New York
Times noted with admiration that Underwood had no "gift of

---

[61] Birmingham *News*, June 7, 1925.
[62] Sholis, "One Young Man"; Birmingham *Post*, August 13, 1937; Davis,
Uncle Hugo, 18; interview with Justice Hugo L. Black, Washington, D.C., September, 1966.

hokum with which to move multitudes" and had never made a rabble-rousing speech. The Birmingham *News* agreed that the senator "never sought to arouse the passions or to play upon the prejudices of the people."[63]

Other newspapers were dismayed by Underwood's departure. The Gloucester, Virginia, *Gazette* said that he had been "drummed out of public life to furnish a triumph for prejudice and intolerance." The Chattanooga *Times* blamed the "demoralizing dangers" of the direct primary. Under the old system of electing senators in state legislatures, the Knoxville *Sentinel* commented, Underwood might have remained in the Senate indefinitely. Frank R. Kent, Washington correspondent for the Baltimore *Sun*, said waspishly that the only person who would profit by Underwood's retirement would be Alabama's other senator, J. Thomas Heflin, because "the contrast between [Heflin] and his colleague will not be quite so marked as before." The New York *World* deplored Underwood's retirement as abandoning Alabama "to the Heflin-Bryan type, a lamentable retrogression."[64]

But the public career of William Jennings Bryan, Underwood's perennial enemy, was also drawing to its close amid the heat and perfervid controversy of the Scopes trial. On July 26, 1925, exhausted by his verbal battles with Clarence Darrow, Bryan died in Dayton, Tennessee. The news, within a single month, that Bryan was dead and Underwood would retire alerted Democrats that the faces of new leaders would be seen in their party as the old guard passed. Contemplating Underwood's forthcoming departure from the Senate, the New York *Herald-Tribune* wondered: "Where will Alabama be able to find his equal?"[65]

---

[63] Birmingham *News*, July 1, 1925; New York *Times*, July 2, 1925; August 30, 1925.
[64] These quotations are from newspaper clippings in the Oscar W. Underwood Papers.
[65] *Ibid.*

VI

⊓⊔⊓⊔⊓⊔⊓⊔⊓⊔⊓⊔⊓⊔⊓⊔⊓⊔⊓⊔⊓⊔⊓⊔⊓⊔⊓⊔

A Pee-Wee Challenges the Royal Bankheads

One month after announcing his Senate candidacy, Hugo Black wrote a brief letter to J. W. Hamilton, Kligrapp, or secretary, of Robert E. Lee Klan No. 1. "Dear Sir Klansman," he scrawled in his own hand. "Beg to tender you herewith my resignation as a member of the Ku Klux Klan, effective from this date on. Yours, I.T.S.U.B., Hugo L. Black." Dated July 9, 1925, the letter was written on the stationery of James Esdale, who, in recognition of his zeal, had been promoted from Cyclops of Robert E. Lee Klan to Grand Dragon for the Realm of Alabama. The initials before Black's signature stood for "In the Sacred, Unfailing Bond." [1]

Guarded about his personal affairs, bound by his Klan oath, and perhaps slightly ashamed, Black had not mentioned his membership even to such close friends as Albert Lee Smith and Ben Ray. Now, in a deliberate act of political strategy, he resigned as secretly as he had joined almost two years before. The Klan was still chary of its members openly seeking political office. If Black's affiliation should become known during the campaign, many voters, particularly Jews and Catholics, would be alienated. Years later Grand Dragon Esdale would recall that he had suggested to Black: "Give me a letter of resignation, and I'll keep it in my safe

---

[1] A photograph of Black's letter of resignation was published in the New York *Times*, September 13, 1937, accompanying a résumé of an article by Ray Sprigle, originally published in the Pittsburgh *Post-Gazette*.

against the day when you'll need to say you're not a Klan member." By resigning, Black had all the advantages of Klan support and none of the disadvantages of membership. But also he had placed in Esdale's hands indisputable proof that he had been a Klansman.[2]

More than forty years after the campaign of 1926, Esdale would reminisce about the era when he had been boss of 148 klaverns and more than 80,000 Alabama Klansmen. The onetime Grand Dragon had fallen from his political pinnacle to the lowly estate of a bail bondsman, whose business was posting bail so that poor clients, mostly blacks, could be released from jail to await their trials. Recalling his heyday, Esdale would relish telling visitors to his dingy office how he had gone about making voters acquainted with a candidate who had never run a statewide race. He arranged for Black to spend six months speaking at klavern meetings on topics of general interest. One topic, Esdale insisted, had been anti-Catholicism. As the primary neared, Esdale's strategy called for Black to make political speeches in courthouse squares and public meetings, while Klansmen mingled quietly with the crowd and whispered the word that this was their candidate.[3]

Black also employed personal techniques, honed in the race for Jefferson County solicitor. To reach lonesome farmhouses and drab, one-street towns in the clay hills, pine barrens, and Black Belt, he invested in two automobiles, one for southern Alabama and one for the northern region. Boarding a cindery day coach in Birmingham, he would munch a box lunch as the train lumbered along or pass the time profitably by introducing himself to fellow passengers. Arriving at the little station where he had parked his Overland Whippet, he would set out over unpaved roads, dusty or muddy according to the season. Residents of Coffeeville, a small town near the Mississippi border, were startled and pleased when

[2] Interviews with James Esdale, Birmingham, January 10, 1967; Albert Lee Smith, Birmingham, September 10, 1969, and Ben Ray, Birmingham, February 11, 1967; New York *Times*, September 13, 1937.
[3] Interview with James Esdale, Birmingham, January 10, 1967; Snell, "The Ku Klux Klan in Jefferson County," 11–12, 125.

this senatorial candidate rolled into town, in spite of the rough roads which isolated them from the rest of their state. Touring Alabama by automobile in the mid-1920s was often unpleasant and sometimes actually perilous. Mildred Black never forgot one stormy night's ride with her uncle over the narrow, winding route between Ashland and Sylacauga, Hugo searching for the roadbed when flashes of lightning illuminated the rain, and Mildred struggling to operate the manual windshield wipers. On such a road Pelham Black had met his death many years before.[4]

Arriving in a county seat, Black made promptly for the courthouse square, shaking the hands of all voters from probate judge, to checker players under the shade tree, to men in overalls lounging on the steps. Not in vain had he spent a boyhood enamoured of rural politics. On Wednesday and Sunday nights, the "noted Bible student" often spoke to church meetings and, afterward, slept at the home of any farmer who invited him. By February, 1926, Black's Overland Whippets had stirred the dusty roads of fifty-seven counties. Of a typical, whirlwind visit, the Abbeville *Herald* reported: "Judge Hugo Black, of Birmingham, who is a candidate for the U. S. Senate, was in Abbeville a few hours Tuesday. Mr. Black is a delightful fellow, an aggressive campaigner, and has the nucleus of a following down this way that might easily grow into formidable proportions."[5]

The Abbeville editor, a shrewd observer of his community, sensed a trend yet unnoticed by more sophisticated Alabamians, who took it for granted that the major Senate contenders would be Thomas E. Kilby of Anniston and John H. Bankhead, Jr., of Jasper. Bankhead aspired to carry on the traditions of his father, John Hollis Bankhead, an old Confederate soldier who had represented Alabama in House and Senate from 1886 until his death in 1920, and of his brother William, already in the House of Rep-

[4] Interviews with Albert Lee Smith, Birmingham, September 10, 1969; George Bentley, Birmingham, October 1, 1969; Davis, *Uncle Hugo*, 64–66.

[5] Interview with Albert Lee Smith, Birmingham, September 10, 1969; Abbeville *Herald*, February 11, 1926; "Investigation by Headlines," *Time*, XXVI (August 26, 1935), 16.

resentatives and building a reputation that would lead him to the speakership. Kilby, prosperous steel manufacturer, former lieutenant governor, and governor; and Bankhead, corporation attorney, coal mine operator, and scion of a wealthy political dynasty, regarded the governor's chair and seats in Congress as fiefs reserved for Alabama's leadership class. It was mildly annoying to Kilby, Bankhead, and Judge Mayfield that Hugo Black should be so presumptuous as to poach upon these exclusive preserves.

Opening his formal campaign, Kilby concentrated his fire on Bankhead. He knew little about Black, he told his audience, except that he had been a police court judge, county solicitor, and prosecutor of prohibition violators. "This record," he said condescendingly, "could hardly be considered as wide enough to warrant his elevation in one step from his law office to the U. S. Senate." To Cash M. Stanley, associate editor of the *Age-Herald*, Mobile *Journal*, Mobile *News-Item*, and Montgomery *Journal*, the candidacy of brash upstarts like Black smacked of class warfare. Black would attempt to draw class and religious lines, Stanley wrote, and "will be designated as the avowed seeker after the Ku Klux Klan vote and . . . his friends are justified in claiming he has most of it." Devoted Hazel Black, campaigning for her uncle in the little town of Montevallo, was told by a merchant: "I'm sorry to say this, Miss Hazel, but I can't vote for a man who tries to arouse one group against another."[6]

As candidates mounted opening sallies, Klansmen in Birmingham inaugurated the election year of 1926 with a spate of activity. Jefferson County, which had spawned the Alabama Klan, now had a network of klaverns: Robert E. Lee Klan No. 1, oldest and largest; Bessemer Klan No. 2; Industrial Cities Klan No. 31, in the steel suburbs of Ensley and Fairfield; Avondale Klan No. 59; Nathan Bedford Forrest Klan No. 60, and a rival, unaffiliated group, both in Woodlawn. The Jefferson County Klan Associ-

6 Birmingham *Age-Herald*, January 4, 1926; Montgomery *Advertiser*, February 7, 1926; Davis, *Uncle Hugo*, 19.

ation, made up of representatives from each klavern, tried to coordinate the forays of these self-appointed, moral watchdogs.[7]

One January evening, patrons of three Chinese restaurants in downtown Birmingham were startled by the appearance of fifteen Klansmen, some masked and others in business suits, who announced that they had warrants to search for liquor. "You had better sit down and behave yourself until we look this joint over," their masked leader ordered. But when the raiders brought in a quarry of citizens, Chief Deputy Sheriff Henry Hill tore up the warrants, declaring "this whole thing was a mistake." The raids were "illegal and disgraceful," county prosecutors protested.

The Birmingham *Post* snapped: "Things have come to a fine pass . . . when citizens are searched and warrants are served by a man masked in a hood." But Sheriff Shirley had a more tolerant viewpoint: "The Klan has no more desire to see American citizens deprived of their rights than it has to see the immorality continue in these Chinese places. . . . While these men were wrong in entering the places as they did, they were at least defending the morals of the city." Four members of the raiding party, found guilty of disorderly conduct, appealed and successfully overturned their convictions. The proprietors of the Chinese restaurants, anxious to protect themselves from further raids, employed Hugo Black and his partner, Crampton Harris, to look after their interests.[8]

In late March, 1926, Hugo Black, just turned forty, triumphantly returned to Ashland to deliver the formal, opening speech of his campaign. His picture decorated every utility pole in town. Neighbors, friends, and relatives handed out small cards displaying his picture and the words: "Hugo Black, candidate for Democratic nomination for United States Senate from Alabama, will appreciate your support and influence." There were printed flyers for those interested in the candidate's views. Black favored

[7] Snell, "The Ku Klux Klan in Jefferson County," 11–12.
[8] *Ibid.*, 109–15; Birmingham *Age-Herald*, January 6, 1926; Birmingham *Post*, January 9, 1926.

veterans' benefits, prohibition, better roads, cheap fertilizer, and limits on immigration. "The shuffling feet of myriads of immigrants fill my heart with dread," Black proclaimed. Optimistically he predicted that "the day of whiskey is doomed" and assured fellow drys, "I have never in my life tasted whiskey." [9]

On the night before the speech, the Klan rallied around Ashland's courthouse, and its candidate, accompanied by his nine-year-old nephew Robert, drove to the square. Recognizing some of his strangely clad neighbors by their size, stance, or shoes, Robert began to greet them by name, until Uncle Hugo remonstrated that they did not want to be recognized. The boy, puzzled by this strange behavior, did not comprehend why the Klan had chosen this night to meet. [10]

On Saturday, March 20, the day Clay County was to launch its native son for the Senate, an air of excitement, like that preceding a county fair or an all-day sing, possessed Ashland. In wagons, buggies, and cars, Clay County farmers and their families began to gather early around the square. Knowing that Ashland's few restaurants could not supply such a crowd, women brought home-prepared dishes to sell. Plied with chocolate cake by his uncle's supporters, James Black, eight years old, found politics greatly to his taste. He and his sister Lucyle, decked out in sandwich signs proclaiming "Hugo Black for U. S. Senator," marched around and around the courthouse. [11]

Black knew his audience well and addressed himself surely and eloquently to their hopes, passions, and prejudices. Echoing the war cries of Populist orators whose voices had rung in this square almost forty years earlier, he castigated concentrated wealth, power trusts, great railroad systems, high tariffs, and cliques in government. In case his Clay County friends might think that he had departed too far from his rural origins, Hugo assured them that, unlike Kilby and Bankhead, he had never been associated

[9] Davis, *Uncle Hugo*, 65–68; a copy of the campaign flyer is in the Hugo L. Black Papers.
[10] Davis, *Uncle Hugo*, 66.   [11] *Ibid.*

with railroads, corporations, or public utilities. True to his Baptist rearing, he was still a stalwart prohibitionist, but he suspected that his opponents were "politically dry but personally wet." Conscious of the hostility with which these hill country farmers and their counterparts, city laborers, regarded the new Catholic immigrants from southern Europe, he proclaimed, "The melting pot idea is dangerous to our national inheritance." [12]

Primarily Black attacked the views of the man whom he astutely judged would be his principal opponent. John Bankhead, he said, advocated that the government pay for completing Wilson Dam on the Tennessee River near Muscle Shoals, and then sell electric power to private distributors. "If you want your great property at Muscle Shoals given away to the Alabama Power Company, or any other privately owned power company," he shouted, "do not vote for me!" Warming to this theme Hugo, once Ashland's outstanding young orator, declaimed:

The electric lights of Mr. Bankhead's vision do not shine far enough. They do not light my way. The vision I see shines from the sunlight of justice to all and special favors to none. In that vision, I see the whole people of Alabama stand equally clear, whether rich or poor, laborer or capitalist, merchant or farmer. In that vision, I see the farmer free from oppression by great monopolies and giant trusts. In that vision, none stand in the electric spotlight of favor or cower in the darkness and obscurity of denied opportunity. [13]

He was not a millionaire like Kilby, Black said; he was not running, as was Bankhead, on his father's reputation. He appealed to the newly enfranchised rural women to help him strike down the idea "that only the rich and powerful sons of the great can serve their state." In peroration, he cried: "Shall the cup of hope be dashed untasted from the lips of all who have not the boast of ancestral office holders, or sufficient money to hire writers to

[12] There is a copy of the opening campaign speech in the Hugo L. Black Papers.
[13] Birmingham *News*, March 21, 1926.

sing their praises?"[14] To the merchant in Montevallo, the editor of major newspapers, and many another Alabamian, such talk smacked of class warfare. But to old-timers gathered around the square in Ashland that March afternoon, it must have seemed as if Joe Manning, Clay County's gifted apostle of Populism, had come home again.

Reporters for the Montgomery *Advertiser* and Birmingham *News*, in Ashland for Black's speech, agreed that the crowd gave him a "splendid reception" and many pledges of support. Reporter Hugh Sparrow of the *News* described the speech as a "vitriolic attack" on Bankhead. But in an editorial a few days later, the *News* said that, although it did not support Black, he had given a "fine speech" and that the *News*, for one, would not be surprised to see him "fool some of the boys in the race."[15]

Evidently fearing that his remarks about Muscle Shoals might have given offense, Black took pains a few days later to clarify his position. In a letter to the *News*, he emphasized that he had always wanted Henry Ford to manufacture cheap fertilizer for Alabama farmers "at this plant built with the people's money." But, if a decision were needed between the alternative of "making some power company a gift of our property for their private profit, or having the government use it for giving the farmer cheap fertilizer," Black said he would prefer to have the government operate Muscle Shoals.[16]

As senatorial candidates headed into the final weeks of campaigning, their careful calculations and plans were upset by the entry of a fifth contender. "Breck" Musgrove, from Bankhead's hometown of Jasper, filed his intention on April Fool's Day, 1926, the final date for qualifying. The entrance of Musgrove, Alabama's foremost knight of prohibition, a friend to labor, and a man who had helped the Klan scare Oscar Underwood out of politics, threatened to attract votes heretofore conceded to Black. In years

[14] Opening campaign speech, Hugo L. Black Papers.
[15] Montgomery *Advertiser*, March 21, 1926; Birmingham *News*, March 21, 25, 1926.
[16] Birmingham *News*, March 23, 1926.

The family of William La Fayette Black, on the porch of their home in Ashland, Alabama, about 1892. Left to right, Orlando, Robert Lee, William La Fayette Black, Hugo, Martha Black, Daisy, Ora, Vernon, Pelham.

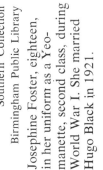

Josephine Foster, eighteen, in her uniform as a Yeomanette, second class, during World War I. She married Hugo Black in 1921.

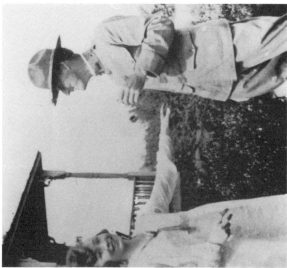

Captain Black, home on furlough, visits his Ashland relatives. With him is a niece, Grace Black, daughter of his older brother, Robert Lee.

Hugo Black, University of Alabama Law School graduate, 1906.

Klansmen appeared
openly on Birmingham
streets in the 1920s.

Birmingham News

Birmingham News

Photograph of a purported meeting of Robert E. Lee Klan Number
One, of which Black was a member.

Black used this photograph in his 1926 Senate campaign literature.

Hat and books in hand, Senator Black boards the train for Washington, D.C., 1927.

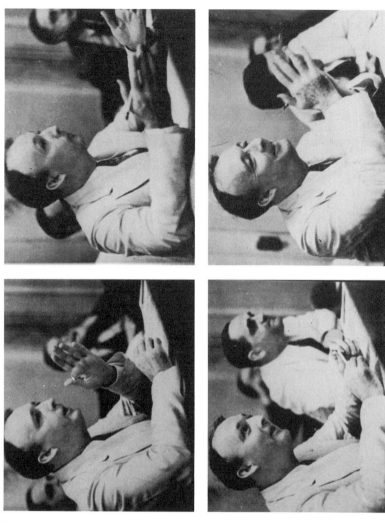

Birmingham News

Chairman Black ca-
joles a witness before
his Senate investigat-
ing committee. To
his left, in the white
suit, is his good friend
Senator Sherman
Minton.

Senator Black and his wife, Josephine, at Birmingham's Terminal Station
before a trip to Washington, D.C.

A happy Hugo Black, Supreme Court nominee, receives the congratulations of Vice-President John Nance Garner.

Colleagues congratulate President Franklin Roosevelt's first Supreme Court nominee, August, 1937. Left to right, Senator Claude Pepper, Black, Senator Sherman Minton, Senator Robert M. La Follette, Jr.

to come, Esdale relished telling the story that Musgrove had come to his office in Birmingham's First National Bank and offered him $125,000 to switch the Klan vote in his favor. Esdale said that he refused, whereupon Musgrove spread the tale that the Grand Dragon had demanded $125,000 as the price of changing candidates. Ben Ray recalled that his friend Hugo confided that he, too, had refused an offer of $125,000 as the price of withdrawal. Whatever financial shenanigans the Musgrove forces may have tried, there was no doubt that the Senate race was a new ball game. The Montgomery *Advertiser* said Musgrove's entry meant, "Look out, money. You're gonna be spent!" [17]

Four of the five candidates, Black, Bankhead, Kilby, and Musgrove, ardently wooed the potent drys and each claimed a share of their allegiance. Only Judge Mayfield was foolhardy enough to advocate local option. If Musgrove were to win blocs of voters, then, he must cut into Black's labor and Klan support. The Montgomery *Advertiser* speculated that Musgrove had little chance to take the labor vote from Black, and that the "organized following which is supporting Mr. Black cannot be swerved from its path," but rumors circulated that a fight was brewing over the Klan vote. [18]

Rival sets of circulars covered the state, each purporting to be the gospel, according to Esdale, on Klan candidates. The earlier circular, allegedly an official document from the office of the Grand Dragon for the Realm of Alabama, appeared genuine enough. It solicited votes for Black, as the only Klansman in the senatorial race, and for Bibb Graves, Cyclops of the Montgomery Klan, for governor. The Grand Dragon requested that these names be read at every meeting and posted in the local klavern. A later circular confused matters by claiming that all senatorial candidates, except Mayfield, were Klansmen. Although there is no evidence that Bankhead and Kilby were members, they certainly did not disavow Klan votes. Refusing to endorse Underwood's stand, Bankhead an-

---

[17] Interviews with James Esdale, Birmingham, January 10, 1967; Ben Ray, Birmingham, February 11, 1967; Montgomery *Advertiser*, April 2, 1926.

[18] Sellers, *The Prohibition Movement in Alabama*, 213; Montgomery *Advertiser*, April 30, 1926.

nounced publicly that he regarded the Klan as a patriotic organization, engaged in good works.[19]

With the Democratic primary only two weeks away, the Birmingham *News* spread the story of Klan infighting by banner headlines on its front page. Imperial Wizard Evans, the *News* reported, had sent his personal representative to threaten Robert E. Lee Klan No. 1 that it must switch from Black to Musgrove or risk losing its charter. M. L. Fox, known as "The Mole" because he specialized in underground maneuvering, reportedly had urged the large Birmingham klavern to support Musgrove in gratitude for his fight against Underwood. But the *News* reported that Esdale had called "the Mole" an imposter, sent by the Musgrove camp, and had refused to budge from his original choice. If Klan votes were pried away from Hugo Black, the *News* predicted that this would be the downfall of Esdale.[20]

Out on the hustings, the five senatorial candidates took no public notice of the Klan's internal quarrel. Only a month before primary day, Bankhead's campaign manager in Anniston confidently reported: "Black's strength seems to be confined to the K.K.K. and the different orders (fraternal) that he belongs to and they all make a big noise as you well know, and for this reason I believe his strength is grossly exaggerated." Considering one another the leading candidates, Kilby and Bankhead set up a series of joint debates, but succeeded only in hurting themselves by swapping political insults. Quick to sense advantage in the situation, Black's supporters hired a mule-drawn dray and Negro driver to parade up and down during a Bankhead-Kilby debate, brandishing the sign: "Bankhead Says Kilby Won't do. Kilby Says Bankhead Won't Do. Both are Right. Vote for Hugo Black!"[21]

[19] Birmingham *Post*, July 2, 1926; Montgomery *Advertiser*, January 4, 1926; Scrapbook of Senator J. Thomas Heflin, Samford University Library.
[20] Birmingham *News*, July 23, 1926.
[21] Montgomery *Advertiser*, June 12, 1926; Joseph J. Willett, Jr., to W. W. Bankhead, July 6, 1926, in Papers of Joseph J. Willett, Sr., and Joseph J. Willett, Jr., Samford University, hereinafter cited as Willett Papers.

With all candidates blaring allegiance to good roads, cheap fertilizer, and some form of liquor control, the campaign, lacking major issues, descended to personalities. Judge Mayfield urged voters to send a lawyer to the Senate and Kilby recommended a businessman. Musgrove implied that the new senator should be a onetime national leader of the Anti-Saloon League of America, and Bankhead thought that he should be a senator's son. Black told blue-collar audiences in rural pockets and workmen's enclaves that the next United States senator from Alabama should be a country boy who spoke their language and understood their problems.[22]

Perhaps to stir up an issue, Black touched off a brouhaha over money, complaining to the Democratic State Executive Committee that his opponents were spending more than $1,000,000 in the senate race, while he stayed within the $10,000 legal limit. Obviously nettled, Bankhead invaded Hugo's stronghold of Jefferson County to strike at what he called the "poor country boy" pose. Black, he said, had earned $30,000 in 1924, not counting the value of his stocks, owned real estate worth $250,000, and in one year alone had paid $20,000 in income taxes. Inspired to one of his rare lively sallies, Bankhead roared: "It would be a great injustice on the part of friends of this 'poor country boy' to reduce him from an annual income of more than $30,000 a year to the $10,000 salary of a senator." Seeing circulars headed "Poor Boy Black is Only Worth Half a Million," Hazel Black was proud to have her relative's success so widely proclaimed and, political tyro though she was, sensed such attacks meant that Uncle Hugo was becoming the man to beat.[23]

If Black's strategy was to focus attention on himself, it succeeded. Kilby and Bankhead, who had once concentrated solely on each other, now turned in chorus upon the outsider in their

[22] Birmingham *Age-Herald*, June 20, 1926; Birmingham *News*, July 12, 14, 18, 1926.

[23] Montgomery *Advertiser*, June 5, 30, 1926; Birmingham *News*, July 31, 1926; Davis, *Uncle Hugo*, 19–20.

race. Black was traversing Alabama "like a prosecuting attorney," Bankhead said, stirring up the people's passions and prejudices and arraying class against class. Both labeled Black a "damage suit lawyer," who "generously" allowed widows and orphans to keep one-half of the judgments he collected in their behalf. "Has he represented the unfortunate on their account or for his own profit?" cried Bankhead. The scion of the Bankhead clan charged Black with capitalizing on his church affiliations and "warming up" the secret orders. "I have never believed," said Bankhead, "that a man should be voted on because he can give a certain sign or grip."[24]

In deserting the high ground and descending to the muddy arena of jibes and name-calling, the former governor and the senator's son were playing word games with a master. Black, whose talent for a rapier retort had won the respect of many a lawyer and the hearts of hundreds of jurors, was in his element, jabbing like a quick, young boxer against older, stodgier opponents. Yes, he acknowledged, he had tried some damage suits. How else could poor men and women afford legal counsel except by offering some lawyer a percentage of the damage award? "I have represented the injured and the broken, the widows and the orphans of men killed beneath the wheels of trains or buried in the falls of rock down in the mines of coal and iron," he told a crowd in Marion. He had as much right to represent these people, Black shouted, as Bankhead had to represent corporations.[25]

To offset Bankhead's claim that he owned real estate worth $250,000, Black offered to sell out for half that amount. When Will Bankhead, speaking for his brother, declared that the Senate was no place for "pee wees and top swimmers," Black told a rally in industrial Bessemer that the Bankheads sought "a line of royal succession." The real question, he said, is "whether the road to

[24] Montgomery *Advertiser*, June 30, August 4, 1926; Birmingham *News*, July 8, 16, 1926.

[25] Birmingham *Age-Herald*, July 31, 1926; Marion *Times-Standard*, August 5, 1926, quoted in Daniel Berman, "The Political Philosophy of Hugo L. Black," 21.

the U. S. Senate shall be paved with gold." In his audience many "pee wees and top swimmers" nodded warm agreement. To Bankhead's charge that he was a "jiner," Black replied: "Yes, I am. I joined the Masons and Knights of Pythias the first meeting after I became twenty-one years of age, and I'm glad of it." But he made no public mention of the secret order from which he had just "resigned." When Bankhead claimed that the majority of the Birmingham Bar Association opposed Black, Hugo good-naturedly replied that it was impossible to get three hundred lawyers to agree on anything. Criticized as being too young for the Senate, he boasted that he would be able to give the best years of his life to public service.[26]

His courtroom experience had taught Black to attack as well as defend. Turning on his critics, he charged that Kilby, an employer, favored admitting more immigrants for cheap labor, and that Bankhead, during a coal strike, once served as a guard against miners. In denying these charges, Kilby and Bankhead only circulated them more widely. Implying that his opponents were political drys but personal wets, Black delighted in this jingle: "There is one little saloon that every man can close, and that is the one that is under his nose." When his opponents, in false humility, claimed that they were running because their friends insisted on it, Hugo boldly declared: "I am running, not because my friends are forcing me, but because I want the job."[27]

As the campaign neared its climax, Bankhead and Kilby helped advertise Black's growing strength by imploring voters to concentrate anti-Black votes on one of them. "Bankhead or Black?" the Bankhead forces advertised daily. Writing to a supporter, John Bankhead admitted that he, Mayfield, and Kilby were competing for the same voters. "Many people," he said, "are waiting to make

[26] Birmingham *News*, July 8, August 4, 1926; Birmingham *Post*, July 8, August 3, 1926; Birmingham *Age-Herald*, July 8, 1926; campaign flyer, Hugo L. Black Papers.

[27] Birmingham *News*, August 4, 1926; Birmingham *Post*, August 3, 1926; Berman, "The Political Philosophy of Hugo L. Black," 22; "Hugo Black," *Newsweek*, II (November 11, 1933), 17.

their decision . . . to find out the strongest man to beat Black." [28]

Black's startling rise from underdog to leading candidate was accomplished without support from the Alabama press and without expensive newspaper advertising. In contrast to Kilby's full-page spreads and Bankhead's frequent, smaller advertisements, Black bought sparsely in the big city papers which opposed him, preferring to spend money on circulars and posters. Bankhead charged that Black, in this manner, did more advertising than any man in the race. Birmingham newspapers plainly indicated favorites by the generosity and bias of their news coverage. Bankhead received the attention of the *News* and the Montgomery *Advertiser*, while the *Post* concentrated on Kilby. Except for headlining the Klan quarrel, there was little mention in Birmingham papers of the local candidate until the *Age-Herald*, late in the race, took note of the fact that Black had spoken at least twice in each of Alabama's sixty-seven counties. In Montgomery, Atticus Mullin, political writer for the *Advertiser*, predicted that Black's chances would rest upon the number of first-choice votes he received, since he would be the second choice of only a few. Seeking to make an asset of his lack of newspaper support, Black assured an audience at Birmingham's Jefferson Theater: "I don't seem to be able to get much in the papers . . . but on August 11 my name will be on the front pages of every paper in Alabama." At one rally, to which all Senate candidates had been invited, only Black and Mayfield were present. He was sorry that the other three couldn't make it, Black said, but the audience could take comfort in the fact that "your next U. S. Senator is on this platform." Plainly he did not refer to Judge Mayfield. [29]

Like Black, Musgrove got short shrift from large Alabama newspapers, but the New York *Times*, assessing the Alabama political scene, mentioned both Klan candidates prominently.

[28] John H. Bankhead to Joseph J. Willett, Jr., July 20, 1926, in Willett Papers.
[29] Birmingham *News*, July 31, 1926; Birmingham *Age-Herald*, July 27, 1926; Montgomery *Advertiser*, June 30, 1926; interview with Charles Harrison, Birmingham, October 28, 1969.

Estimating that the Klan was split fifty-fifty between Black and Musgrove, the *Times* said that Black, in an effort to hold Klan votes, had devoted part of his final campaign to attacking New York Governor Alfred E. Smith. Only two days before the primary, the *News* quoted a representative of the Klan's Imperial Kloncillium as claiming that the entire Klan strength had been swung to Musgrove. "Backed by no political machine, aided by no paid workers," Black advertised.[30]

At the end of the long campaign, there was little left to do except file statements of expenses and await the voters' decision. All candidates claimed to have stayed within the legal limit; Black posted a figure of $6,510.86, including depreciation of $600 on two automobiles. Months earlier he had confided to his friend Hugh Locke that he planned to spend on his campaign the $10,000 fee which he received for handling the divorce case of a prominent Birmingham woman. As the summer of 1926 drew to a close, there were many diverting topics for conversation: the deaths of Rudolph Valentino and of Robert Todd Lincoln, the remarkable news that John D. Rockefeller had attained his eighty-seventh birthday, and that Gertrude Ederle had swum the English Channel. But Alabamians talked of little else that August except who would be their new governor and senator. Few even paused to reflect upon a poignant photograph of Senator Oscar Underwood and his wife Bertha departing for a European vacation.[31]

In the humid dusk of August 10, a crowd gathered early before the *Age-Herald* building where returns would be posted. As votes rolled in from all parts of Alabama, one bystander exclaimed excitedly to the spectator next to him: "I'd like to be the first to congratulate you, Senator Black!" As Atticus Mullin had predicted, Black piled up an overwhelming lead of first-choice votes. Bankhead, Mayfield, Musgrove, and Kilby, in that order, trailed far

[30] New York *Times*, August 9, 1926; Birmingham *News*, August 8, 1926.

[31] Birmingham *Age-Herald*, August 6, 8, 1926; Birmingham *News*, August 5, 1926; Montgomery *Advertiser*, August 7, 1926; interview with Hugh Locke, Birmingham, February 14, 1967.

behind. When finally tallied, the vote was: Black, 71,916 first choice, 12,961 second choice; Bankhead, 49,841 and 14,024; Mayfield, 34,325 and 16,668; Musgrove, 30,454 and 12,598; and Kilby, 29,123 and 10,587. Those who kept track of political feats were amazed to note that, of sixty-seven counties, Black had carried forty-two; Bankhead, nineteen; Mayfield four; and Kilby and Musgrove one apiece.[32]

Although Black won only 32 percent of the votes, there was no runoff. Under the primary rules adopted in 1915, the candidate polling the highest total of first- and second-choice votes won. Commenting on the voting pattern, the *News* noted that Black was not the choice of a majority or even of one-third of the voters, but that he polled a much larger vote than any one of his opponents. He was "the beneficiary of divided allegiance," the *News* explained, although conceding that the "brilliant, young attorney" had run a remarkable race. "Mr. Black will be heard from in the Senate, make no mistake about it," the *News* predicted. The Montgomery *Advertiser* was frankly disappointed that an "untried man" had been chosen Democratic nominee over such experienced opponents, but said that Black, "the darling of the Klan," had held on to his votes in spite of Musgrove. Because Kilby, Mayfield, and Bankhead drew their support from the same group, it was inevitable, the *Advertiser* contended, that "a fiery go-getter of the Black type should overwhelm them." The majority of Alabamians "do not regard Mr. Black as the most suitable man to succeed the great Underwood and they voted against him," said the *Advertiser*, "only they divided their votes." Analyzing his brother's defeat, Representative Will Bankhead wrote a Washington friend: "He [John] was up against one radical [Black] and a Ku Klux [Musgrove]." Senator Tom Heflin heard from a brother in Alabama that "the KKK stuck to Black and Graves too all over the state. . . . It is in every way best for you in a political way that Black won." The Opelika *Daily News* credited the victories of Black and

---

[32] Childers, "Hugo Black, Always an Alabamian"; *Alabama Official and Statistical Register* (1927), 358–59.

Graves to their personalities, "coupled with certain affiliations which proved to be very formidable attachments."[33]

Black's 84,877 votes came uncannily close to the estimated total of Klan membership in Alabama in 1926. The New York *Times*, which had predicted a fifty-fifty split between Black and Musgrove, explained that many observers viewed Black's victory as a repudiation by the Alabama Klan of its national organization. In a four-man contest for the gubernatorial nomination, Colonel Bibb Graves, Cyclops of the Montgomery Klan and a paid Klan lecturer for the preceding four years, won over his three opponents. Graves, like Black, had pitched his campaign to plain Alabamians, forging a similar coalition of veterans, drys, labor, and the Klan, and advocating that corporations be taxed to provide funds for education and social services. The outcome of the primary, forecast the *Times*, might hurt the presidential hopes of Alfred E. Smith because Alabama would send a Klan-controlled delegation, opposed to Smith, to the 1928 Democratic convention.[34]

In a telephone interview shortly after the primary, Grand Dragon Esdale exuberantly told an *Age-Herald* reporter: "We licked 'em clean in the election and I've got 150,000 men who will scratch Al Smith's name if they put him up for President next year." Dr. Lewis C. Branscomb, president of the Alabama Anti-Saloon League, rejoiced that Hugo Black, "bone dry and born dry will take a wet man's place in the Senate," and agreed with Esdale that the primary showed Alabama's attitude toward "that wettest of all aspirants . . . Al Smith." Esdale, evidently deciding that he had been imprudent, later repudiated his statement, but Alabama Republicans were already happily anticipating 150,000 bolters from Democratic ranks and the possibility of carrying the state

[33] Birmingham *News*, August 15, 1926; Montgomery *Advertiser*, August 13, 1926; Opelika *Daily News* quoted in Birmingham *Post*, August 18, 1926; William B. Bankhead to Kenneth Romney, August 18, 1926, in W. B. Bankhead Papers, Alabama Department of Archives and History, Montgomery, hereinafter cited as W. B. Bankhead Papers; R. L. Heflin to J. Thomas Heflin, August 12, 1926, in Papers of J. Thomas Heflin.

[34] New York *Times*, August 11, 1926; August 12, 1926; Moore, *History of Alabama*, 769–70.

for the first time since Reconstruction. In order not to offend potential allies, Republicans, at their state convention, beat down an anti-Klan resolution.[35]

Men who bet on long shots cleaned up on Black. Two of his friends made sizable sums, Black recalled years later, by taking four-to-one bets against him early in the campaign and later taking one-to-two bets for him. Judge Joseph J. Willett, an ardent Bankhead supporter, noted ruefully that he paid off bets of twenty-five dollars on Bankhead over the field, a hat that Black would not run ahead of Bankhead, twenty-five dollars that Black would not win, and a hundred dollars that Bankhead would win. On an Anniston street corner, a Kilby supporter told Black's friend Albert Lee Smith that he couldn't understand how Calhoun County could vote for a man like Black when its native son, Kilby, had been one of Alabama's finest governors. At Smith's suggestion, they asked two men in overalls how they had voted. They voted for Hugo Black, the workmen said, because they knew him personally and had shaken his hand, but they had never laid eyes on their fellow townsman Kilby. In Birmingham, Smith joshed a prominent corporation lawyer who lamented Black's election, "I thought all you corporation lawyers voted for Black to get him out of Alabama." [36]

Three weeks after the primary, Klansmen from over Alabama converged upon Birmingham for a joyous victory celebration, starting with a parade of three thousand masked and hooded men through downtown streets. Titans from three provinces, fifty cyclops, and Imperial Wizard Hiram Evans came for the occasion. On the stage of the great klavern on Twentieth Street, Grand Dragon Esdale introduced Governor-nominee Graves and Senate-nominee Black to the cheering crowd as "the men who have been chosen by the Klansmen of Alabama to come out into the forefront." Dr. A. D. Ellis of Tuscaloosa presented Graves and Black

[35] Birmingham *Age-Herald*, August 15, 1926; Birmingham *News*, August 14, 1926; Birmingham *Post*, August 17, 18, 1926.
[36] Interviews with Hugo L. Black, Washington, September, 1966; Albert Lee Smith, Birmingham, September 10, 1969.

with "grand passports" of Klandom, explaining: "They are good as long as you are good, and your fellow Klansmen of the Realm of Alabama will put the date of retirement upon those certificates for you when you yourselves make such action necessary and not until then." Black's passport read:

Grand Klan of the Invisible Empire. Knights of the Ku Klux Klan, Realm of Alabama. To all exalted cyclops, greetings. The bearer Kl. Senator Hugo L. Black is a citizen of the invisible empire and to him is given this Grand Passport that he may travel unmolested throughout our beneficent [sic] domain and grant and receive the fervent fellowship of Klansmen. By this authority you will pass him throughout the portals of your klavern to meet with klansmen in konklave assembled. Signed and sealed this 2nd day of Sept., 1926. James Esdale, Grand Cyclops.[37]

Accepting the gold card, Black told his enthusiastic audience:

This passport which you have given me is a symbol to me of the passport which you have given me before. I do not feel that it would be out of place to state to you here on this occasion that I know that without the support of the members of this organization I would not have been called, even by my enemies, the "Junior Senator from Alabama." I realize that I was elected by men who believe in the principles that I have sought to advocate and which are the principles of this organization.[38]

He digressed briefly from politics to pay tribute to his old teacher Judge Hiram Evans, father of the Imperial Wizard. "Some of the greatest inspirations that have come into my life," he told Dr. Evans, "I received from your father."[39]

To the assembled Klansmen, Black said:

I desire to impress upon you as representatives of the real Anglo-Saxon sentiment that must and will control the destinies of the Stars and

---

[37] Birmingham *News*, September 2, 1926; New York *Times*, September 15, 1937.

[38] Ray Sprigle of the Pittsburgh *Post-Gazette* published in 1937 a stenographic transcript of the klorero proceedings. The New York *Times*, September 15, 1937, reprinted the transcript.

[39] *Ibid.*

Stripes, that I want your counsel. . . . My friends, I thank you. I thank the Grand Dragon. He has stood by me like a pillar of strength. . . . The great thing I like about this organization is not the burning of crosses, it is not attempting to regulate anybody—I don't know, some may do that—but, my friends, I see a bigger vision. I see a vision of America honored by the nations of the world.

In a profuse burst of oratory, Black concluded:

I thank you, friends, from the bottom of my heart. With my love, with my faith, with my trust, with my undying prayer that this great organization will carry on sacredly, true to the real principles of American manhood and womanhood, revering virtue of the mother of the race, loving the pride of Anglo-Saxon spirit—and I love it—true to the heaven-born principles of liberty which were written in the Constitution of this country, and in the great historical documents, straight from the heart of Anglo-Saxon patriots, with my love and my faith, and my hope and my trust, I thank you from the bottom of a heart that is yours.

A Klan stenographer, taking down the speech, noted: "Great applause."[40]

That evening Klansmen paraded again through Birmingham and convened in the Municipal Auditorium to hear Imperial Wizard Evans. Marchers removed their hoods as they entered the auditorium, wrapped them in newspapers, and took their seats. Evans spoke of preserving America for Americans, enforcing the Monroe Doctrine, and avoiding the World Court. He proposed to place control of the government in the hands of "native-born, white, gentile, Protestant Americans," such as Klan members. Still crowing over the downfall of Underwood, Wizard Evans said the senator had betrayed southern traditions. "That is all this great fight is," Evans told his robed audience and hundreds of other Alabamians gathered around their home radios. "It is a question of white supremacy."[41]

As customary the November general election was anticlimax. Republicans contented themselves with nominating Judge Ed-

[40] *Ibid.*
[41] *Ibid.*, September 16, 1937; Birmingham *News*, September 3, 1926; Birmingham *Age-Herald*, September 3, 1926.

mund H. Dryer, a Birmingham lawyer and federal referee in bankruptcy, to offer token opposition to the Democratic nominee for senator. Dryer had come to public notice as umpire between unions and operators in the postwar coal strike, in which he had ruled that operators were under no obligation to reemploy union labor. On November 2, 1926, Hugo Black was elected United States senator by 91,843 votes over 21,712 for Dryer.[42]

Although his Klan support was widely known, there was little awareness in Alabama at the time, except within the secret confines of the Klan, that the new senator-elect had actually been a member. His opponents dared not raise the question publicly, and Black had no need to bring his formal letter of resignation out of Esdale's safe. The possibility that this letter and his extravagant speech of gratitude would come back to haunt him seemed remote. Esdale, after his triumphant outburst, subsided into his accustomed role of a behind-the-scenes manipulator, whose influence upon his state was little known to many Alabamians. Submitting to a rare press interview just before the November, 1926, election, the Grand Dragon, all innocence, told a reporter for the Birmingham *News,* "I never meddle in politics."[43]

[42] *Alabama Official and Statistical Register* (1927), 391–92; Moore, *History of Alabama,* 474.
[43] Birmingham *News,* October 31, 1926.

VII

Let Al Smith
Tote
His Own
Skillet

Flamboyant "Cotton Tom" Heflin, string tie askew and face flushed, brought to a stemwinding close a sample of the southern oratory for which he was famous. If his Senate colleagues sometimes found Heflin a windy bore, tourists in the gallery tittered appreciatively at his expansive gestures, frock coat, and folksy stories. After his speech on December 26, 1926, the Alabama senator performed the routine duty of presenting to the Senate a certificate of election for his new colleague, Hugo Black.[1]

Midway through President Coolidge's term, control of the Senate had slipped from the hands of Old Guard Republicans and now hung in a precarious balance of power. Of fifty-six Republican senators in 1924, only forty-eight remained, and these included such undependable mavericks as George Norris of Nebraska; Hiram Johnson of California; William E. Borah of Idaho; and Robert M. La Follette, Jr., of Wisconsin. Across the aisle sat forty-seven Democrats. Henrik Shipstead of Minnesota was the lone Farmer-Laborite. It was particularly galling to Republicans that every Democratic senator who faced an expiring term in November, 1926, had been reelected with the sole exception of the old titan Oscar W. Underwood, who had "voluntarily" retired under circumstances well-understood by his friends in the Senate. Rumor had reached Capitol Hill that Underwood's replacement was a

[1] *Congressional Record*, 69th Cong., 2nd Sess., 738.

forty-year-old hillbilly lawyer, placed in their midst by the Ku Klux Klan in another example of the unfortunate effect of the Seventeenth Amendment upon the membership of their exclusive club.[2]

Compared to most of his newly elected colleagues, the junior senator from Alabama was indeed politically green. David I. Walsh, an Irish-Catholic Democrat who had upset former Republican National Chairman William Butler in Coolidge's own state of Massachusetts, was a former senator and had twice governed his state. Robert F. Wagner, who had replaced Republican James W. Wadsworth, Jr., in New York, had been a judge of the New York Supreme Court and Democratic leader in the state senate. Carl Hayden of Arizona, Elmer Thomas of Oklahoma, Alben W. Barkley of Kentucky, and Millard F. Tydings of Maryland were all moving over from seats in the House. John James Blaine was a former Progressive governor of Wisconsin; Smith W. Brookhart, Iowa Republican, had previously served in the Senate; and William S. Vare had been Republican boss of Philadelphia.[3]

Surveying this promising crop of new senators, the New York *Times* could find little to say about Hugo Black, whose name it placed at the end of the list. Noting that Black had been supported by the Klan, the *Times* added: "He is a bundle of activity, physically and mentally. As a lawyer, he has made a specialty of looking after the interests of workmen injured in the Alabama mines."[4]

Although the Seventieth Congress officially came into being March 4, 1927, Coolidge made no move to call it into extraordinary session and it did not meet until December. The President's leisurely pace was fortunate for Black. Conscious of his complete lack of experience in legislative service, he set about to make himself master of the Senate's rules and traditions. Smarting perhaps from the realization that his colleagues regarded him as

[2] John D. Hicks, *Republican Ascendancy, 1921–1933* (New York, 1960), 129; Charles Michelson, *The Ghost Talks* (New York, 1944), 184.
[3] New York *Times*, December 12, 1926.
[4] *Ibid.*

a rube and upstart, he sought to fill the gaps in his education left by Ashland College and a two-year law course. He would become conversant with the political theories of Montesquieu, Rousseau, Locke, Spencer, and Veblen; he would enrich his speeches with a knowledge of Herodotus, Thucydides, Plutarch, Seneca, and Cicero; particularly he would absorb American history, beginning with the records of the Constitutional Convention.[5]

In the thirteen months between his election and the taking of his senatorial oath, Black read more voluminously than ever before in his life. In the torpid Coolidge administration, he found few demands on his time other than workaday favors for his constituents. Underwood accompanied him to pay his respects to the President, and Coolidge, in turn, invited the freshman senator from Alabama to one of his famous White House breakfasts. Upon his doctor's advice, Black even began what was to be a ten-year abstinence from tennis, his favorite form of exercise.[6]

Adjusting to life in Washington, the Blacks also retrenched from the forty thousand dollars which Hugo had made in his last year of full-time law practice to the ten-thousand-dollar salary of a senator. He announced that he was buying "on the installment plan" a modest house in the District of Columbia. Josephine, with her talents for decorating and gardening, was to transform it into a home of charm and distinction, befitting a senator and his family. This task and the needs of her two young sons would absorb most of Josephine's energy, leaving little time for capital social life. At twenty-seven, she was the youngest senate wife, and the prettiest. Noting the seating arrangement at one formal dinner party, Josephine, once yeomanette third class, was amused to see that she now outranked an admiral.[7]

On December 5, 1927, opening day of the Seventieth Congress, Vice-President Charles G. Dawes administered the oath of office

[5] Frank, *Mr. Justice Black*, 45–47.

[6] *Ibid.*; Montgomery *Advertiser*, April 19, 1952; "Black, A Man of Parts: Senator, Investigator and Individual," *Newsweek*, VII (March 14, 1936), 21.

[7] "Black, A Man of Parts," 21; "Mrs. Hugo Black—Glamor in Politics," Birmingham *News*, April 4, 1941.

to the new member from Alabama. Senator Black was appointed to the committees on claims, interstate commerce, and military affairs. Within less than two months, his quick, incisive manner of speaking, so persuasive to Alabama jurors and voters, would impress fellow senators too, if not always favorably, at least with cautious respect. But Josephine, wearing a new dress bought for the occasion of her husband's maiden speech in the Senate, was dismayed to find that there were only four listeners lounging at their desks. "These new senators are always bores," an elderly doorman explained.[8]

While Hugo Black was studying Montesquieu in Washington, Imperial Wizard Evans and Grand Dragon Esdale were battling to hold Alabama in the political grip of the Klan. As a result of the 1926 Democratic primary, Alabama, one political observer wrote, was "the most completely Klan-controlled state in the union." Its candidates and friends occupied the governor's chair, both senate seats, and hundreds of minor state and county offices. But when Charles C. McCall, attorney general-elect and a Montgomery Knight, announced that he planned to appoint Esdale as assistant attorney general, he created such a furor that the Grand Dragon withdrew his name. In Montgomery the Klan suffered another setback when its candidate for mayor was soundly defeated by William A. Gunter, who had challenged the voters to decide whether they wanted "to be governed by an invisible empire or by a government of, for, and by the people."[9]

"Our governor," as many Klansmen referred to Bibb Graves, was to be inaugurated in Montgomery on January 27, 1927. To demonstrate its triumph, the Klan offered to adorn the occasion with the biggest parade of hooded men in the history of the South. When the inaugural committee refused to permit them to use Montgomery streets, Klansmen blamed Mayor Gunter. "Can

[8] *Congressional Record*, 70th Cong., 1st Sess., 3, 481–82.
[9] Charles N. Feidelson, "Alabama's Super Government," *Nation*, CXXV (September 27, 1927), 311–12; Arnold S. Rice, *The Ku Klux Klan in American Politics* (Washington, D.C., 1962), 47, 65–66.

any 2 x 4 mayor of a Jew-owned town prevent 50,000 per cent Americans from jubilating over our great victory?" Nathan Bedford Forrest Klan No. 60 of Birmingham, complained to Montgomery Klan No. 3.[10]

The issue aroused a two-hour debate in the Montgomery klavern. McCall urged that the Klan be allowed to demonstrate on the state-owned capitol grounds, but Cyclops Graves opposed such a public admission of his political debt. Before even taking their oaths, two of the Klan's top beneficiaries appeared to be at odds. On inauguration day Imperial Wizard Evans and Grand Dragon Esdale sat on the speakers' platform in mute testimonial to their role in Graves's victory.[11]

If Alabama were the Eden of the Klan, as one writer put it, combining the Bible and Greek mythology, apples of discord were ripening. Disputes within its klaverns were widely publicized in the Birmingham *Age-Herald*, while a Grand Tribunal of twelve members sought vainly to discover who was leaking the secret proceedings of their order. Many Klansmen had been rebuked for drinking, the *Age-Herald* revealed, and attendance at klaverns had sharply declined. At one heated meeting, a knight proposed that "in order to govern not only the United States but the whole world," the Klan adopt harsher punishments for those it considered traitors. Evidencing a growing distaste for flogging, another urged fellow members to follow the nonviolent methods of Christ.[12]

But thousands of Klansmen were not yet satiated with the dark excitement which tarring, feathering, branding, and flogging lent to their drab and otherwise insignificant lives. In January four unmasked men administered twenty-five lashes to a Birmingham man whom they accused of drunkenness, wife beating, and of having improper relations with his invalid daughter. In March the

[10] Snell, "The Ku Klux Klan in Jefferson County," 136–37.

[11] *Ibid.*, 139–40.

[12] Feidelson, "Alabama's Super Government," 311; Snell, "The Ku Klux Klan in Jefferson County," 143–51.

German proprietor of a small Birmingham grocery was beaten with heavy sticks, and his sixteen-year-old daughter lashed with tree branches. His assailants told the grocer that they were punishing him for allowing his daughter to work in a store patronized by Negroes. Outside an Oneonta church one Sunday night in June, robed Klansmen seized mildly intoxicated Jeff Calloway, an illiterate white orphan in his early twenties, and whipped him with an automobile fan belt until his back was covered with welts and his legs blue with blood clots. As they lashed, they drank the whiskey which they had found on their victim.[13]

The brutal flogging of Jeff Calloway stirred Alabamians as had no other case since Dr. Dowling was whipped in 1922. "Alabama must not be crucified upon a cross of masked malevolence," the *Age-Herald* declared, chiding Governor Graves and Senators Black and Heflin for not crying out long ago "against this hideous rule of lash and mask." Dr. Henry M. Edmonds, prominent minister of a wealthy Presbyterian congregation in Birmingham, called on its members to fight, as Jesus would, against the "whipping of a defenseless boy by a group of men." Dr. J. E. Dillard, pastor of the largest Baptist church in the city, suggested that an antimasking law would uncover "evil-minded persons" in Klan ranks. In Montgomery another Presbyterian minister, Dr. H. V. Carson, exhorted his congregation: "Let us say to the midnight riders: you shall not crucify the freeborn men of America upon a fiery cross."[14]

O. D. Street, Grand Master of the Masons, and Dr. L. C. Branscomb, president of the Alabama Anti-Saloon League, denounced mob violence, but the majority of Protestant ministers kept a prudent silence concerning the Calloway case. Years later Grand Dragon Esdale would estimate that 51 percent of these ministers and of their congregations were Klan members or sympathizers.[15]

[13] Snell, "The Ku Klux Klan in Jefferson County," 156–58; Birmingham *News*, June 26, 1949.
[14] Snell, "The Ku Klux Klan in Jefferson County," 157–62.
[15] *Ibid.*, 162.

Public pressure was intense enough, however, to compel the attention of Governor Graves and Attorney General McCall. The governor ordered an investigation of the Calloway case, and McCall demanded, without success, that Esdale give him the names of those responsible. On a sultry August day in Oneonta, law officials brought to trial, charged with the assault on Calloway, seven Klansmen from Tarrant City, a working-class suburb of Birmingham. One week later a Blount County jury, convinced by the testimony of a Klan informer, convicted the first defendant, Eugene Doss, and sentenced him to eight to ten years in prison for kidnaping. After a second defendant received the same sentence, the remaining five pleaded guilty to assault and battery and were sentenced to six-month jail terms and five-hundred-dollar fines. These were the first convictions for such offenses in forty years, and the first ever definitely linked with the Klan. "The Bastille of Masked Tyranny has fallen," crowed the *Age-Herald*.[16]

Henry D. Clayton, federal judge for middle and northern Alabama, openly called upon law-abiding men to sever their relations with the Klan. It was a suggestion which many eventually would heed, but not until 1927 ended in a crescendo of violent incidents. While her children watched in horror, a divorced farm woman who had married a divorced neighbor, was thrashed by Klansmen, who then presented her with a bottle of vaseline for her wounds. A Greek commercial artist had his back "beaten to a poultice" because the Klan objected to his marriage. In Birmingham a Negro was thrashed by masked men until he agreed to sell for nine hundred dollars property valued at six thousand dollars. The property was later purchased by W. J. Worthington, a prominent local realtor and onetime Cyclops of the Avondale Klan. Attorney General McCall urged Alabamians who had been "lashed or terrorized by mobs" to report these incidents to his office and within a few days seventy cases were catalogued. Twenty floggings, some

---

[16] Feidelson, "Alabama's Super Government," 311; William G. Shepherd, "The Whip Hand," *Collier's*, LXXXI (January 7, 1928), 8–9, 44–45; Snell, "The Ku Klux Klan in Jefferson County," 164–67.

fatal, were reported from Crenshaw County. McCall said a virtual "reign of terror" existed there.[17]

In the first year of the Graves administration, relations between the governor and his attorney general worsened. Politically ambitious himself, McCall broke openly with the Klan and with Graves. He resigned publicly from Montgomery Klan No. 3, announcing: "I do not feel that I should follow longer behind the banner and under the leadership of those leaders of the Klan in Alabama who . . . are placing themselves at war with constituted authority." Seeking to prosecute the Crenshaw County floggers, McCall found himself blocked at every turn. In a courtroom at Luverne, he dramatically withdrew one hundred two flogging indictments, declaring that a "mysterious power" was interfering with his prosecutions. Governor Graves, it soon appeared, was the "mysterious power" McCall had in mind. The attorney general made public a letter from Esdale to Ira B. Thompson, Exalted Cyclops of the Crenshaw County Klan, in which the Grand Dragon promised to persuade Governor Graves to hamstring McCall.[18]

Rising opposition to the Klan was reflected in two stalemates in the Alabama legislature. An antimask law was defeated by the "bed-sheet block" in both houses. Klan opponents, in their turn, blocked a bill to widen the libel laws and muzzle press criticism of the Invisible Empire. One newspaper observer charged that Governor Graves had worked behind the scenes to defeat the antimask law and to pass the libel law, thereby revealing "the extent to which he speaks for the Klan."[19]

Late in the fall, outraged protests from such prestigious daily newspapers as the *Age-Herald* and the *Advertiser*, spokesmen for the twin Bourbon interests of industry and Black Belt agriculture,

[17] Snell, "The Ku Klux Klan in Jefferson County," 168; Shepherd, "The Whip Hand," 8–9; Birmingham *News*, June 26, 1949.

[18] Rice, *The Ku Klux Klan in American Politics*, 65–66; Shepherd, "The Whip Hand," 44–45; William G. Shepherd, "The Whip Wins," *Collier's*, LXXXI (January 14, 1928), 10–11, 30, 32.

[19] Moore, *History of Alabama*, 774–77; Feidelson, "Alabama's Super Government," 311–12.

galvanized public opinion in Alabama against the Klan. Lawlessness, the newspapers sensed, was an Achilles heel where the Klan might be mortally wounded, and its surging political movement of small farmers from the hill country and workmen in the cities, reminiscent of Populist days, turned back. At a statewide meeting of Alabama's Baptists, heretofore neutral, tolerant, and even friendly toward the Klan, it was evident that the newspapers were winning converts. "Punishment inflicted outside the law is anarchy," the Baptists declared, urging Christians to repudiate publicly acts of masked violence. "The Baptists have spoken the sentiment of the state . . . and recreant public officials may as well take sober note of it," rejoiced the Mobile *Register*. "Too long," the *Age-Herald* reminded Baptists, "have church organizations allowed some ministers to toy and flirt with the pleasures of the mask." Small-town papers began to join the city press in demanding that floggers be punished.[20]

In a desperate attempt at a show of strength, Esdale called for a "victory parade" of 50,000 Klansmen in Birmingham on December 15 to celebrate two acquittals in the Crenshaw County flogging trials. But even the elements seemed against him. Delayed by heavy rain, the parade finally straggled forth. A reporter counted 828 men, 103 women, four children, two automobiles, and one float labeled "Poor, Little Orphan" and bearing a live reenactment of the Calloway flogging. Drivers of other cars, impatient at the traffic snarl, honked angrily at the thin line of marchers. After a short dinner meeting with his drenched followers, Esdale left Municipal Auditorium without commenting to newspapermen. But it was obvious that the "victory parade" had fizzled and that his organization, so potent only a year earlier, was on the skids.[21]

Membership in the Alabama Klan slipped from a total of 94,301 members in 1926 to 10,431 by the end of 1927. One

[20] "Alabama's Floggers," *Literary Digest*, XCV (October 29, 1927), 11–12; "Moral Lashes for Alabama Floggers," *Literary Digest*, XCV (December 17, 1927), 32.
[21] Snell, "The Ku Klux Klan in Jefferson County," 182–83.

explanation for this startling drop was advanced by a writer who came to Alabama to describe the goings-on for *Collier's*. Floggers had grown "wilder with each dose of degenerate excitement they enjoyed," he said; having started to whip for immorality, they went on to punish for personal grudges, and then for mere criticism. The next step, he predicted, would be to use the whip in a socialistic, even Bolshevistic class fight against the well-to-do. Perhaps the same suspicion had begun to grow in the minds of those white-collar Alabamians who had joined the Klan for political expediency. Finding themselves outnumbered by thousands of combustible, working-class members, recruited in the great drive for ten-dollar memberships, respectable, middle-class members began quietly to slip away.[22]

As Hugo Black was serving his first weeks on the Senate floor, it was evident that Klan alliance, instead of being an asset, might become a political liability. The story even circulated in Alabama of a minor public official who arranged a masked and hooded raid on his own house, complete with fiery cross, to convince the neighbors that he was now anti-Klan. Early in 1928 Wizard Evans instructed his followers that henceforth no mask or visor was to be worn with Klan regalia, a voluntary move interpreted as an effort to forestall state and city antimasking laws. "The beginning of the end," trumpeted the Montgomery *Advertiser*.[23]

But, confronting the prospect of Catholic Al Smith as Democratic nominee for the presidency, the Invisible Empire mustered its dwindling ranks for one last fight. "The time has come," Hiram Evans exhorted, "when the legions of the Klan must go forth to battle for the preservation of that Americanism so dear to every loyal son of the Republic. . . . Shortly you will receive a Fiery Summons from the Exalted Cyclops of your Klan. . . . The Imperial Wizard is depending on you to answer that call." To impress Montgomery Klansmen with the gravity of the mission

---

[22] Birmingham *News*, November 23, 1930; Shepherd, "The Whip Hand," 44–45.
[23] New York *Times*, September 13, 1937.

ahead, Esdale, on a visit there, donned his sword and his best white uniform, embroidered with a dragon. Because of the Klan's waning popularity, it was rumored that its candidates for seats on Alabama's delegation to the Democratic convention of 1928 would be disguised as prohibitionists and supported also by the 150,000 members of Alabama's Anti-Saloon League.[24]

At first there was every indication that Hugo Black would be in the front ranks of the anti-Smith campaign in his state. In September, 1927, he and Heflin attended a Montgomery conference at which plans were laid to elect a delegation opposed to Smith. Governor Graves, on his way to Washington in January, wrote Heflin that he was coming "to talk with you and Hugo on the political situation in Alabama, with special reference to the delegation to be selected in May." Black told the Mobile *Register* in March that Smith's views were in direct conflict with the "settled opinion of the Democratic South" and that his nomination would disrupt the party.[25]

Shortly before Alabama's Democratic primary, Esdale instructed the Klan's Washington representative, W. F. Zumbrunn, to confer with Heflin and Black on whether both senators should come home to make political speeches. Noting the national attention which Heflin was attracting by his virulently anti-Catholic speeches on the Senate floor, the Grand Dragon advised that "it might be well to leave our Senators in a position that they can act at a time when most needed. . . . and be fresh on the subject." Under Heflin's congressional frank, thousands of copies of his Senate speeches were mailed to Alabama voters from Klan headquarters in Birmingham. As the Grand Dragon had anticipated, Alabama Democrats, in a relatively quiet campaign, elected a twenty-four-member delegation unanimously opposed to the nom-

[24] Letter from Imperial Wizard Hiram W. Evans to members of the Ku Klux Klan, January 18, 1928, in Papers of J. Thomas Heflin, University of Alabama Library, Tuscaloosa, hereinafter cited as Heflin Papers; Hugh Dorsey Reagan, "The Presidential Election of 1928 in Alabama," 96–98.

[25] Reagan, "The Presidential Election of 1928 in Alabama," 73, 105; Bibb Graves to J. Thomas Heflin, January 27, 1928, in Heflin Papers.

ination of a Catholic Yankee who, said the *Alabama Baptist*, was "as wet as the ocean."[26]

More than a year after his election and five months after his first appearance on the Senate floor, Black was still regarded by many of his colleagues as somewhat of a pariah, tainted with his Klan association and unworthy to succeed the respected Underwood. His principal tormentor was a fellow Democrat, William C. Bruce of Maryland, wet, Catholic, and a caustic critic of the lower South. Black and Bruce engaged in several, sharp exchanges, with Bruce pointedly expressing his regret that Alabama was no longer represented by "a man worthy to hold a seat in any parliamentary assembly in the world, Senator Oscar W. Underwood . . . a true statesman." Confronting Black in May, 1928, Bruce declared bluntly: "I have heard it said that the junior senator from Alabama owes his seat in the Senate to the Ku Klux Klan." With the verve of his courtroom days, Black retorted, "That is absolutely untrue." He added quickly: "I got all the Ku Klux votes I could get . . . and all the Catholic votes I could get, and all the Jew votes I could get, and all the Baptist votes I could get, and all the others, and I have no apology to make for it, and I am here representing them."[27]

Inevitably Black was also associated in the minds of many with the buffoonery and fanaticism of his colleague "Tom-Tom" Heflin, who toured the country in 1928 thundering against the "Roman candidate" and urging voters to choose between "the God of white supremacy or the false god of Roman social equality." To Black's embarrassment, Heflin jousted with feisty Joe Robinson of Arkansas, Smith's Protestant running mate, over the Catholic issue, and threatened Robinson that he would be tarred and feathered if he campaigned in Alabama. Robinson took their dispute to a caucus of Democratic senators and won a thumping

[26] James Esdale to W. F. Zumbrunn, April 14, 1928, in Heflin Papers; James Esdale to J. Thomas Heflin, April 14, 1928, in Heflin Papers; Sellers, *The Prohibition Movement in Alabama*, 196.
[27] *Congressional Record*, 70th Cong., 1st Sess., 8815.

thirty-three-to-one vote of confidence. Senator Black prudently abstained from voting.[28]

As the date of their party's June convention neared, Alabama Democrats contemplated the dilemma which seemed certain to confront them: whether to desert the party or risk supporting a wet, Catholic candidate. J. Bibb Mills, superintendent of the Alabama Anti-Saloon League, advised Representative William B. Bankhead: "You will have to vote for [Smith] or be awfully sick, and as you are on the ticket yourself, you will hardly be sick . . . because you will have to be mighty busy . . . to keep a Republican from being elected." Heflin's brother warned the senator: "Don't say that you will not vote for Smith if he is nominated, for you must keep your record straight as a Democrat." Hugo's relatives, the Lee Blacks, talked it over one moonlit summer evening on their porch. "Hugo's ruined," his brother opined. ". . . he can't make the people of Alabama swallow New York's whiskey governor . . . the South will never vote for a Catholic for President." But heedless of southern protests, Democrats at Houston gave Smith an overwhelming endorsement.[29]

In the laboring man's community of Wahouma near Birmingham, Klansmen lynched an effigy of the Democratic nominee, plunged a knife in its throat until red mercurochrome poured out and dragged it around the hall for knights to kick. The Women's Christian Temperance Union of Alabama pledged that a million women would vote against Smith. Meeting in Birmingham on August 13, dissident Democrats formed the Alabama Conference of Anti-Smith Democrats, led by Hugh A. Locke, prominent attorney and member of the Democratic State Executive Committee, and Horace Wilkinson, Klansman and chairman of the state boxing commission. Edmund W. Pettus, chairman of the Dem-

[28] Tindall, *The Emergence of the New South*, 245; J. Mills Thornton, III, "Alabama Politics, J. Thomas Heflin, and the Expulsion Movement of 1929," *Alabama Review*, XXI (April, 1968), 83–112.

[29] J. Bibb Mills to William B. Bankhead, April 9, 1928, in W. B. Bankhead Papers; John T. Heflin to Senator J. Thomas Heflin, May 24, 1928, in Heflin Papers; Davis, *Uncle Hugo*, 22–23.

ocratic State Executive Committee, warned them sternly that Democrats who voted against their party's presidential nominee would be barred from the Democratic primary of 1930, when a governor would be chosen and Tom Heflin himself would come up for reelection.[30]

Sensing a golden opportunity to garner Alabama's electoral votes for Herbert Hoover, Republicans entered the confused political arena. In an obvious bid for the votes of Democratic bolters, Republicans listed twelve widely known Democrats as their candidates for presidential electors. Rumor had it that the names had been chosen at headquarters of the anti-Smith Democrats, with Hugh Locke and Horace Wilkinson nodding approval. "The Klan Names Them," declared the *Advertiser*, charging that Judge O. D. Street, Republican state chairman and Masonic leader, was "walking arm-in-arm with Grand Dragon Esdale and Dr. L. C. Branscomb, president of the Anti-Saloon League—another Catholic-hating organization. They are out to nail Al Smith to a crucifix while Judge Street holds the torchlight."[31]

Genuinely fearful that their state would deposit its electoral votes in the Republican column for the first time in Alabama history, regular Democrats rolled out the ancient heavy artillery of racism. W. B. Oliver, chairman of the Democratic campaign committee, appealed to would-be bolters to think before joining a party that "brought the black heels of the ex-slaves down on the throats of Southern men and women following the War Between the States." Another loyal Democrat chanted: "You ask what my party stands for. My answer it shall be. It stands for the rule of white men. White men like you and me." For good measure, he added: "God meant Alabama to be a white man's state, and the Democratic party has been His instrument in keeping it a white man's state." Judge B. M. Miller reminded voters that, although

[30] Rice, *The Ku Klux Klan in American Politics*, 87; Sellers, *The Prohibition Movement in Alabama*, 199–210; Reagan, "The Presidential Election of 1928 in Alabama," 206–10. Pettus was a grandson of Senator Pettus.

[31] Sellers, *The Prohibition Movement in Alabama*, 202–203; Reagan, "The Presidential Election of 1928 in Alabama," 228–29.

122 Negro delegates helped nominate Hoover, "no nigger helped nominate Al Smith. He was nominated by more than 900 Anglo-Saxons." Republicans fought fire with fire. The slogans "Negro-lover" and "Negro bootlicker" were hurled at Smith in full-page ads and circulars. The Democratic nominee was blamed for mixed marriages and integration in New York.[32]

To further inflame the voters' gut emotions, Democrats, bolters, and Republicans unfurled the tawdry banners of sinful alcohol and religious hatred. If Smith were elected, Republicans and bolters predicted that prohibition would be repealed and the South so overrun with drunken Negroes that "no white person would be safe." To critics of Smith's Catholicism, Democrats retorted that Hoover was a Quaker. They quoted the *Encyclopaedia Britannica* to describe Quakers as having no baptism, formal creed, Holy Sacrament, or regular ministers, and as conscientious objectors who refused to take civil oaths. But when the campaign neared the wire, it was the old rallying cry of white supremacy which rang loudest and most often in dusty courthouse squares of Alabama and saved the day for loyal Democrats.[33]

The major speechmaker for bolters and Republicans was Tom Heflin. Despite his brother's warning and the threat of Democratic Chairman Pettus, Heflin threw out colorful hints that he would bolt. "They have asked me if I could take my crow and eat it," he thundered. "I can. But I cannot eat buzzard served with Tammany sauce." On September 21, egged on by a cheering crowd of five thousand supporters in Montgomery's Cramton Bowl, Heflin laid the fat on the fire. "So help me God, I will vote against Al Smith if they read me out of the Democratic Party and drive me from every Senate committee!" Although he could not know it from the emotional response of the audience, "Cotton Tom" had sounded the death knell of a thirty-year political career.[34]

[32] Hugh Dorsey Reagan, "Race as a Factor in the Presidential Election of 1928 in Alabama," *Alabama Review*, XIX (January, 1966), 5–19.

[33] *Ibid.*

[34] Moore, *History of Alabama*, 782; Sellers, *The Prohibition Movement in Alabama*, 203.

Although all Alabama was stirred by the hottest presidential campaign in its history, two prominent figures remained strangely quiet. "I hear the question asked everywhere," a man from Talladega wrote the Birmingham *News*. "Why do we not hear from Hugo Black in this campaign?" A Birmingham citizen wrote the *Age-Herald*: "How about Senator Black? How about it, Governor Graves? Are you and your regiment of public pieeaters on the hustings doing your bit for the old home state? Or are you and they listening to the whispers of Wizard Evans?" At a Democratic rally in Anniston, a man reported hearing many ask where Hugo Black stood. Speaking to another loyalist rally in Birmingham's Municipal Auditorium, Mabel Jones West, a grandniece of Alexander H. Stephens, vice-president of the Confederacy, declared heatedly: "Since I'm not a United States Senator, I need have no fear of the Ku Klux Klan, and so far as I am concerned, the Ku Klux Klan can go to the devil!" [35]

Black was attempting to walk a tightrope of party regularity without giving offense to his recent supporters, the Klan and the drys. Unlike the feckless Heflin, he took seriously the warning of Edmund Pettus that Alabama Democrats would expel the bolters. With the Klan on the wane, where else would Black find support for his own reelection but within the folds of the regular Democratic organization? Another consideration argued against alliance with the bolters. Powerful Democrats in Washington, who would hand out choice committee seats in the next Congress, viewed the defection of Heflin with extreme disfavor. If a freshman senator were to follow such a defiant course, the doors of opportunity in the Senate would slam shut.

Vacationing in Geneva, Wisconsin, far from the heat of Alabama politics, Senator Black wired the Montgomery *Advertiser* that Smith's views, except on the issue of immigration, constituted "a clarion call to progressive democracy." He deplored making prohibition the dominant issue, thereby creating "a noisy division

[35] Birmingham *News*, October 21, 28, 1928; Birmingham *Age-Herald*, October 28, November 6, 1928.

of wets and drys, submerging party issues of Jeffersonian progress and equal opportunity as opposed to Hamiltonian reaction and special privilege." But beyond this statement, Black dared not venture. The sight of their 1926 protégé actively stumping for a Catholic and a wet would have been more than his Klan and dry friends could have forgiven.[36]

He accepted a place on the Democratic campaign committee, but when Josephus Daniels, who had been Wilson's navy secretary, visited Birmingham in behalf of the cause, the *Age-Herald* noted that Senator Black did not attend the dignitaries' breakfast. Other prominent Democrats, at considerable risk to their own political futures, stumped the state in a frenetic effort to outpoll Republicans and bolters. "Bill, for God's sake, don't make any more speeches for the party," a friend implored Representative William Bankhead. "Let Al Smith tote his own skillet."[37]

Lister Hill, W. B. Oliver, and Henry Steagall, other members of the state's delegation in the House of Representatives; John Bankhead, Lieutenant Governor William C. Davis, and Attorney General McCall exhorted voters to remain safe within the traditional embrace of the Democratic Party. For reinforcement the regulars called in tub-thumping Senator Theodore G. "The Man" Bilbo from Mississippi. Despite Heflin's threat of tar and feathers, Joe Robinson came from Arkansas to lend his voice to the cause. But Hugo Black appeared only once on the speakers' platform that fall, not to endorse Al Smith but to urge Birmingham citizens to support their Community Chest. Years later his friend Ben Ray recalled Black's plight in the 1928 election. "Hugo," Ray said, chuckling, "was really in the middle."[38]

Vowing white supremacy, Alabama's regular Democrats won the state's electoral votes by a narrow margin of 6,971 votes. In Florida, Texas, Tennessee, North Carolina, and Virginia, where

[36] Montgomery *Advertiser*, August 24, 1928.

[37] Birmingham *Age-Herald*, October 17, 20, 1928; letter from S. W. Williams, to William B. Bankhead, October 14, 1928, in W. B. Bankhead Papers.

[38] Birmingham *Age-Herald*, November 2, 6, 1928; Birmingham *Post*, October 22, 1928. Interview with Ben Ray, former chairman of the Alabama Democratic Executive Committee, February 11, 1967.

Democrats were not so energetic and Republicans more numerous, electoral votes went to Herbert Hoover in the first breakup of the Solid South since the end of Reconstruction. As in Populist days, the slim margin of victory in Alabama had been provided by eleven Black Belt counties, which reported heavy majorities for Smith.[39]

When the votes were in, the Montgomery *Advertiser* scolded Graves and Black for their "total indifference and neglect" of a party which had supported them in 1926, although both had been nominated by a minority of Alabama Democrats. In their party's hour of need, said the *Advertiser*, both Graves and Black refused to write a newspaper statement or make a speech urging their friends to support the ticket. Chiding Heflin also for "open hostility," the paper declared: "The hold of the Ku Klux Klan upon these three men was so tight that they could not bring themselves to discharge their plain duty to the Democratic party."[40]

But the Klan did not win Alabama for Hoover. Nor did it begin the resurgence its leaders hoped would result from a Republican victory. Never again did the Invisible Empire wield the political power in Alabama that it displayed when it named the leading Democratic office holders in 1926. Instead, membership and prestige continued to dwindle. Dissension divided its ranks and the depression cut into its dues. The Alabama Anti-Saloon League also began to lose political potency as sentiment grew for revoking the Eighteenth Amendment. These two forces, so influential in launching the career of Senator Hugo Black, were rapidly losing their hold upon the Alabama electorate. In the future Black would have to depend upon the whims of unorganized followers or forge new political affiliations.

Their new young colleague from Alabama puzzled Senate veterans. Underwood's successor was certainly no twentieth century Bourbon, defending the status quo. Obviously he was no "Tom-

[39] *Alabama Official and Statistical Register* (1931), 511–12; Reagan, "Race as a Factor in the Presidential Election of 1928 in Alabama," 19.

[40] Montgomery *Advertiser*, November 5, 18, 1928.

Tom" Heflin, addicted to racist jokes and displays of anti-Catholic spleen on the Senate floor. Almost from the first day that Hugo Black appeared in his seat, he seemed at ease with the complex procedures of the Senate. He was self-assured, even cocky, in floor exchanges with men who had been national figures when Judge Black was handing down five-dollar fines in a dingy, Birmingham police court.

His accent was undeniably southern, but this newcomer, reputed to be a hillbilly, surprised the Senate by displaying a scholar's acquaintance with world history and literary classics. Amid the heat of floor debate, he could momentarily stun an adversary by tossing in an apt quotation from Aristotle, a reference to the French Revolution, or advice from Thomas Jefferson. While Calvin Coolidge napped in the White House, members of the Senate were becoming acquainted with an atypical Southerner, who spoke with the assurance of a Bourbon but the fiery passion of a Populist.

In his first months on the Senate floor, Black occasionally lapsed into the rhythmic prose of his campaign days. On a pleasant day in May, 1928, William Bruce of Maryland, inveighing against the Eighteenth Amendment, provoked Black by remarking that most Southerners voted dry but drank wet. In defense of southern honor, the freshman treated the Senate to a sample of those hypnotic cadences which had so fascinated jurors and voters back home in Alabama:

Let the Senator from Maryland hurl his darts and charges thick and fast. Let him drop his loaded shrapnel into their midst, and still, when the din of the explosion is ended, the people of the South will be there, back in their homes on the hillsides and in the valleys, responding to the same old Anglo-Saxon principle of loyalty to law and decency and government which seems to entitle them to be the particular object of the animadversions of the Senator from Maryland.

I did not know that there was any longer any line which separated the so-called Confederate States from the others. I thought that line had been washed away by the blood of patriots. I thought, when Wheeler and Dewey met together on the battle field, when we were at

war with Spain, and when the boys from the North and the boys from
the South joined hands to fight the battles on the blood-soaked fields
of France, that old lines were gone. . . .

I have no apology to make for being from the "Confederate states,"
as my colleague terms them. I am proud of the fact that I come from
those states. There repose the ashes of my ancestors. When the time
shall come to join the throng across the unknown shore, I hope that
I, too, shall there lie down to rest peacefully under the calm sunshine
of Dixie. Yet these Southern states are mentioned from day to day as
though it is a crime or a disgrace for a man to be a citizen of the South.[41]

After this outburst, Black may have concluded that his Washington audience was too sophisticated for such sentimentality. His
floor manner turned more toward the rapierlike courtroom fencing at which he was a master. Obviously the new Alabama senator
was attracted by the congressional weapon of investigation. As a
young lawyer in the early twenties, Black had followed newspaper
accounts of the Teapot Dome hearings, admiring the tenacity of
Montana's Thomas J. Walsh who had conducted them. In his days
as Jefferson County solicitor and scourge of the Mobile liquor
ring, Black, too, had tasted the satisfaction and notoriety of being
a dogged prosecutor for the public weal. So it was natural that he
should be drawn again to this role, so well suited to one who passionately wanted to defend the little man against his predators.
Senate investigations not only uncovered serious wrongdoing in
public affairs but also focused national attention on the investigator, be he Montana's Walsh or Burton K. Wheeler, or, in years to
come, Alabama's Black.

The first subject to attract Black's crusading eye was the United
States Shipping Board. In an effort to stimulate the flagging American merchant marine, the board was selling war-surplus ships at
bargain prices to private operators. Black sought an investigation.
When Republicans blocked him, he lambasted the agency from
the Senate floor. The board, he complained indignantly, had paid
large salaries to forty-seven lawyers who handled only 258 cases

41 *Congressional Record*, 70th Cong., 1st Sess., 8687–91.

in 1927. "Five reasonably good lawyers," he fumed, could easily manage such a case load; spending the taxpayers' money to employ people who have "nothing to do" was "rank, organized robbery."

Somewhat to their own surprise, a majority of senators found themselves agreeing to amendments offered by this neophyte to limit to ten thousand dollars the salary which the Shipping Board might pay a lawyer, and to cut the board's appropriation for legal counsel so sharply that it could not afford more than ten lawyers. It was a small victory, but the board was to hear much more from Senator Black.[42]

Black's mentor Tom Walsh asked the Senate to investigate the power industry, particularly its efforts to influence public opinion against government power projects. Administration leaders sought to shunt off the investigation to the Federal Trade Commission, a less public arena than a Senate hearing and possibly more congenial to power interests. Although Nebraska's George Norris bluntly told the Senate that such an inquiry would be no investigation at all, the Senate voted to turn the job over to the FTC. Norris noted with pleasure, however, that the newcomer from Alabama, unlike many fellow Southerners, voted for a Senate inquiry. When this was defeated, Black sponsored a successful amendment to open the FTC investigation to the public. It must have occurred to Norris that these were hopeful portents. Perhaps he could win Senator Black's alliance in his long fight for government operation of Muscle Shoals.[43]

But it took time for Black and George Norris to reconcile their views on Muscle Shoals. The Nebraska Progressive visualized a great, government-operated development on the Tennessee River to provide the benefits of cheap, electric power, soil rehabilitation, and flood control to poverty-ridden farmers of Alabama and Tennessee. But Harding and Coolidge preferred to turn over to pri-

---

[42] *Ibid.*, 2423–24.
[43] *Ibid.*, 3029–30; Preston J. Hubbard, *Origins of the TVA: The Muscle Shoals Controversy, 1920–1932* (Nashville, 1961), 219–21.

vate enterprise the government's partially completed dams and two nitrogen plants at Muscle Shoals, built during the World War to furnish synthetic nitrogen for explosives. Their most promising offer came from Henry Ford, who proposed to take a hundred-year lease on Wilson Dam and Dam No. 3, if the government would complete them, and to pay $5,000,000 outright for the nitrate plants which had cost $82,000,000. Although Ford insisted that he wanted to render a public service, Norris and other critics claimed that the automobile magnate sought an "undisguised subsidy" for his private interests. The very possibility that Ford might put his Midas touch on North Alabama and cause a new Detroit to arise launched a real estate boom akin to the Florida Bubble.[44]

On the issue of Muscle Shoals, Underwood had experienced several changes of heart. In the last year of the Wilson administration, he supported the idea of a government-owned corporation to manufacture nitrogen for fertilizer. When his friend Harding succeeded to the presidency, Underwood advocated Ford's offer. But Ford, piqued by the long controversy over his bid, suddenly withdrew it in 1924. With the collaboration of President Coolidge, Underwood introduced a bill to lease the Muscle Shoals facilities to private fertilizer producers. Heflin, who had also been a Ford supporter, allied himself with Underwood. Norris' plan for government operation, Heflin declared, was "socialistic" and "Bolshevistic." In turn, Norris and his followers charged that Underwood was a tool of the "power trust" in general and of Alabama Power Company in particular. All these interests, Norris said, were posing as friends of fertilizer in order to block a government-operated power program. Eventually Norris defeated the Underwood bill.[45]

While campaigning for the Senate, Black had told Alabamians that he favored leasing Muscle Shoals to Ford. If this could not be arranged, he declared that he would rather have it run by the federal government than by the Alabama Power Company. Above all he wanted cheap fertilizer to restore the impoverished soil and

[44] Hubbard, *Origins of the TVA*, 28–47.
[45] *Ibid.*, 16, 48–49, 147–69.

people of his state. Consequently in the first weeks of the Seventieth Congress, he opposed Norris' plan for comprehensive development of the Tennessee and supported a bid by the American Cyanamid Company to take over the property and manufacture fertilizer. The American Cyanamid proposal, Norris retorted, was insincere and another cover-up for private power interests.[46]

In his first major Senate speech, Black employed his considerable talents of persuasion and drama in behalf of what he thought to be the farmers' best interests.

"The farmers are asking for the bread of nitrate," he cried, "and they get the stone of power. . . ."

When the farmer comes in after a hard day's work following a mule on some red-clay hillside and finally puts his tired limbs to rest on an old-fashioned feather bed, he can lie there and pass into dreamland, with the sweet hope and fancy that his children's children's children may someday get fertilizer as cheaply as they are getting it in Germany today. . . . We care nothing for power. . . . I beg and plead with . . . those who really have the interests of the farmers of America at heart, to find something better than a mere experiment for ten years.[47]

But gradually Black and Norris moved toward harmony on Muscle Shoals. They discovered their mutual antipathy to private power interests and sometimes joked about it on the floor. Had the junior senator from Alabama ever known the Alabama Power Company to reduce its consumer prices, Norris would ask innocently. "No," Hugo would thunder, "and that is the reason he does not want to turn over the rest of it [Muscle Shoals] to them for ten years or fifty years." Even the staid *Congressional Record* made note of Senate laughter when Black, in mock horror, asked Norris: "The Senator did not understand me to say we should let the Alabama Power Company have it, I hope." [48]

To win Black and other Southerners, Norris enlarged his pro-

---

46 *Ibid.*, 184, 211.
47 *Congressional Record*, 70th Cong., 1st Sess., 4088, 4189–90.
48 *Ibid.*, 3437, 3528.

gram to provide for fertilizer manufacture. But Black was not yet satisfied. Alabama, he contended, should receive compensation for the taxes it would lose if Muscle Shoals were converted to a government power project rather than leased to private, taxpaying fertilizer interests. He argued:

"What is the state? Has it no right at all? It cannot get any taxes under this plan. Somebody has to pay the taxes. Where should the taxes come from? They will have to come from the poor, hard-working overburdened farmer. Yet we are told that any person or corporation or government that is big enough may come into the state of Alabama and put its hands on that which is justly ours and take from us the right to collect taxes and rob the state of Alabama of the last right which has been left it under the rapidly disappearing rights of the sovereign states of America.[49]

When Norris' joint resolution came to a Senate vote in March, 1928, Black announced that he would vote for it because it now included fertilizer. "Legislation," he remarked to the Senate, "is a matter of compromise." To Senate veterans, it must have seemed audacious to hear this Alabama freshman, only four months on the Senate floor, speak of compromise with a legislative giant who had been striding the halls of Congress since 1903. After Congress adjourned in May, Coolidge silently pocket-vetoed the Norris resolution. It remained to be seen how the Great Engineer, to take office in 1929, would react when Norris stubbornly pressed his case.[50]

The lame duck session of the Seventieth Congress, which convened in December, 1928, had little purpose other than to mark time. Herbert Hoover was to be inaugurated in March, and a new Congress, with comfortable Republican majorities in both houses, would come into being. During this short session, the hobgoblins

---

[49] Ibid., 4537.
[50] Ibid., 4634. Preston J. Hubbard, a careful student of the Muscle Shoals controversy, concluded that, unlike Underwood, Black did not oppose public operation of the river project, although on occasion he paid lip service to the principle of private enterprise.

of liquor, immigration, and Romanism, which haunted the dreams of so many Americans, arose in Congress.

When championing a dubious cause, Black's tactic was to put forth the most respectable and aggressive arguments he could muster and to follow literally the old adage that a good offense was the best defense. Urging harsher penalties for prohibition violators, he warned the Senate that it would bring all laws into disrespect if enforcement of the Eighteenth Amendment were allowed to become a farce. Answering those who argued against spending more money trying to enforce a grossly violated law, he cried: "Do we hear any hue and cry that we should repeal the law against murder?" Every law should be enforced, he insisted, "especially where it is written into the Constitution of the United States."[51]

Proposing that all immigration be suspended for five years, Black called economic arguments to the fore, but the spectre of Anglo-Saxon nativism lurked in the background. He told the Senate that native-born Americans must be protected from the competition of cheap, foreign labor. He did not advocate bringing in newcomers while four million Americans were jobless. In reply to those who claimed that Americans would not stoop to manual labor, he cited low wages. His fellow countrymen, he said, would perform any work for decent pay.[52]

But in a radio speech later that spring, Black said: "We must and will determine the character of those who enter our country upon a basis of rapid and successful assimilation with our present citizenship. We have closed our doors to certain Asiatic people because of this consideration. The time is coming when we must extend this prohibition in defense of racial purity and national traditions."[53]

Evidently Black could find no plausible arguments in favor of cutting off government financial aid to Howard University or sid-

[51] *Congressional Record*, 70th Cong., 2nd Sess., 1818–19.
[52] *Ibid.*, 380.
[53] *Ibid.*, 71st Cong., 1st Sess., 1903–1904.

ing with Heflin in his newest paranoia. Without comment, but obviously with political survival in mind, he joined thirteen southern colleagues voting to rescind federal aid to the Negro university in Washington, D.C. He voted with nine colleagues in favor of an amendment offered by Heflin to forbid the Navy to fly a pennant bearing St. George's Cross above the American flag during church services aboard ship. Although the Navy insisted that the pennant was nondenominational, Heflin saw it as a menacing Catholic symbol.[54]

The second session of the Seventieth Congress had its more elevated moments. With a majority of his colleagues, Senator Black voted for the Kellogg-Briand peace pact, and for the construction of Boulder Dam on the Colorado River, leaving open the possibility of government operation. He favored the withdrawal of Marines from Nicaragua and Norris' amendment to do away with lame duck sessions of Congress. He argued that the Senate should end its custom of voting on presidential nominees in closed session. On this topic, Black and Samuel Shortridge, a California Republican, vied with one another to display their knowledge of American history. Did the "scholarly senator from Alabama," asked Shortridge, believe secret sessions were contrary to the spirit of democracy. Black did. "I suppose," Shortridge persisted, "the Senator will agree with me that Washington and Franklin believed in the true spirit of democracy?" But Black spotted the intended trap. "I will agree with the Senator to that extent," he interrupted, "and further state that I agree with Mr. Jefferson in his criticism as to holding the Constitutional Convention in secret." Shortridge had the last word. If the theory held by Jefferson and Black had been followed, he told the Senate, "we would never have had a Constitution."[55]

In March, 1929, Americans inaugurated a new leader, confident that Herbert Hoover, who epitomized rugged individualism, was fully capable of directing their destiny. The President imme-

[54] *Ibid.*, 70th Cong., 2nd Sess., 505, 2853, 4116.
[55] *Ibid.*, 603, 1731, 2519, 4119.

diately called Congress into extraordinary session to deal with farm relief and tariff. It seemed a vigorous and auspicious beginning. When committee assignments of the Seventy-first Congress were made public, Senator Black, perhaps in reward for party fidelity in 1928 and as evidence that he was no longer a greenhorn, moved from interstate commerce to the more prestigious foreign relations committee.[56]

Floods and storms prostrated much of the South that spring. On the Senate floor, Black and Heflin pleaded for flexible government loans so that stricken farmers could buy horses and mules as well as fertilizer and feed. But the Alabama senators argued in vain to a Congress dominated by Hoover's creed of individual initiative. What was the point, Black asked sardonically, of lending money to a farmer to buy feed for a mule which had drowned?[57]

As summer heat moved on Washington, squabbles of the Seventy-First Congress became intense. Hordes of lobbyists ascended Capitol Hill to pressure members for higher tariff rates. Congress finally gave Hoover his Federal Farm Board, but only after beating down a determined effort in the Senate to include "export debentures." By this agrarian relief plan, farm leaders had hoped that domestic prices on key agricultural commodities could be kept above the world price through bounties paid out of the government's customs receipts. With other members of the "farm bloc," Black had fought for export debentures. It was a method, he said, "by which the farmers could reasonably get the benefit of the tariff."[58]

Carpenters hurried to install a "cooling apparatus" as Senate tempers mounted over a proposal to reapportion the House of Representatives for the first time since 1911. Under the plan, Alabama was to lose one representative. Other predominantly rural areas would face similar losses, reflecting the ebbing of population away from American farms. Drys feared that new, big city representatives would favor modifying or abolishing the Eighteenth Amendment.

[56] *Ibid.*, 71st Congress, 1st Sess., 246.
[57] *Ibid.*, 811–14.   [58] *Ibid.*, 4599.

Black became a leader in the fight against this bill. He insisted that it was not because Alabama would lose a representative. He did not mention the prohibition issue. His objection, he told the Senate, was that the President would be given a power which the Constitution reserved to Congress. Under the plan, the President was directed to submit to Congress in December, 1929, two sets of computations. One would compute representation in the House by a formula called equal proportions, and the other under a formula called major fractions. Supposedly the major fractions formula favored large, populous states. Black announced that he could not vote for a measure which would "change prematurely the great balance of legislative power in the nation from the rural districts into the great metropolitan areas." Further, he argued that the bill put more power "into the already overflowing hands of the Chief Executive."

Cried Black:

The followers of Hamilton, the followers of that man who believed in a rule not by the people but in a rule by the privileged classes are in the saddle, booted and spurred, riding roughshod over the privileges of the people as they whittle and whittle away from their representatives and place in the hands of one man. . . . One by one, their rights are being taken away; little by little, inch by inch, gradually, as the stones of the earth are worn away by the beating water, the legislative functions have been sacrificed as additional powers have fallen into the basket of the Executive.[59]

Black offered an amendment to forbid the President to declare a reapportionment in the event Congress failed to do so. Opponents of the bill had considered his proposal their most effective move, but it was rejected by a margin of seven votes. The reapportionment plan passed both Houses and was signed by President Hoover.[60]

In September, 1929, the New York *Times* deemed it newsworthy that a United States senator appeared in the Washington,

[59] *Ibid.*, 70th Cong., 2nd Sess., 4243–49; 71st Cong., 1st Sess., 1334–36; New York *Times*, May 30, 1929.
[60] New York *Times*, May 25, 30, June 8, June 19, 1929.

D.C., police court as the chief complainant in a hit-and-run case. A driver had hit Senator Hugo Black's car and fled. But witnesses knew his license number, and Black indignantly pursued the case. In court he identified the culprit, who was promptly sentenced to sixty days or a two-hundred-dollar fine. Unfortunately for the defendant, he had collided with a former police court judge and a stern believer in obedience to law. On its front page the *Times* had weightier news to report. The stock market had begun to exhibit ominous signs. In the weeks ahead, Americans seemed propelled inexorably toward the financial chaos of Black Thursday, October 24.[61]

While these storm clouds gathered, Black set after prey more elusive than hit and run drivers. Washington, he told the Senate, was infested by a mass of lobbyists who pretended to have patriotic motives but actually were employed by "powerful interests and combinations intent upon special privilege, public pillage, and public plunder." He proposed laws requiring them to name their employees and report the amount of their expenditures. Even United States senators, he declared, were not safe from the "reckless statements bandied about by secret agents of special privilege seekers." One lobbyist had gone so far as to imply that nine of the twelve senators who voted that past February against Coolidge's proposal to build fifteen new Navy cruisers had Communist ties. Among the twelve were the Senate's frequent Republican mavericks, Norris, Borah, and Gerald P. Nye; the Farmer-Laborite Henrik Shipstead; and Black himself. His onetime Klan affiliations must have been far from Black's mind when he told a reporter for the New York *Times*: "Men and groups who work behind a mask deserve no sympathy and no quarter. They are enemies of true government or they would not fear public knowledge." [62]

While lobbyists spent lavish sums, Black felt that average Americans were too poor to make their wishes known to Con-

---

[61] *Ibid.*, September 5, 1929.
[62] *Congressional Record*, 71st Cong., 1st Sess., 3948; New York *Times*, September 26, 1929.

gress. He and Reed Smoot tangled in floor debate over the right of the public to be represented at Tariff Commission hearings. Black said that hundred of Alabamians, who could not afford the railroad fare to Washington, had written him to protest against tariff increases on sugar and leather. He was attempting to represent individuals, he said, by protesting logrolling, tariff hikes, and higher living costs. He did not approve of tariffs on products of the Philippines. The plight of these islands reminded him of the American colonies before their own revolution. "I believe in immediate, unequivocal independence for the Philippine Islands," he told the Senate.[63]

As Hoover's first year in the White House drew toward its close, the Senate sat in judgment upon a senator-elect and two of the President's nominees. It refused to seat William S. Vare, Republican boss of Pennsylvania, because of allegations that more than a million dollars had been spent in his campaign. Black, who had accused his own Senate opponents in Alabama of excessive expenditures, voted against Vare. He told the Senate that he could not support a man who had attempted to "buy the nomination." Years later George Norris would describe the successful fight against Vare as "one of the most satisfying struggles in that era of reaction."[64]

Black took sharp exception to Hoover's nominees for a federal district judgeship and a seat on the Interstate Commerce Commission. As a onetime attorney for union miners, he found it unthinkable that Richard J. Hopkins should become a federal judge in the face of accusations that he was blatantly antiunion. It was charged in the Senate that Hopkins, while attorney general of Kansas, had fired district attorneys who refused to prosecute striking miners for vagrancy. To misuse a vagrancy statute in order to prevent a man from bettering his working condition, Black told the Senate,

[63] *Congressional Record*, 70th Cong., 1st Sess., 3844; *ibid.*, 71st Cong., 1st Sess., 4419, 4599, 4622.

[64] *Congressional Record*, 71st Cong., 1st Sess., 3521–22; George W. Norris, *Fighting Liberal, The Autobiography of George W. Norris* (New York, 1946), 234.

was a flagrant abuse of the rights of free speech and free action.[65]

Although Hopkins was confirmed, Black won his fight against Robert M. Jones, a corporation lawyer nominated to the Interstate Commerce Commission. The nomination, he had charged, was being rushed through the Senate "like a third-class postmastership." He suspected that Jones had railroad affiliations. At Black's insistence, the matter was referred back to committee. Jones later withdrew his name from consideration.[66]

Bewildered Americans were glad to see the last of 1929. Surely a new decade would find the economy swinging upward again toward "normalcy." But which were the magic nostrums? Should tariffs be raised or lowered? How deal with mounting agricultural surpluses and falling farm income? How feed the hungry, create jobs for the swelling ranks of unemployed, revive the sagging industrial machine? All these complex dilemmas lay ahead for Hoover and Congress as the turbulent thirties began.

[65] *Congressional Record*, 71st Cong., 2nd Sess., 846–938.
[66] *Ibid.*, 893–94; 3922.

VIII

Set
a Steel Trap
for Tom

Hugo and Josephine Black were seldom seen at large noisy Washington parties. Capital hostesses discovered that this senator had no fondness for idle chatter and took prohibition literally. Josephine, by nature shy and reserved, was absorbed in her home and garden, her sons, and her husband's career. Occasionally the Blacks appeared at gatherings of fellow Alabamians or gave small parties at home, inviting guests who would make interesting conversation after dinner.

Like his farmer forebears, Hugo got up early. In these quiet morning hours, he annotated the works of Thomas Jefferson, or studied the French Revolution, a subject which particularly intrigued him. He had kept his schoolboy ability to read and retain a page at a glance. But in the works of Carlyle and Macaulay, he paused to underline those passages describing Turgot's vain effort to get the French nobility and clergy to relinquish some privileges in order that the monarchy might survive. He seldom read fiction. It was a waste of precious time which might more profitably be spent on Aristotle's *Politics* or an economic treatise by John Stuart Mill. If Black could be said to have a hobby in those early Senate years, it was reading and collecting books. Josephine valiantly tried to find space for them in the house.

In the brief hours he allotted to recreation, the senator played golf with his wife or pitched baseballs to his sons. On some Sundays they went out for family picnics. Even this frivolity could be made worthwhile by visiting a Civil War battlefield or an historic Virginia home. When excitement was brewing in the Senate, Black often summoned his wife to watch from the gallery. On the rare evenings when he came home early, he might help his sons with their homework or pick out folksongs by ear on the piano or violin. A visitor from Alabama was startled one night to watch his host wrap himself in a large apron and disappear into the kitchen to cook dinner.[1]

His diligent program of self-education, reflected in Black's floor debates, impressed his colleagues. When Alexander Legge, chairman of Hoover's Federal Farm Board, tentatively proposed that agricultural production be limited, Hugo found guidance in Jefferson. "While I cannot quote the exact language . . ." he told the Senate, "Mr. Jefferson in one of his letters stated that when the time came that he could be directed from Washington when to sow and when to reap and how much to plant and how much to reap, the days of the independence of the farmer would be at an end."[2]

Jefferson's philosophy also inspired Black in opposing an amendment to the Smoot-Hawley tariff which would have allowed customs inspectors to ban certain books from entering the country. "I have an inherent opposition—" he told the Senate. "I presume it comes from reading a great deal of Thomas Jefferson's philosophy—against vesting in the hands of an individual judicial power on matters of supreme importance with reference to the dissemination of human knowledge." Utah's Reed Smoot equated bad books with opium, but Black quickly objected. "Oh no. All opium is bad, but all books are not bad." He agreed to the amendment after it was modified to refer disputes to court action, and to narrow the category of questionable books to those which urged

---

[1] These descriptions of the Black's family life are derived from numerous press articles, particularly interviews with Josephine Black which appeared in Birmingham newspapers.

[2] *Congressional Record*, 71st Cong., 2nd Sess., 1497–1500.

such illegal actions as treason, rebellion, insurrection, or forcible resistance. Reminding his colleagues of the Alien and Sedition Acts of 1798, Black remarked that he hoped the same unfortunate consequences would not follow the tariff ban.[3]

As the Smoot-Hawley bill made its tortuous way through Congress, Black heeded pleas from home. Graphite mining, Clay County's sole industry, was being threatened by imports from Madagascar, "dug out of the ground," Black reported indignantly, "by women and children at seven cents per day." When his amendment for a tariff on graphite failed, Black declared it was because big crucible manufacturers opposed it. Graphite, he told the Senate, was too minor a business to produce large contributors to Republican campaign funds.[4]

If Republicans sincerely wanted to help workingmen, Black suggested that they support his amendment for an "ironclad law" against importation of "cheap, unorganizable Mexican labor in inexhaustible quantities to compete with American labor." Unable to get action on his bill to suspend all immigration for five years, he attempted to ban all Mexican migrants. He charged:

> Foreign immigration has been utilized by the big business interests of the country as a direct weapon to break down . . . wages. . . . We do not want a caste system in our country. We do not want one class of people who live down on a lowly order of intelligence like serfs and peons . . . while we have at the same time a great aristocratic class . . . to uphold the traditions of aristocracy and wealth and power.[5]

When the amendment failed, Black commented sardonically that the same Republicans who favored high tariff for manufactures would not vote for a tariff on cheap labor.

Indiana's James E. Watson, the Republican floor leader, charged that Democrats like Black had been inconsistent by voting for some tariff increases but against the final bill. In a heated reply,

[3] *Ibid.*, 5418, 5517.
[4] *Ibid.*, 3660, 8838.
[5] *Ibid.*, 7138, 7328–29, 7614.

Black pointed out that, of 234 votes taken on tariff increases, he had supported only four. These applied to the agricultural products of cotton, dates, cattle, and casein. He pointed out to the Senate that he had voted against increases on pig iron, cement, and lumber, all important to Alabama. Watson, he said, was seeking to throw up a smoke screen by charging that "because some Democrats happened to vote for a tariff on mustard seed and a tariff on dates in packages . . . it is their duty to swallow the entire iniquitous tariff scheme . . . this Grundyized and greedy gouge of the people of this country." [6]

When the bill finally passed in June, 1930, raising American import duties to an all-time high, Watson told the Senate confidently. "The sun again will shine and bring prosperity and happy days back to the people of the United States." But the Republican tariff had exactly the opposite effect. In an election-year radio speech that July, Black did not hesitate to taunt Watson and his fellow Republicans with the memory of that optimistic prediction. "Ten years' trial is enough," Hugo exhorted his radio listeners. "It is time to restore the government to the hands of the people!" [7]

Floor fights over two Supreme Court nominations and another nominee for the Interstate Commerce Commission erupted in the Senate early in 1930. When Hoover nominated Charles Evans Hughes for chief justice, cries of dismay arose from Republican mavericks and a number of Democrats. Hughes, they objected, had represented wealthy corporations in a number of cases before the high court. They predicted that his economic views would be colored by these legal affiliations, and his political ideas by his close ties with the Republican Party. Twenty-six senators, Black among them, voted against Hughes. But fortunately for his future relationship with the chief justice, Black took no part in floor debate over the nomination. [8]

Shortly after the Hughes debates, Hoover sent to the Senate the

6 *Ibid.*, 8838.
7 New York *Times*, July 14, 1930.
8 *Congressional Record*, 71st Cong., 2nd Sess., 3591.

name of John J. Parker of North Carolina to be an associate justice. This time the Senate balked. Rejecting a Supreme Court nominee for the first time in thirty-three years, the majority labeled Parker antiunion and anti-Negro. The nominee, they said, had once rendered an opinion upholding the legality of a "yellow dog" contract. During a gubernatorial campaign in North Carolina, Parker was said to have made disparaging remarks about Negroes. Although Black had little to say about Parker, he voted against him.[9]

Commenting on the Senate's rejection of Parker, a New York *Times* correspondent called it a victory for those senators who believed that the high court "must be composed, in greater part if not wholly, of men who would interpret the laws in a spirit that was not influenced entirely by strictly legalistic reasoning." It would probably have seemed almost inconceivable to members of the Senate in the Hoover years that the name of their fiery colleague from Alabama would one day come before this same body for approval as a Supreme Court justice.[10]

When Hoover nominated Hugh Tate to the seat on the Interstate Commerce Commission, originally offered to Robert M. Jones, Black led the opposition. In a ninety-minute speech, he railed against the President's choice of two men with corporation and railroad affiliations. Tate's firm represented the Electric Bond and Share Company and the Southern Railway System. Black thought it was "ridiculous and fantastic" to claim that Tate would not be influenced by big interests. A lawyer's clients, he argued, are his firm's clients. Furthermore he objected to Tate because he was a Republican and would give that party a majority of seven to five on the supposedly bipartisan ICC. But despite Black's opposition, Tate was confirmed. Years later, when the suitability of Senator Black for a seat on the Supreme Court was under question, a writer for the New York *Times* would recall Black's words during the Tate debate: "Show me the kind of steps a man made

[9] *Ibid.*, 7807, 7934, 7949, 8181, 8195, 8196, 8342, 8343, 8432.
[10] New York *Times*, May 11, 1930.

in the sand five years ago, and I will show you the kind of steps he is likely to make in the same sand five years hence."[11]

Still unresolved, the issue of Muscle Shoals reappeared in the Seventy-First Congress and gave Black his first experience as a Senate investigator. Before the Senate was a new Norris joint resolution, identical to the one vetoed by Coolidge except that it now provided for compensating Alabama and Tennessee with a percentage of the gross proceeds from the sale of power. Conceding to the arguments of Black and of Tennessee's Kenneth D. McKellar, Norris had agreed that compensation was only fair, because both states would be deprived of taxable resources by the federal program.[12]

From January until April, 1930, a subcommittee of the Senate judiciary committee probed the thicket of Washington lobbyists, looking for unethical practices by those pushing for higher tariffs and for private operation of Muscle Shoals. Thaddeus Caraway of Arkansas was chairman. Beside him sat Tom Walsh and Hugo Black. Black had suggested that Muscle Shoals lobbyists be scrutinized and, although he was not a member of the judiciary committee, Chairman Norris invited him to sit with the subcommittee.[13]

The stormy probe has been described as "marked by ill temper on the part of both witnesses and committee members." Caraway, Walsh, and Black were said to have "treated some of the witnesses in a rather brusque manner." At one session Black almost came to blows with an Alabama newspaper editor, J. H. Pierce of the Huntsville *Times*, because he charged Pierce with accepting a thousand-dollar bribe to change his editorial policy to favor the American Cyanamid offer instead of government operation. The editor called the senator "a contemptible cur." Black replied hotly: "I'll see you outside about that. Everybody knows you are by na-

[11] New York *Times*, February 20, 1930; September 17, 1937; *Congressional Record*, 71st Cong., 2nd Sess., 3353–4005.

[12] Hubbard, *Origins of the TVA*, 249; *Congressional Record*, 71st Cong., 2nd Sess., 6400.

[13] Hubbard, *Origins of the TVA*, 257; *Congressional Record*, 71st Cong., 2nd Sess., 6438.

ture a coward." But Walsh intervened and adjourned the hearings until tempers cooled.[14]

As Norris suspected, Senate probers found that efforts had been made, even by Coolidge himself, to assure private power companies that the American Cyanamid Company did not plan to compete with them in the power business. Caraway and Walsh attempted to show that the cyanamid company was owned by the "power trust" but they were unable to obtain stockholder records to prove this charge. However, the investigation convinced the public that deals had been made behind the scenes, and embarrassed the Farm Bureau by revealing that its Washington representative had lobbied for the cyanamid offer and against the Norris plan.[15]

The hearings spoiled any chance that Congress would accept the Cyanamid proposal. Even Heflin withdrew his support from American Cyanamid, and Black, who had been lukewarm, denounced the offer. When the Norris plan passed the Senate in April, several newspapers credited the victory to the investigations and predicted that public opinion would now turn toward federal power projects. Norris was publicly grateful to Black for his part in the hearings. "We cannot praise the senator from Alabama too highly," he told the Senate. "He has been of almost invaluable assistance." [16]

When the Norris plan became deadlocked in conference with the House, Black and Norris bluntly blamed President Hoover. "Why is Muscle Shoals legislation held up?" Black roared from the Senate floor. "In order that 2,000 to 3,000 per cent profits may continue to go into the pockets of the Power Trust and that out of every dollar's income 92 cents can go to dividends and profits." As the deadlock dragged on, he charged that "the Republican administration is 100 per cent responsible for the failure to operate Muscle Shoals." [17]

[14] Hubbard, *Origins of the TVA*, 257; Birmingham *News*, April 8, 1930.
[15] Hubbard, *Origins of the TVA*, 257–65.
[16] *Ibid.*, 265; *Congressional Record*, 71st Cong., 2nd Sess., 6438.
[17] *Congressional Record*, 71st Cong., 2nd Sess., 11673, 12383.

During the summer of 1930, Black embroiled himself in controversy with the War Department over its refusal to sell surplus power from Wilson Dam to the nearby town of Muscle Shoals, while agreeing to sell to the Tennessee Electric Power Company. In mixed anger and amusement, he read to the Senate this message from the city fathers of Muscle Shoals: "Telegram you received from Muscle Shoals this morning framed by city fathers, in City Hall, by light of kerosene lamps though within 2 miles of tremendous power tumbling to waste over Wilson Dam with administration's consent." [18]

Black suspected the administration of refusing to sell power to Muscle Shoals in order to discourage municipally owned power systems. He told the Senate:

With vetoes coming thick and fast on the ground of economy and on the ground that some poor, disabled soldier may get a few dollars for himself and his hungry wife and babies, the administration remains silent and permits $4,000,000 per year to go to waste in the form of power, for the benefit of the power companies, when the evidence shows that their associates made a profit of 3,012 per cent in the year 1927 on their investment in that company. [19]

Despite his protests, Black lost. The Senate passed his resolution to require Secretary of War Patrick J. Hurley to sell Muscle Shoals power to municipalities which applied for it, but the measure died in the House. [20]

In the fall of 1930, Norris himself and a number of outspoken congressional opponents of power companies were reelected. "Tuesday [election day] was a bad day for the utilities," commented the New York *Times*. With election results fresh in their minds, House conferees at last came to agreement with the Senate, approving a compromise which contained all of Norris' power provisions. Cleared through both houses, the conference bill went to Hoover's desk. [21]

[18] Hubbard, *Origins of the TVA*, 277.
[19] *Congressional Record*, 71st Cong., 2nd Sess., 11966.
[20] *Ibid.*, 11763–64; Hubbard, *Origins of the TVA*, 277–78.
[21] Hubbard, *Origins of the TVA*, 284–89.

Unlike "Silent Cal," Hoover met the issue head-on. "The power problem," he lectured Congress, "is not to be solved by the Federal government going into the power business." In the Senate Norris and his cohorts received the President's veto with bitterness. Hoover had deliberately misled the people of the Tennessee Valley, Black declared, because he had implied during his presidential campaign that he would support government operation. "Thousands of people in the South voted for Mr. Hoover . . . ," he told the Senate, "because he came into their midst and made statements which would have led any reasonable man to believe that he would sign a measure such as he today opposed." Norris called the President's rejection of his proposal "his cruel, his unjust, his unfair, his unmerciful veto." Followers of Norris tried to override the veto but failed. In the House no attempt was made. While Hoover occupied the White House, Norris would not realize his dream.[22]

Although the Muscle Shoals fight seemed futile, it had proven invaluable to the seasoning of Senator Black. Watching the dogged Norris at work, he absorbed practical lessons in patience, persistence, craftiness, and compromise. In later years, when Black pursued his own pet cause of limiting work hours and raising wages, he would remember the long ordeal and final victory of George Norris. Working together, the young Democrat and the old Bull Mooser found that despite party labels, their basic ideals were much the same. It was the beginning of an association of mutual respect and admiration which would be broken only at Norris' death.

But other Senate colleagues did not always share Norris' fondness for Senator Black. Opponents who had met him in debate had good reason to fear his sharp tongue. Black and Millard Tydings of Maryland amused the Senate one day by a spirited debate over whether farmers should be allowed to keep hard cider in their storehouses and city people keep beer in their basements. Each urged the other to end this "evasion of the spirit of the law." Sud-

---

[22] *Congressional Record*, 71st Cong., 3d Sess., 7070–75.

denly switching tactics, Black began to chide Tydings for taking up the Senate's time to discuss "dandelion wine and rhubarb beer" while five to six million people in the nation were unemployed. "Let me be prosecuting attorney for a moment," the beleaguered Tydings pleaded.[23]

Many a conventionally educated senator respected Black's self-acquired background in economics and history, which enabled him on one occasion to quote Washington, Madison, and John Quincy Adams in support of his arguments that all negotiations leading up to the London Naval Treaty of 1930 should have been made available to the Senate.

"I have always been and am still opposed to secret diplomacy," he lectured Hoover and Secretary of State Henry L. Stimson. "The Senate is entitled to all the information there is to be had in order that it may pass intelligently on treaties."[24]

Although he was primarily interested in domestic affairs, Black made it known in the Foreign Relations Committee that he had little use for colonialism. Debating with Samuel Shortridge, he told the Californian that the United States, "not by a bona fide vote of the people but at the point of a bayonet," had once forced Haiti to adopt a new constitution "in order that Americans might own land."[25]

Large meat packers were also wary of Senator Black. He accused them of coloring margarine with the yellow fats of old cattle rather than artificial coloring in order to avoid the higher tax on colored oleo. Unsuccessfully he sought to tax oleo which had been colored by yellow fats. Packers urged an annulment of the consent decree of 1920, which had forced them out of business activities such as food store chains and railroads. Again they aroused Black's ire. Such mergers, he told fellow senators, would deprive thousands of workers of their jobs in order to build up "huge monopolies to fleece the public." He protested, "We are rapidly becoming

[23] *Ibid.*, 71st Cong., 3d Sess., 5004–5005.
[24] New York *Times*, June 11, 1930.
[25] *Congressional Record*, 71st Cong., 2nd Sess., 7511–12.

a nation of a few business masters and many clerks and servants";
Americans, in their "wild craze for efficiency," were building up a
"caste system." [26]

In the fall of 1930, as bread lines in the cities of America grew
longer, alarmed and bitter voters began to turn against an administration which seemed powerless to reverse the tide of depression. When midterm election results were in, it was obvious
that Republicans had lost control of both houses of Congress. The
new Senate would have forty-eight Republicans to forty-seven
Democrats and one Farmer-Laborite, with the balance of power
resting again with Republican insurgents. In the House 214 Republicans were to face 220 Democrats and one farmer-Laborite.[27]

Political soothsayers found other omens in the mid-term election
results. Wets appeared to be gaining. Franklin D. Roosevelt won
an impressive victory in his reelection to the governorship of
pivotal New York State. Little national notice was given the fact
that Alabama Democrats had turned Tom Heflin out of his Senate seat and replaced him with John H. Bankhead, Jr., thereby
elevating Hugo Black to the heady title of "senior senator from
Alabama."

Early in 1930 Tom Heflin had no intention of relinquishing the
fellowship of the Senate nor his role as its jester. But the threat by
Edmund Pettus to read out of the party all who had voted for Al
Smith hung like the Damoclean sword over his head. Hugh A.
Locke, his partner in the bolt of 1928, wanted to run for governor.
Alabama Democrats waited uneasily for their executive committee
to clarify the muddled political picture.

At first Will and John Bankhead were anxious for a harmonious
ruling. Will, a member of the House since 1917, represented a
congressional district in the hills of northwest Alabama where a

---

[26] *Ibid.*, 9551, 9547; Hugo L. Black, "Should the Meat Packers be Permitted
to Enter the Chain Store Field?" *Congressional Digest,* IX (August–September,
1930), 209–10.
[27] Hicks, *Republican Ascendancy,* 239.

tradition of Republicanism had stubbornly persisted since the Civil War. Will glimpsed the possibility that his promising career might end in defeat if anti-Smith Democrats, driven from their own party, made common cause with these Republicans.

John, who had yearned for a Senate seat since his defeat by Hugo Black in 1926, planned to run against Heflin. His brother and other strategists convinced John that his best chance would be to fight it out within Democratic Party ranks. "If he [Heflin] can't be beaten in a primary in which Republicans can't take part, he certainly can't be beaten in a general election with all the Republicans voting for him," Congressman George Huddleston of Birmingham advised the Bankhead brothers.[28]

Supporters of Heflin and Locke also sought harmony. On behalf of the two leading bolters, Ben Ray, a member of the Democratic executive committee, asked Alabama's congressional representatives to express their views on the situation. His friend Hugo was the first to answer. Recalling the Populists of the 1890s, Black reminded Ray that these earlier defectors from Democratic fealty had been allowed to return to their party. Democrats of 1930, Black felt, should also resolve their differences within ranks and "not force life-long members to the formation of a new party or to affiliation with the Republican party."[29]

In Montgomery in December, 1929, party nabobs made the long-awaited ruling. To bar as voters the estimated one hundred thousand Alabama Democrats who had voted for Hoover would be too risky a course. But Black Belt politicians, wets, and other leaders of the traditional Democratic hierarchy could not pass up this chance to purge two major figures in the Klan-dry coalition which had swept control of the state from their hands in 1926 and almost delivered Alabama to Republicanism in 1928. By a vote of 27–21, the executive committee decided to permit wayward

[28] George Huddleston to William B. Bankhead, October 4, 1929, in W. B. Bankhead Papers.

[29] J. Thomas Heflin to Ben F. Ray, October 12, 1929, in Heflin Papers; Vincent J. Dooley, "United States Senator J. Thomas Heflin and the Democratic Party Revolt in Alabama" (M.A. thesis, Auburn University, 1963), 39.

Democrats to vote in 1930 but to bar as candidates for state, district, federal, or circuit offices any person who "either voted a Republican presidential ticket in November, 1928, or openly and publicly opposed the election of the Democratic nominees, or either of them." [30]

Jouett Shouse, chairman of the Democratic National Committee, feared this move would endanger the southern solidarity so essential to his party. Alabama newspapers voiced their political loyalties. The Montgomery *Advertiser* and Selma *Times-Journal*, vehicles of the Black Belt hierarchy, strongly approved barring the bolters. The Birmingham *News* agreed. Only by "year-round and life-round party fidelity," the *News* declared, had the South saved itself from "domination by the enemy." But the Mobile *Register*, published by Frederick I. Thompson, charged that "wet Smith" elements, corporation lawyers, and the "power trust" were seeking control of the Democratic Party in Alabama by restricting constitutional rights and setting rules so that John Bankhead, "the corporation candidate," would have no primary opposition. The Mobile *News-Item*, Alabama *Journal*, and North Alabama dailies in Florence and Sheffield sided with Thompson.[31]

Black was quick to lambaste the ruling but, typically, he first sought legal ammunition. The Alabama Code of 1923, he found, specified that qualified voters should have the right to participate in primary elections "subject to such political and other qualifications as may be prescribed for its candidates." Black stated:

The law does not contemplate a special privileged class to run for office, and a subordinate class who can vote but not hold office. Citizenship carries with it the right of an elector to vote and hold office. An attempt to abridge the sacred rights of citizenship is fundamentally un-American. If a citizen is barred as a candidate for political office as

[30] Dooley, "United States Senator J. Thomas Heflin," 43–48; Ralph Melvis Tanner, "James Thomas Heflin: United States Senator, 1920–1931" (Ph.D. dissertation, University of Alabama, 1967), 162–63; "Punishing Hoovercrats in Alabama," *Literary Digest*, CXXIV (January 4, 1930), 9.

[31] "Punishing Hoovercrats in Alabama," 9; Alabama *Journal*, November 16, 1929; Moore, *History of Alabama*, 785.

a party's punishment, he must be barred as a voter. If barred as a voter, he must be barred as a candidate.[32]

During an automobile ride in Washington early in 1930, Black and Will Bankhead discussed their party's plight. Describing this conversation to John Bankhead, Will said that Hugo expressed great "anxiety" over the situation and seemed to think that the action was also aimed at him. He proposed to Will that Democrats who were dissatisfied with the ruling should become candidates for seats on the party executive committee. If they won a majority of committee seats in the forthcoming August primary, they could declare that primary null and void and call a new primary in which bolters would be allowed to run as candidates. Will Bankhead thought the idea "fantastic" and wrote John that he would try to get the senator "tamed down."[33]

Supporters of Heflin and Locke tried legal action and propaganda. Circulars, headed "The Coward's Declaration," accused the committee of being afraid to let Democratic voters choose between Bankhead and Heflin. At a mass meeting in the Birmingham Municipal Auditorium, eight thousand Heflin-Locke supporters roared agreement with a resolution from Ben Ray demanding that the committee's action be rescinded.[34]

When party leaders ignored them, the bolters sought a court injunction to forbid the holding of a Democratic primary in Jefferson County. The case reached the Alabama Supreme Court. Heflin and Locke were represented by Horace Wilkinson, who had defended the floggers of Jeff Calloway, and by Crampton Harris, who, with his partner Hugo Black, had defended the slayer of Father Coyle. The Democratic Executive Committee was rep-

[32] This public statement by Black was quoted in Heflin's testimony before a special Senate investigating committee during the Heflin-Bankhead contest. Copies of these hearings are in the Papers of George Norris, Library of Congress, Washington, D.C. Black made similar statements in the Mobile *Register*, December 21, 1929, and Birmingham *News*, December 21, 1929.

[33] William B. Bankhead to John H. Bankhead, January 8, 1930, in W. B. Bankhead Papers.

[34] Dooley, "Senator J. Thomas Heflin," 60, 74–79; Tanner, "James Thomas Heflin," 177–82.

resented by Forney Johnston, Underwood's close adviser who had touched off a near-riot at the Democratic convention of 1924 by openly condemning the Klan.[35]

Like Black, Wilkinson and Harris protested that the committee had no right to distinguish between qualifications for voters and those for candidates. Black wrote Wilkinson that he hoped the supreme court would declare the ruling illegal: "I have always taken the position that when a citizen is admitted into an election or primary, none of his constitutional rights could be abridged." But in April, 1930, the Alabama Supreme Court affirmed a lower court ruling that it had no jurisdiction over such party squabbles. Faced with this setback, Heflin and Locke decided to offer themselves as independent "Jeffersonian Democrats" in the November general election.[36]

It first appeared that John Bankhead would be unopposed in the August primary. Earlier there were rumors that Lister Hill, the personable young congressman of prominent Montgomery antecedents, had aspirations to be a senator. But Hill was persuaded by the Bankheads that Democrats should concentrate on one candidate to defeat Heflin. An intriguing rumor reached the Montgomery *Advertiser* that Heflin would drop out and run, instead, for Black's seat in 1932.[37]

But Bankhead had opposition in the primary after all. Frederick I. Thompson, the Mobile newspaper publisher, entered late but waged a vigorous campaign. He taunted Bankhead as a spokesman for the Alabama Power Company who would seek to block government development of Muscle Shoals. Owners of rival newspapers in Mobile and Montgomery attacked Thompson as a secret ally of Republicans.[38]

As in the 1928 election, Black shrewdly remained silent. After

---

[35] *Ibid.*

[36] A photographic copy of Black's handwritten letter to Horace Wilkinson, dated April 14, 1930, was published in a political advertisement in the Birmingham *News*, June 5, 1932.

[37] Telegram from Montgomery *Advertiser* to J. Thomas Heflin, June 16, 1930, in Heflin Papers.

[38] Moore, *History of Alabama*, 79–84.

the supreme court ruling, neither side was sure just where he stood, although Hugh Locke had been one of his ardent supporters when John Bankhead was his chief opponent in 1926. Locke suspected that Black and other members of the Alabama delegation in Congress would support Thompson. But if Thompson were defeated, Locke wrote Heflin, "most all of them might be our friends." Only a month before the primary, the Birmingham *News* wondered: "Will Senator Black Speak at the Heflin-Locke Meeting?" [39]

William Bankhead advised John to continue reminding voters that Black and Graves, "both recognized as KKK sympathizers and . . . ultra dry," had supported the Democratic ticket in 1928. "This will cut a good deal of ground from under Heflin," Will said. One of Black's supporters warned the senator not to ally himself "with the very men who opposed your election four years ago and who very likely will oppose you again in 1932." If Black made such an alliance, his friend warned, he would become the puppet of a "hide-bound, conscienceless, Bourbon type of partisanship." [40]

Just before the primary, Black spoke. Keeping to the cautious path of party loyalty, he urged voters to remain true to the Democrats as the South's only hope against Republican greed. He mentioned no candidate by name. Praising the speech, the Birmingham *News* asked: "Does Tom Heflin dare to attack Hugo Black because Hugo Black manfully defends the party and loyally pleads for Democratic solidarity?" Years later Black told an interviewer that he had voted for Thompson. [41]

Excluded from the Democratic primary, Heflin urged his friends to make this the "smallest primary vote in the history of Alabama." When the total vote was in, it fell forty thousand short of that cast in the 1928 general election. Bankhead was

[39] Hugh Locke to J. Thomas Heflin, July 9, 1930, in Heflin Papers; Birmingham *News*, June 22, 1930.

[40] William B. Bankhead to John H. Bankhead, April 25, 1930, in W. B. Bankhead Papers; O. H. Stevenson to Hugo L. Black, July 11, 1930, copy in Heflin Papers.

[41] Birmingham *News*, August 3, 1930; Tanner, "James Thomas Heflin," 194.

nominated for senator by a sizable majority. In the governor's race, Judge Benjamin M. Miller, from the small Black Belt community of Camden, defeated William C. Davis, lieutenant governor under Bibb Graves. Miller had waged a vigorous anti-Klan campaign. In his final speech he promised: "Make me governor of Alabama and . . . you will not have to make a sign or symbol to enter my office." Labelling Black, Graves, Heflin, and Davis as "Kluckers," Miller urged voters to drive out government "of, by and for the Klan."[42]

Gleefully the Birmingham *News* predicted a Bankhead victory in the November general election. "It is surely not news that the Ku Klux Klan is waning . . . ," the *News* declared. "After November 4, the KKK will be as dead politically as its darling Tom Heflin himself will be." But the newspaper warned that the Klan would ally with Republicans to make "its last bid for political power."[43]

No politician was more aware than was Hugo Black of waning influences and changing alliances in Alabama politics. The Klan was in eclipse. Labor was divided, although it was generally conceded that Heflin had a majority of these votes. Even the drys' strength seemed diluted. The Alabama Anti-Saloon League supported Heflin, but the *Alabama Baptist* and the Methodist *Christian Advocate*, once noisy supporters of the dry cause, remained silent on the senatorial race. Old war cries of white supremacy and anti-Catholicism seemed to have lost some of their potency. On the other hand, regular Democrats were organizing enthusiastically to face this second challenge from the Klan and Republicans. They were supported by most daily newspapers in Alabama and a large majority of the weeklies.[44]

With these factors in mind, Black faced a choice between the remnants of those forces which had placed him in the Senate or the rejuvenated regulars. His opponents would later charge that

[42] Out of a total of 164,000 votes, Bankhead received a 44,553 majority. Dooley, "Senator J. Thomas Heflin," 96; Birmingham *News*, August 9, 1930.
[43] Birmingham *News*, October 3, 1930.
[44] Dooley, "Senator J. Thomas Heflin," 129–33.

he took no role in the Heflin-Bankhead race until he "made a trade" with Democratic leaders—he would help elect John Bankhead in return for their support in his own reelection campaign of 1932. One irate citizen wrote the *News* that Hugo had weakened "under the . . . lash of the machine which had fought him in 1926" and had deserted his allegiance to the "God-fearing Democrats who sent him to the Senate."[45]

"Black Unsheaths Sword in Defense of Party Ticket," trumpeted the Birmingham *News* in October, 1930. To a large crowd in the North Alabama town of Guntersville, Black was introduced as "Alabama's junior senator who will be senior senator after November 4." He did not mention Heflin or Locke, but harangued against Republicans as advocates of "mergers, monopolies, corporations and chain business." Black promised to speak frequently. In Montgomery on the following day, he urged voters not to desert the party of Jefferson, Jackson, Cleveland, Wilson, Robert E. Lee, and Stonewall Jackson for that of Hamilton, Grant, Thaddeus Stevens, Harding, Daugherty, Coolidge, and Hoover. "We cannot," Hugo exhorted, "we will not, we must not destroy the party which brought the sunlight of peace, happiness, and security to the white men and women of Alabama."[46]

For the first time in his political career, Black's speeches were covered prominently and enthusiastically in Birmingham newspapers. The *News* spoke of his "flow of eloquence," and the *Age-Herald* said he "took the high ground for the honor and triumph of the Democratic party." In Bessemer the senator acknowledged that he had originally protested against barring bolters from the primary, but had accepted the decision of the party "which sent me to the Senate." Two days before the election, Governor Graves belatedly added his voice in support of party regularity.[47]

In a heavy vote on November 4, Alabamians elected John Bankhead to the Senate and Benjamin Miller to the governorship.

[45] Birmingham *News*, October 11, 1930, June 5, 1932; Birmingham *Post*, May 21, 1932; Montgomery *Advertiser*, May 21, 1932.
[46] Birmingham *News*, October 6, 8, 1930.
[47] Birmingham *News*, October 11, November 2, 1930; Birmingham *Age-Herald*, October 7, 28, 1930.

Bankhead defeated Heflin, who won only ten of the state's sixty-seven counties, by a majority of 50,033 votes. Miller had a majority of more than 59,000 over Hugh Locke and won all but seven counties. It was a stunning victory for the party regulars who had managed to hold their state in the Democratic column by a bare 7,000 votes two years earlier. The coalition of Klan, prohibition, and labor, joined for expediency by Republicans, had been decisively defeated. Three weeks after the election, James Esdale, the once powerful, behind-the-scenes manipulator whose whim could elect a governor or senator, gave up the robes of Grand Dragon and resigned from the Klan. Control of Democratic politics in Alabama had returned to traditional hands.[48]

Tom Heflin took defeat hard. The election, he stormed, had been "one of the most fraudulent and corrupt ever held in Alabama." He threatened to seek a Senate investigation. "I trust he does not repeat his charges on the floor," Black wrote Curran S. Goodwin, of Birmingham. "You can rest assured that if he does . . . I shall take the floor." Goodwin urged Will Bankhead and other members of the House delegation to "get cocked and primed . . . to make a monkey out of Heflin if he starts anything. . . . Now you boys get together up there and set a steel trap for Tom and catch him by the hind leg."[49]

The Birmingham *News*, long an ardent supporter of Bankhead, commented that "Cotton Tom" had never been a credit to his state, but at least had behaved respectably until 1926. "After that . . . ," said the *News*, "he became an intolerable figure. . . . The old, genial Heflin passed out of the picture. He apparently became cursed with fears and hatreds, coupled with delusions of grandeur and of persecution." Now the *News* urged Heflin to "take his beating like a man and not persist in his absurd insinuations of election fraud."[50]

[48] Bankhead received 150,985 votes to Heflin's 100,952. *Alabama Official and Statistical Register* (1931), 511–12, 568–69, 575; Snell, "The Ku Klux Klan in Jefferson County," 219.

[49] Hugo L. Black to Curran S. Goodwin, Curran S. Goodwin to William B. Bankhead, December 4, 1930, in W. B. Bankhead Papers.

[50] Birmingham *News*, November 3, 8, 1930.

In the Senate Black requested the clerk to read a resolution of the Alabama legislature condemning Heflin's "very poor sportsmanship." Heflin retorted that he would never be good sport enough to condone fraud. But it would take "wholesale fraud and corruption," Black replied, to steal an election in fifty-seven of sixty-seven counties. Heflin challenged his colleague to tell the Senate whether he would object to having the Senate Committee on Privileges and Elections look into Alabama's ballot boxes. He had no objection to investigation of any case, where *prima facie* fraud was charged, Black replied; but he did not favor inviting people to come into Alabama on the assumption that "there was such wholesale fraud and corruption as to make a change of 150,000 out of 250,000 votes." Dramatically Black told the Senate:

I deny the right of the Federal Government to go down into the State of Alabama, sir, and tell the people who shall vote or who shall not vote. We had entirely too much of that in the days when the carpetbagger and scalawag were running the State. I do not favor, sir, the extension by one inch or one particle of an inch of the rights of the Federal Government to enable it to invade the sacred rights of franchise in the Southern States of this Union or in any other States of this Union. I am opposed body, soul, mind, and spirit, to any additional step which gives the Federal Government the right to go into my state.[51]

Many senators secretly sympathized with Heflin. "Tom-Tom" amused the Senate with his jokes and harangues. For all his foolishness and bigotry, he was an insider, a member of their club. Black, brash and often waspish, had won respect but not affection. Even George Norris, who had bolted the Republican Party himself to support Smith in 1928, believed that Heflin had been illegally excluded from the Alabama Democratic primary. When Norris offered a resolution authorizing an investigation of Alabama's ballot boxes, the Senate agreed.

[51] *Congressional Record*, 71st Cong., 3d Sess., 3473.

That reminded him of a story, Heflin said. Senators perked up and gallery spectators leaned forward eagerly. "Cotton Tom" was about to perform. Mr. Jones had lost a ninety-pound shoat, Heflin related. Looking for the shoat, Mr. Jones and the sheriff went to Rastus' cabin. There was Rastus, rocking a pine cradle covered with quilts. "Dere you go, accusin' the ole nigger of stealing," said Rastus, "but I welcomes a search." Asked the sheriff, "What you got in that cradle?" Rastus replied, "It's my baby, and he's got pneumonia. If the air hits him, he's gone." But the sheriff insisted on looking in the cradle, and Rastus lit out across the fields. "When they pulled the quilts back," Heflin roared, "there was old Rastus' baby, Mr. Jones' shoat. Make this investigation in Alabama, and we will take the quilts off their baby!" The Senate chamber rang with laughter.[52]

While Senate investigators probed the Alabama election, Black attacked Hoover's economic policies, earning some national repute as a Democratic gadfly. The New York *Times*, which had described him in 1927 as a damage suit lawyer, now sought his tart comments on Republican palliatives for the worst depression in American history. The Democratic National Committee happily helped publicize Hugo's caustic words.

None of Hoover's tentative efforts to deal with the depression pleased Senator Black. When the President reluctantly embarked on a public works program late in 1930, Black complained that the government was awarding contracts to firms which paid sub-standard wages to imported labor. These contractors, he told the Senate, employed bricklayers for forty cents an hour when the prevailing rate was ninety cents. While Hoover was imploring industry not to cut wages, Black charged that "that same government is . . . beating down the wages paid labor in the erection of public buildings in every section of this country."[53]

Sarcastically, Black described Hoover's well-known abhorrence for the dole: "The dole seems to consist in relieving the distress of those who are in poverty and poor; but if the amount is large

---

[52] *Ibid.*, 2243.   [53] *Ibid.*, 681.

enough to relieve those who have great power, it is not a dole—it is an act of statesmanship." The President approved of aid to "starving steamship companies" in the form of mail subsidies, Hugo said, but considered it "very bad to give assistance to the starving unemployed."[54]

During the great drought of 1931, with the Red Cross able to provide only four dollars a week for needy families, Hoover still insisted that the problem of feeding hungry Americans should be handled by private charity. On the Senate floor, Black read excerpts from testimony by Hoover himself, in the role of postwar humanitarian, asking a House committee to appropriate twenty million dollars to feed Russians benighted by a similar drought. Why was it all right then to use public money to feed starving Russians, Senator Black demanded, but wrong to use it now to feed starving Americans? Mockingly he described Hoover as insisting that "we must adhere to the ancient method of passing the hat." Behind Hoover's pious talk of individual effort, Black said, lay fear that a federal relief program would mean higher taxes on business. Urging the Senate to appropriate twenty-five million dollars to be distributed to drought sufferers by the Interior Department, Black declared: "The great heart of America is more interested in providing relief than whether that relief is supplied by voluntary contributions or taxation."[55]

Black also leaped at the chance to deride Hoover's "pet idea" of a Federal Farm Board. Congress, he said, had enacted exactly what Hoover asked, but prices of cotton, corn, and wheat had gone down instead of up. The scheme, he said, "has proved to be an absolute and complete failure . . . a miserable farce." He objected particularly to Farm Board dealings in futures or in partial payments. If the government were going into gambling, he suggested sardonically that it employ professional gamblers. Otherwise, Black predicted that board funds would find their way into the pockets of slick investors in New York and Chicago. "It is perfectly all right to devote $100,000,000 to them," he cried, "but

---

[54] *Ibid.*, 2437, 5032.   [55] *Ibid.*, 2361–62; 3253–54.

not to offer $25,000,000 for people who are starving." In August the board proposed that cotton growers plow under a third of their 1931 crop. Hugo called the idea "impossible and unsound."[56]

When an uprising in Nicaragua threatened the lives of Americans in that country, the New York *Times* sought the reactions of members of the Senate Foreign Relations Committee. "The inevitable product of Coolidge-Hoover dollar diplomacy," Black telegraphed the *Times*. "People will be satisfied with nothing less than a clear and unequivocal abandonment and repudiation of this entire policy, and a return to the American principle of non-interference with the internal affairs of foreign governments, both great and small."[57]

The *Times* also inquired about Senator Black's reaction to Hoover's proposal of a one-year moratorium on war debt payments. "A gift to European customers . . . to increase their purchasing power," Hugo snorted. The plan would not put six million unemployed American citizens to work, nor shorten next winter's bread lines. "Our crisis," he told the *Times* crisply, "is not in Europe. It is in America."[58]

Midway through 1931, Black went home to check his own political fences. He spoke to high school graduating classes and meetings of the American Legion. He told a reunion of Confederate veterans that the real cause of the "War Between the States" was not slavery but states' rights. "It was to preserve her constitutional rights that the South established the Confederacy," Hugo assured the old Confederates.[59]

There was gossip as to who might oppose the senior senator in 1932, most of it centering around Hugo's friend Congressman Lister Hill. Both men were reported to be strong with the American Legion. But the Birmingham *Post* noted that many citizens who opposed Black in 1926 were now his supporters.[60]

Race feelings ran high in Alabama during the sultry summer of

[56] *Ibid.*, 4146, 4304; New York *Times*, August 14, 1931.
[57] New York *Times*, April 19, 1931.   [59] Birmingham *News*, June 17, 1931.
[58] *Ibid.*, June 21, 1931.   [60] Birmingham *Post*, June 12, 1931.

1931. Eight Negroes, the famous "Scottsboro boys," were under death sentences and a ninth, only thirteen years old, faced life imprisonment. On March 25 they had been hoboes aboard a freight moving slowly through North Alabama. In a fight with some white riders, the blacks threw several white youths off the train. When the freight stopped at Paint Rock, sheriff's deputies clambered aboard and arrested the nine ragged Negroes. To the deputies' surprise, they found two white girls dressed in men's overalls. Wild rumors began to circulate as to what had happened aboard the Chattanooga to Memphis freight. Within less than three weeks, the "Scottsboro boys" had been convicted of rape. Their cases were destined to ascend from hot, dingy Alabama courtrooms to the state supreme court in Montgomery and the nation's highest court in Washington, D.C. It would be almost twenty years before the last "Scottsboro boy" would be freed.[61]

In 1931 the Communist Party of the United States, through its legal arm, the International Labor Defense, determined to make the "Scottsboro boys" symbols of economic oppression and southern racism. The National Association for the Advancement of Colored People, vying with the ILD for control of the legal defense, sought to employ well-known Alabama attorneys to represent the defendants. Walter White, NAACP executive secretary, announced that his organization had retained the best criminal law firm in Birmingham—Fort, Beddow, and Ray. William E. Fort, Hugo's ally in courthouse feuds before the World War, had presided over the Stephenson case and for a short time had been Black's law partner. He and Ben Ray were not eager to publicize their association with the case. Roderick Beddow, considered Alabama's most talented criminal lawyer, was to handle the actual appeal. But bitter squabbles ensued between the NAACP and the ILD. Finally the NAACP and its Birmingham attorneys withdrew from the case.[62]

[61] Dan T. Carter has written a definitive account of these lengthy legal proceedings in *Scottsboro: A Tragedy of the American South* (Baton Rouge, 1969).
[62] Carter, *Scottsboro*, 51–103.

The affair attracted Communist attention to Alabama. In August, with temperatures soaring in the nineties, white citizens of Tallapoosa County were terrorized by a rumor that carloads of "Negro reds" were advancing from Chattanooga, determined to arouse the "oppressed black peasantry" and to form a sharecroppers' union. Blacks, too, were terrorized by the realistic fact that armed whites patrolled county roads, determined to break up any "radical meeting." When two hundred Negro sharecroppers gathered in a Camp Hill church to draft a resolution of protest on the Scottsboro case, law officers broke up their gathering. In the process a sheriff and deputy were wounded and a Negro killed. Before Tallapoosa County calmed down, sixty Negroes had been arrested, a few had mysteriously disappeared, and the church where the sharecroppers had met was burned to the ground.[63]

But the hot summer violence had not yet ended. In Birmingham three young girls, daughters of prominent citizens, were riding one afternoon when a Negro jumped on the running board of their car and ordered them to drive to a deserted wooded area. He raped the girls and later harangued them about how white people had mistreated his race. When one girl lunged for his pistol, he shot wildly, killing her and seriously wounding the other two before he fled. Several hours later, a second girl died. In the hospital the sole survivor told officers that their assailant was "very educated" and apparently from "up North." She constantly described his talk as a "radical harangue." Indignant whites insisted that the unrest in Tallapoosa County and the shootings in Birmingham were due to the influx of "reds" in their state. As long as the Scottsboro "negro rapists" remained alive, one citizen wrote Governor Miller, they would be "used by the reds to incite our colored people to riot, rape and kill."[64]

The Klan sought to pile more fuel on these hot coals of racial hatred. Hiram Evans came to Birmingham to address a rally at East Lake Park. There would be a free barbecue dinner, the Klan advertised, and small statues of Klansmen would be given away

[63] *Ibid.*, 123–27.   [64] *Ibid.*, 129–32.

as souvenirs of the occasion. Klanswomen and junior Klansmen, wearing their robes, were especially urged to attend.[65]

Prudently Alabama's senior senator abstained from comment on his state's latest paranoia. Instead Black concentrated on the deepening economic crisis. With seven million now reported unemployed, the nation prepared to celebrate Christmas as best it could. Senator Black proposed a billion-dollar public works program. If something were not done, he warned the administration, the clamor for a public dole would become irresistible. But his proposal got nowhere. During that dreary December, Black also filed an affidavit that he had supported Democratic nominees in the Alabama election of 1930 and announced his candidacy for a second Senate term [66]

[65] Birmingham *Post*, November 19, 1931.
[66] Birmingham *News*, December 19, 1931.

IX

Mixing
in Political
Beds

Birmingham, so long a fief of the United States Steel Corporation, was prostrated by the depression. Congressman George Huddleston testified to a House committee early in 1932 that 25,000 of his city's 108,000 wage and salary earners were out of work, and most of the rest were working short time. Birmingham's Community Chest, accustomed to helping 800 families each winter, made a valiant effort to feed 9,000 families. When the city advertised for a few men to clean its parks at $2 a day, 12,712 applied. Automobile sales in Alabama fell 85 percent from the levels of 1929; fertilizer sales, 72 percent. Owners of department stores and life insurance firms watched helplessly as business dropped 50 percent. In each category Alabama sales fell further than those in the country as a whole. Hoping to seduce blue-collar whites as well as black sharecroppers, the Communist Party opened a Birmingham office in 1930 and began to publish the *Southern Worker*.[1]

With Alabama so stricken, champions of federal relief were surprised when her senior senator led the floor fight against a new relief proposal. Robert M. La Follette, Jr., the progressive Republican from Wisconsin, and Edward P. Costigan, Colorado Democrat, had offered a bipartisan bill authorizing a Federal

[1] *Congressional Record*, 72nd Cong., 1st Sess., 3522; Tindall, *The Emergence of the New South*, 359; Carter, *Scottsboro*, 151.

Emergency Relief Board to allocate $375,000,000 to needy Americans. Hoover set himself stubbornly against the measure. It was even rumored that Joe Robinson, the Democratic floor leader, had promised to help defeat the bill in exchange for a Supreme Court nomination. But Robinson stayed in the background while Black openly led the fight. Calling up the shade of Jefferson, Black inveighed against concentration of power in Washington:

> How much more in line it is with the principles of Jefferson . . . not to say that the money shall be distributed in Alabama and Colorado . . . according to rules established by a Washington bureau but to let them have the money directly, and then trust the States and the people to distribute it as they should. . . .
> The natural tendency of a bureau is toward immortality. It knows no end to its greed. When it has once dipped its hands in the Federal treasury and felt the greedy touch of gold, it knows no end to its avarice and ambition. When you have created a horde of Federal employes, it is to their interest to . . . perpetuate themselves.[2]

Although cloaked in the finery of Jeffersonianism, Black's rhetoric veiled the old southern animosity toward a federal program which might upset racial mores. He offered a substitute bill authorizing states to distribute the relief money, but it was defeated. Then the La Follette-Costigan bill, too, went down to defeat at the hands of administration regulars and southern Democrats. Deep in the winter of 1932, federal relief was stalemated.[3]

Remembering Black's fight a year earlier for drought sufferers, fellow senators called him inconsistent. The Birmingham *Post* hinted that, with reelection at stake, Black had altered his political views to please powerful new friends back home. Describing the defeat of the La Follette-Costigan measure for the *Nation*, Paul Y. Anderson, a veteran Washington newspaperman, was harsh in his judgment: "Black of Alabama . . . became hysterical over the

[2] *Congressional Record*, 72nd Cong., 1st Sess., 3321, 4046; Harris Gaylord Warren, *Herbert Hoover and the Great Depression* (New York, 1959), 203–204.
[3] *Congressional Record*, 72nd Cong., 1st Sess., 4044, 4052; Warren, *Hoover and the Great Depression*, 204.

prospect of a federal relief plan which might feed Negroes as well as whites, and gave an exhibition which brought a blush to the face of Tom Heflin, lurking in the rear of the chamber."[4]

Hoover's sensibilities were not offended by the thought of spending billions to revive distressed corporations. At the President's recommendation, a bill creating the Reconstruction Finance Corporation glided smoothly through both houses. Black tried to amend the bill to forbid loans to any company paying an official more than $15,000 a year, which was the salary of the Vice-President. When this was defeated, he raised the barrier to $100,000. But his colleagues shouted down his amendments. When the Senate approved RFC, Black did not vote. Later, one rival for his Senate seat taunted him for failing to vote against RFC after he had fought La Follette-Costigan on the ground that it would create a new federal bureau. John M. Burns cackled, ". . . [RFC] was a bureau to make you sit up and take notice."[5]

Black unsuccessfully tried to block an authorization of forty million dollars in RFC funds to finance sales of farm products abroad. While Americans were hungry, he fumed, the Agriculture Department was asking forty million dollars "for the privilege" of giving away food. When tornadoes whipped through the South, creating havoc in rural areas such as Clay County, Black demanded that RFC distribute five million dollars to the stricken states. The Senate agreed, although Kentucky's M. M. Logan jested that citizens would now telegraph their favorite senator: "Get your resolution ready. I think we are going to have a storm."[6]

George Norris asked Black to represent drys that winter on a special subcommittee studying modification of the Eighteenth Amendment. The Senate should spend all its time trying to remedy unemployment, Black protested, instead of listening to personal opinions on prohibition. "But neither side will be satisfied without

[4] Birmingham *Post*, February 5, April 23, 1932; Paul Y. Anderson, "Democracy at Work," *Nation*, CXXVIII (March 2, 1934), 252.

[5] *Congressional Record*, 72nd Cong., 1st Sess., 1694, 1705, 2633, 2641–42; Birmingham *Post*, April 26, 1932.

[6] *Congressional Record*, 72nd Cong., 1st Sess., 7656, 7665, 13644.

it," said Norris resignedly. The Birmingham *Post* noted that many Alabama drys, recognizing the futility of enforcing prohibition, now favored modification. "If Senator Black will face the facts squarely," the *Post* predicted, "he, too, may change his mind."[7]

Prohibition was to be the central issue of the Alabama Democratic primary. Four aspirants challenged Hugo Black for his seat: former Governor Thomas E. Kilby of Anniston, his old foe of 1926; Charles McCall of Montgomery, embattled attorney general of the Graves administration; John M. Burns of Selma; and Judge Henry L. Anderton, a Birmingham attorney. Sensing a shift in the political wind, Kilby, a dry in 1926, and McCall came out in favor of a referendum to allow Alabamians to vote on the future of the Eighteenth Amendment. Burns was "a dripping wet." Anderton boasted that he was drier than talcum powder in a desert. There was no sign that Black planned to change his well-known "arid dry" sentiments.[8]

Confident that he had more to gain as Bankhead's defender, Black chose to campaign from the Senate floor. William Bankhead helped spread the word. "I hope that all of our friends . . . will support Senator Black. . . . He has stayed away from Alabama during the campaign purely to help John . . . and I hope that his interest will not suffer among our friends. I shall thank you to pass this word out . . . ," Will urged a Bankhead stalwart.[9]

For more than a year, Senate investigators had probed the Alabama election. When all votes were painstakingly recounted, except those in three counties where ballots had been destroyed, Bankhead still held a 47,706 majority. But the subcommittee, splitting along party lines, voted 3–2 to unseat Bankhead. In the majority report, Chairman Daniel Hastings, a Maryland Republican, declared the Alabama Democratic primary of 1930 had

[7] Birmingham *Age-Herald*, December 30, 1931; Birmingham *Post*, January 1, 1932.

[8] New York *Times*, March 20, 1932; Sellers, *The Prohibition Movement in Alabama*, 213–25; Montgomery *Advertiser*, April 8, 1932.

[9] New York *Times*, June 12, 1932; William B. Bankhead to Murray Cannon, April 26, 1932, in W. B. Bankhead Papers; Moore, *History of Alabama*, 787.

been illegal because it had adopted different qualifications for candidates than for voters. As for the election itself, Republicans estimated that 39,000 votes had been improperly cast. They charged that, among other irregularities, hat boxes had been used as ballot boxes; absentee ballots had been cast without the consent of voters; poll taxes had been paid for some; and poll watchers for Heflin had been threatened.[10]

Democratic senators on the subcommittee stressed that Bankhead had a clear majority, even after the recount, and that he had not been accused of responsibility for any of the irregularities. To void the election because of technical matters, Democrats said, would frustrate the popular will. Alabama newspapers joined the fray, declaring that Republicans were out to "get Bankhead" in revenge for the Senate's rejection, two years earlier, of Republican Senators-elect William S. Vare of Pennsylvania and Frank L. Smith of Illinois, because of their exorbitant campaign expenditures. The Mobile *Register* accused Republicans of trying to declare a Democratic seat vacant in order to alter the delicate Senate balance of power in their favor.[11]

By a one-vote margin, the full Senate committee on privileges and elections recommended that Bankhead be seated. The fight then went to the Senate floor. Black was Bankhead's most eloquent defender. He accused Republicans of "bowing at the shrine of technicality instead of trying to get to the justice of the case." He described the irregularities as "petty, trivial, small, trifling." He contended that it was not illegal for a political party to pay poll taxes for voters unless the party was trying to influence votes. Hastings interrupted to ask if a political party ever paid a poll tax for any reason except to influence a voter. "I do not know," Hugo counterattacked. "They might think they would get his vote; but I imagine they would not always get it. Of course, the practice was most common up in DeKalb County, where the probate judge is a Republican." Black insisted that the Senate face the "irresistible

[10] Dooley, "United States Senator J. Thomas Heflin," 184–88.
[11] *Ibid.*, 193–98.

conclusion" that 60 percent of Alabama voters had put their cross marks by Bankhead's name, and 40 percent had marked their ballots for Heflin.[12]

Heflin himself was the climactic speaker of the long contest. His former colleagues voted 33–31 to grant Heflin the unusual privilege of addressing the Senate, even though his old seat was already occupied by Bankhead. Black had voted against allowing Heflin to speak.[13]

For Heflin's last hurrah, the Senate and its galleries were packed. House members crowded the rear of the small chamber. Long lines of hopeful spectators, sensing that this might be their final taste of Heflin's oratory, waited outside. "Cotton Tom" wore a long, black tailcoat, white vest, and flowing tie. To dramatize his arguments, he frequently clapped his hands and uttered his familiar cry: "My God, Senators, think of that!" At the end of the two hours allotted to him, Heflin was just getting under way. George Norris moved that he be given unlimited time.[14]

During most of his speech, Heflin faced the friendly Republicans or addressed himself to the sympathetic galleries. But several times he turned toward the Democratic seats to point an accusing finger at Black, calling him "my one-time friend" and "the junior senator from Alabama." He read aloud Black's denunciation of the ruling which had excluded Heflin from the primary. "Senator Black," Heflin shouted, "was strong against the machine then; he fought it to the bitter end, and issued a statement against its conduct that while he lives will ring around the state." Black was supporting Bankhead, Heflin charged, to please the "machine" and the Alabama Power Company. Insisting that the election had been stolen, Heflin implored the Senate to support him. "I am fighting to smash the worst political machine outside of Tammany and Pittsburgh and Philadelphia," he roared.[15]

---

[12] *Congressional Record*, 72nd Cong., 1st Sess., 8770–79.
[13] *Ibid.*, 8877.
[14] Birmingham *News*, April 26, 1932.
[15] *Ibid.*; *Congressional Record*, 72nd Cong., 1st Sess., 8918–45.

After five hours and thirteen minutes, Heflin reached his crescendo: "Alabama shall be free; my State will walk again with unfettered step; her voters will vote as they choose and, by the eternal God, every ballot shall be counted as cast. I thank you, Senators." The galleries exploded with applause.[16]

Next day John Bankhead, son of a former senator and brother of a well-known House member, made his first Senate speech. In marked contrast to Heflin, Bankhead was calm and solemn. He reminded the Senate that he had originally supported Heflin's right to run in the primary. He denied that a political machine ran Alabama. Answering Heflin's charge that he was a tool of the Alabama Power Company, Bankhead said that he had resigned as a power company attorney eight years earlier because he differed with the company over Muscle Shoals. Finally Bankhead urged senators not to vote on the basis of old friendship for Heflin, but on the merits of the contest.[17]

When Bankhead finished, George Norris, Heflin's old ally on the Farm Bloc, arose. "Cotton Tom's" most powerful friend in the Senate was still troubled by the exclusion of Heflin from candidacy in the Democratic primary. On this ground Norris urged the Senate to unseat Bankhead. The Constitution, he said, provided that the Senate should be the sole judge of the qualifications of its members; therefore it was not bound by any decision of the Alabama Supreme Court. Key Pittman of Nevada countered that in 1921 the United States Supreme Court had denied the right of the Senate to sit in judgment on a primary. Georgia's Walter George made a plea for Bankhead, stressing his moral qualities in contrast to the charge that Smith and Vare had condoned illegal expenditures.[18]

In April, 1932, a year and a half after the disputed election, the Senate voted 65–18 to recognize Bankhead. Joe Robinson and Walter George had succeeded in keeping every Democrat in line.

[16] *Congressional Record*, 72nd Cong., 1st Sess., 8918–45.
[17] *Ibid.*, 9021.
[18] Dooley, "United States Senator J. Thomas Heflin," 212–14.

Twenty-two Republicans and one Farmer-Laborite, apparently unconvinced that irregularities had changed the outcome of the election, also supported Bankhead. George Norris and seventeen other Republicans, including some of the old Farm Bloc, opposed Bankhead. Watching from the rear of the chamber, Heflin seemed stunned by the overwhelming rejection of his contest. He rose, looked reproachfully at his former colleagues, and left the Senate.[19]

Four days before the 1932 primary in which he was a candidate, Hugo Black arrived home, acclaimed by the press as a hero who had saved Alabama from the disgrace of a voided election. Joe Robinson and fellow Senate Democrats had praised his "able handling" of Bankhead's case and assured him of their support in his campaign for renomination. The Birmingham *News* wrote admiringly of the "irrefutable logic and withering ridicule" of Black's answer to Hastings. "He had to bear the burden of defending his state," declared the *News*. "How admirably he bore it, every Alabamian knows." Friends of the Bankheads were busy in his behalf. J. J. Willett, Jr., an influential newspaper publisher in Anniston and a Bankhead supporter in 1926, wrote Black: "Your demonstrated efficiency calls for your reelection."[20]

One sour note marred the homecoming. Former Governor Kilby trumpeted the charge that Black's wife was on the senator's payroll. "It is hard to know just exactly how a man should restrain himself under an attack like this," Hugo wrote a friend. "I can frankly state that I am glad I was not in Alabama when I first read it." When Kilby and Black met by chance in an elevator, Kilby shrank behind other passengers, evidently afraid that Black would attack him physically. Dr. Sterling Foster was outraged at the use of his daughter's name in a political campaign.[21]

19 *Ibid.*, 214–16; Tanner, "James Thomas Heflin," 231.
20 Birmingham *News*, April 29, 1932; Joseph J. Willett, Jr., to Hugo L. Black, April 9, 1932, in Willett Papers.
21 Hugo L. Black to Joseph J. Willett, Jr., April 17, 1932, in Willett Papers. Justice Black, in an interview with the author in September, 1966, recalled the elevator incident and the fury of his father-in-law.

Black denounced the "false charge" that his wife was currently on the government payroll. It was conceived, he said, by the same "cunning mind" which pressed false charges against Alabama in the Senate. The "cunning mind" to which Black referred was that of Horace Wilkinson, who had presented Heflin's case in the Senate hearings. Black then acknowledged that Josephine had received pay during the summer of 1931 when one of his regular secretaries could not accompany the Blacks to their summer retreat in Mentone, Alabama. He reminded his constituents that Josephine had done stenographic work as an enlisted member of the United States Navy during the World War. "She earned her money then," he declared. "She earned every penny she received during those few months she did temporary work." Later Kilby denied that he had said Mrs. Black was currently on the senator's payroll. He said he had quoted government records showing her on the payroll at $2,200 a year from April 1, 1931 to June, 1931, when the government report ended.[22]

Black was not the only Alabama legislator accused of nepotism. The LaFayette *Sun* reported that Senator Bankhead employed his son-in-law as a secretary at $3,900; Representative William Bankhead's wife was listed as a clerk at $2,000; two other representatives had their wives on their payrolls; and Cora Grant, wife of Black's secretary, Hugh G. Grant, was employed by Senator Black at $1,800 a year. In the midst of major unemployment, the *Sun* protested, "it is adding insult to injury for congressmen and senators to be employing members of their own families when they are already amply paid."[23]

Kilby's charge of nepotism sputtered and died. The former governor had violated an old taboo. Names of southern ladies were not to be dragged in the political mud. "Certain people seek to emphasize pigmy questions," Black commented scornfully.[24]

[22] Birmingham *News*, April 30, May 11, 1932; Hugo L. Black to Joseph J. Willett, Jr., April 17, 1932, in Willett Papers.

[23] LaFayette *Sun*, April 13, 1932, copy in scrapbook of Hugo L. Black, in Hugo L. Black Papers.

[24] Birmingham *News*, May 1, 1932.

Prodded by Governor Miller, the Alabama legislature had rid its state in 1931 of the "minority primary," adopted in 1915 by drys seeking political power. Under that system of adding first- and second-choice votes to determine the leading candidate, Black had won his first senatorial nomination without a runoff and without the support of a majority of Alabama Democrats. Determined that minority groups should no longer control state politics, Miller's legislature passed a new primary law. There would be no more second-choice votes. If no candidate received a majority, there would be a runoff.[25]

On May 3, 1932, Hugo Black came within 659 votes of a majority. In the same primary, Alabama chose a slate of delegates pledged to Franklin D. Roosevelt as Democratic nominee for the presidency. Commenting on Black's race, the Birmingham *News* said it was "almost unheard of" for a candidate to come so close to a majority against four opponents. Kilby, the runner-up, lagged 35,000 votes behind. "The size of his vote is a handsome tribute to Senator Black," said the *News*. But the Montgomery *Advertiser* remembered that Black had been nominated in 1926 by a minority, mostly of "Kluxers," and that in 1928 he had "denied his party's candidate for President the benefit of his active support." Alabama Democrats, the *Advertiser* concluded, had evidently decided to let bygones be bygones.[26]

Despite Black's commanding lead, Kilby challenged the senator to a June runoff, demanding to know Black's views on prohibition, Muscle Shoals, and economic problems. "Mr. Black," Kilby said, "seems to be constitutionally opposed to taking a definite stand on any issue." Black retorted that Kilby was costing Alabama taxpayers fifty thousand dollars by insisting on a runoff even though his opponent had won 49.64 percent of the primary vote.[27]

Kilby's campaign theme was "wily Hugo." He called Black the

25 Moore, *History of Alabama*, 787; New York *Times*, June 12, 1932.
26 The vote was Black, 92,930; Kilby, 57,875; Burns, 15,528; McCall, 11,376; and Anderton, 9,467. *Alabama Official and Statistical Register* (1935), 468–70; Birmingham *News*, May 4, 9, 1932; Montgomery *Advertiser*, May 5, 1932.
27 Birmingham *News*, May 8, 17, 1932.

"arch deserter" of the Democratic Party in 1928; and he accused him of refusing to speak for the party in 1930 until he "made a trade" with Democratic leaders to support his own renomination. He declared that Black had tricked the drys by waiting until after the primary to announce that he favored a nationwide referendum on the Eighteenth Amendment. "By his false stand," Kilby charged, Black had received thousands of votes from strict prohibitionists who might otherwise have supported "powder dry" Anderton. During the climax of his attack, Kilby waved a photostatic copy of the Grand Passport, presented to Black by the Klan in 1926. "He would double cross the Ku Klux Klan too," Kilby shouted, "except for the fact that he is a life member of that order."[28]

Leaders of Alabama's Anti-Saloon League, who had supported Black in the primary, were outraged by his tardy endorsement of a referendum on prohibition. They met to consider dropping Black and supporting Kilby. After hours of debate, the frustrated drys adjourned without endorsing either candidate. Now that both Senate aspirants favored a referendum, drys "had nowhere to go," commented the Montgomery *Advertiser*. Henry Anderton, the "powder dry," would have had an opportunity to win antireferendum votes, the *Advertiser* said, if Black had announced his stand before the primary. The Birmingham *Post* called Senator Black "an opportunistic politician." Defending himself, Black said he was a Jeffersonian Democrat who believed that the people themselves should decide the fate of prohibition.[29]

Kilby also attacked Black for his "indefensible" stand against the La Follette-Costigan bill. Speaking to the Alabama Federation of Labor, Black explained that he favored direct relief for the needy, but wanted funds to be administered by states rather than by a federal bureau. He said the La Follette-Costigan bill would

[28] Montgomery *Advertiser*, May 21, 1932; Birmingham *Post*, May 21, 1932.
[29] Sellers, *The Prohibition Movement in Alabama*, 214–15; Birmingham *Post*, May 19, June 2, 1932; Montgomery *Advertiser*, May 18, 1932; Birmingham *News*, May 17, 1932.

have "given the right to a Washington bureau to dictate the terms upon which every pound of food distributed in Alabama would have been given out." Late in the campaign, he charged that the bill was "pork barrel legislation" to provide Republican campaign funds. At Kilby's request, La Follette and Costigan replied that their bill was proposed solely to relieve human suffering and "had no partisan purpose whatever." The Birmingham *News* approved Black's view, but Tom Heflin called Black's vote against La Follette-Costigan "a cruel act." [30]

Challenged by Kilby to explain his current stand on Muscle Shoals, Black said that he favored a new bill offered by Representative Lister Hill of Montgomery. The bill purported to be a compromise between the approach favored by President Hoover and that of Norris, but contained little of the Norris program. It provided for government operation of Muscle Shoals power plants, but surplus power was to be sold at the switchboard only, not through transmission lines. Preference would be given to state, county, and municipal customers. Under the Hill plan, nitrate plants were to be leased to private operators. The Birmingham *Post*, Black's most outspoken press opponent, charged that he was abandoning the Norris plan for a "makeshift measure under the spell of the power interests." His change, the *Post* said, "helps explain the support he is now receiving from some interests which in the past have fought him bitterly." [31]

Barraged by criticism, Black returned the fire. He declared that Kilby, as governor, had raised tax assessments to become "the tax adjuster's patron saint and the taxpayer's regret." He accused Governor Miller of permitting state employees to campaign for Kilby at public expense. He declared that Kilby was allied with Republicans, and that Kilbyites were fighting him because he had supported the Democratic Party. "I have a letter in my files," Black

[30] Birmingham *Post*, May 9, June 2, 11, 1932; Birmingham *News*, June 16, 1932.

[31] Birmingham *News*, May 17, 1932; Birmingham *Post*, May 19, 1932. The fact that the Hill bill provided for any public power cost it the support of the Hoover administration and it died in committee in July, 1932. Hubbard, *Origins of the TVA*, 305–307.

confided to a Montgomery audience, "warning me that if I dared to raise my voice in defense of the Democratic party in the contest, I would be defeated in the next primary."[32]

As the campaign grew more heated, puzzling political lineups emerged. Atticus Mullin, veteran political writer for the Montgomery *Advertiser*, told his readers he had never known "such mixing in political beds." Kilby repeatedly charged Black with deserting his party in 1928, yet Edmund Pettus, chairman of the Democratic State Executive Committee, openly backed Black. It was reported that twenty-two of the committee's twenty-seven members were also Black supporters. "Where does this leave Kilby?" asked the Birmingham *News*. "It leaves him in the infamous company of those who, out of spite against Black for his valiant services to the party, are out to 'get' him." Black was the choice of both Mayor William Gunter of Montgomery, a Klan foe and a leader in the campaign for Smith, and of former Governor Bibb Graves, onetime Klansman and a reluctant Smith supporter. Labor, regarding Kilby as an antiunion employer, remained faithful to Black; William Green, of the American Federation of Labor, and chiefs of twenty-one railroad labor organizations urged his reelection.[33]

Kilby was supported by Horace Wilkinson and Forney Johnston, who had represented opposite sides in the suit against the Democratic Executive Committee's ruling to bar the bolters. Although he hammered away at the theme that Black was a onetime Klansman and a party deserter, Kilby was also backed by the Klan itself and by Tom Heflin, the main bolter of 1928. "Why did Black Sulk in His Tent?" asked a full-page, Kilby advertisement in the Birmingham *News*. Forney Johnston, sponsor of the advertisement, repeated the charge that Black had originally encouraged the 1928 bolters but later decided to stick with the Democratic

[32] Birmingham *News*, May 17, 1932.
[33] Montgomery *Advertiser*, June 9, 1932; Jesse B. Hearin to Joseph J. Willett, Jr., June 6, 1932, in Willett Papers; *Labor*, June 7, 1932, published in Washington, D.C., by Associated Recognized Standard Railroad Labor Organizations, copy in Hugo L. Black Papers, Washington, D.C., Birmingham *News*, June 9, 1932.

Party. Johnston and Kilby insisted that Black had received "fine" committee assignments in the Senate as a reward from Democrats for remaining faithful and from Republicans for not actively supporting Al Smith. They reminded voters that Black had criticized the ruling to bar the bolters as candidates in 1930, but later championed Bankhead. Johnston, once a leading foe of Heflin and Locke, said the bolters "at least had the courage to square their shoulders and take the lightning." [34]

All three defeated candidates lined up with Kilby. The Birmingham *News* commented with wonder that Kilby had "linked the antipodes of prohibition sentiment" in John M. Burns, the "dripping wet," and Henry Anderton, the "powder dry." But prohibitionists were divided and confused. One observer thought that "between Kilby's frankness and Black's apparent sail-shifting, they were inclined to prefer Kilby." Charles McCall, who had broken with the Klan in 1927, now supported Kilby. Atticus Mullin summed it up: "If Solomon were . . . asked to . . . unscramble the political alignments in Alabama, he would grab the butcher knife and probably cut his own throat." [35]

Kilby tried to taunt Black into a series of debates. He would not consider it, Hugo replied firmly; Kilby was only attempting to get an audience for himself. Black was afraid to face embarrassing questions, Kilby retorted. But one June day, the two candidates met on the same platform at Scottsboro. It was "trading day," an annual occasion when farmers came from miles around to swap mules, hound dogs, and political gossip. Before the rape trials had made its name known to the world, Scottsboro's main claim to fame had been trading day. About fifteen hundred farmers and their wives were waiting to hear Senator Black. Even the *Advertiser* admitted that he was one of the best political speakers heard in Alabama in many a decade. [36]

Moments before Black was to begin, Kilby clambered onto the

[34] Birmingham *News*, June 5, 1932.
[35] Birmingham *News*, May 25, 1932; New York *Times*, June 12, 1932; Montgomery *Advertiser*, June 9, 1932.
[36] Montgomery *Advertiser*, June 4, 1930.

platform, offering to debate. Black told the crowd he refused "to stoop down in the mud like the gentleman who challenged me." Turning to Kilby, he declared: "You speak to your crowd, and I'll speak to mine." There was nothing for Kilby to do but step down and listen while Black harangued the North Alabama farm people for more than an hour. Then the senator left immediately to speak in nearby Florence. Kilby jumped to the platform and tried to rekindle the crowd by calling Black "the great double-crosser who has ever flashed athwart Alabama's political horizon." But twilight was falling on trading day and farmers were beginning to drift toward home. The Birmingham *News*, ardently for Black, thought Kilby's attempt "undignified," but the *Advertiser* described Black as "brought to bay" and the Birmingham *Post* said the senator virtually "took to his heels." [37]

At the end of the campaign Black wryly told a capacity crowd in Birmingham's Jefferson Theater: "Kilby and Horace [Wilkinson] . . . have already accused me of everything except murder." To wind up his plea, Kilby dispatched a hundred speakers over the state. Black spoke for himself by radio.

When the votes were in, Black had won renomination by a majority of more than twenty-nine thousand. He carried fifty-two of Alabama's sixty-seven counties. The *News* and the *Advertiser* agreed that the size of Black's victory was "a vote of confidence." Kilby had lost, the *Advertiser* believed, because of "the protective armor which Senator Black had fabricated in the Bankhead-Heflin contest." The *Post* consoled itself that Kilby had forced Senator Black to take public stands on issues. By cautious, intricate maneuvering, Hugo Black had successfully navigated the political shoals upon which "Tom-Tom" Heflin had wrecked his senatorial career. [38]

Black returned briefly to Washington. He was there in July when

---

[37] Montgomery *Advertiser*, June 7, 1932; Birmingham *News*, June 7, 1932; Birmingham *Post*, June 7, 1932.

[38] Birmingham *News*, June 13, 1932; Birmingham *Post*, June 13, 1932; Montgomery *Advertiser*, June 16, 1932. The vote was Black, 103,453; Kilby, 74,039. *Alabama Official and Statistical Register* (1935), 491.

Hoover ordered Douglas MacArthur to evict the bonus marchers from their shacks on the Anacostia Flats. Seeking comment on the clash which left two veterans and two policemen dead, the New York *Times* found that Black, a veteran himself, was the only senator who would speak out publicly against Hoover's use of force, although other senators privately criticized the President's action. "Wholly unnecessary and ill-timed," Black told the *Times*. "As one citizen, I want to make my public protest against this militaristic way of handling a condition which has been brought about by wide-spread unemployment and hunger."[39]

Black was not so forthright, however, when it came to controversy in his own state. Four college girls from Vassar and Wellesley called on the senator to protest the Scottsboro case. Later Black told reporters that he had informed the girls there was plenty of crime in northern cities to engage their sympathies. He said he would be glad to discuss the case after the girls had read the legal transcripts.[40]

Democrats that August, milling about in the heat of Chicago Stadium, voted resoundingly in favor of repealing the Eighteenth Amendment and nominating Franklin D. Roosevelt. "The party wants repeal, your candidate wants repeal, and I am confident the United States of America wants repeal," Roosevelt declared candidly in his acceptance speech. Black wrote the nominee, "I am subject to your call from now until the last vote is counted." Roosevelt replied, "Keep in touch with Farley."[41]

During much of the fall, Hugo Black was away from Alabama campaigning for the national ticket. Although he and all nine Alabama representatives were opposed by Republicans, the *News* assured them: "Alabama Democrats are concerned not with whether they will win but only with how great the margin of

[39] New York *Times*, July 30, 1932.
[40] Montgomery *Advertiser*, April 2, 1932.
[41] Sellers, *The Prohibition Movement in Alabama*, 222; Hugo L. Black to Franklin D. Roosevelt, undated; Franklin D. Roosevelt to Hugo L. Black, August 11, 1932, in Franklin D. Roosevelt Papers, Franklin D. Roosevelt Library, Hyde Park, New York, hereinafter cited as Roosevelt Papers.

victory will be." Despite the distress of drys over the repeal plank, Roosevelt carried Alabama by 207,000 votes to 34,000 for Hoover. Black was overwhelmingly reelected. The Montgomery *Advertiser* hoped that the Roosevelt victory meant the end of prohibition. Alabama's strange alliance of bedsheet and Bible had been vanquished. Her troubled people, seeking a way out of their economic slough, were ready to hail the New Deal.[42]

[42] *Alabama Official and Statistical Register* (1935), 503–508; Birmingham *News*, November 4, 1932; Sellers, *The Prohibition Movement in Alabama*, 224.

X

ЛЛЛЛЛЛЛЛЛЛЛЛЛЛЛЛЛЛЛЛЛЛЛЛЛЛЛЛЛ

When Are
These
Air-mail Killings
Going to Stop?

North Alabama farmers lined the main streets of little towns in the Tennessee Valley on a bleak January day in 1933 for a glimpse of the man who was soon to be the nation's new leader. It heartened them to see Franklin Roosevelt smile and wave as he rode through their desolate trading centers and the impoverished land which barely sustained their lives. The New York *Times* reported that Roosevelt, at Muscle Shoals, inspected "a $150,000,000 white elephant . . . which has troubled two administrations." In the President-elect's party, Alabamians easily recognized Senator Hugo Black, but few could identify a small, white-haired member of the entourage. To George Norris, from faraway Nebraska, the tour symbolized victory after a long, stubborn fight. This new Democratic President would transform the "white elephant" into a government development beyond Norris' dreams. "He plans to go even farther than I did," Norris told newsmen happily.[1]

Black's presence in this tour emphasized his transition from a freshman minority senator and gadfly of Republican administrations to a seasoned, majority senator in a congenial political atmosphere. Committee chairmanships and national attention

---

[1] New York *Times*, January 8, 1933; Arthur M. Schlesinger, Jr., *The Coming of the New Deal*, Vol. I of *The Age of Roosevelt* (Cambridge, Mass., 1958), 454.

would reward New Deal stalwarts, and Senator Black would make the most of these opportunities.

During the lame duck session of Congress, Black voted for the Twenty-First Amendment, which was to end the sham of nation-wide prohibition. He told the Senate he favored resubmission of the Eighteenth Amendment to the voters only if states were assured of the right to prohibit liquor sales within their boundaries. In July, 1933, Alabamians, at the urging of their influential newspapers and of Roosevelt himself, voted to repeal the Eighteenth Amendment. But dry militancy, stealthily aided by bootleggers, was far from dead.[2]

To the dismay of many who had just cast their votes for his reelection, Black launched in December, 1932, his startling scheme to cut the work week in industry to thirty hours in hope of creating more jobs. By using the power of Congress to regulate commerce, he proposed to prohibit the shipment, between states or abroad, of products made by workmen employed longer than a five-day week of six-hour work days. Such a panacea, radical for 1932, came to Black out of his readings in economic theory and perhaps because of the prompting of organized labor.[3]

From reading G. D. H. Cole, Arthur Dahlberg, and Stuart Chase, Black had become acquainted with the "technocratic" theory that machines had brought the capitalistic system to its peak, creating a permanent labor surplus which could be relieved only by spreading employment thinner. But while machines were taking the jobs of men, the average work week of those who remained in factories was getting longer, he pointed out, instead of shorter. In southern mills, for example, spinners and weavers worked 53.6 hours a week in 1930, 55.7 hours in 1932. In open-pit mines, workers in 1932 had averaged 56 to 64 hours a week. Labor-saving machines, Black told a radio audience in January,

[2] *Congressional Record*, 72nd Cong., 2nd Sess., 4231; Sellers, *Prohibition Movement in Alabama*, 227–43.

[3] *Congressional Record*, 72nd Cong., 2nd Sess., 820. In an interview with the author, Justice Black said that the thirty-hour bill was his own idea.

1933, were created for the public good and not to exact 50, 60, or 70 hours a week from some, driving others into unemployment and poverty.

Voicing his conviction that the depression was caused by a lack of consumers, Black cited the example of a Washington, D.C. charity which had just appealed for seven hundred pairs of used shoes at a time when American shoe factories had the capacity to produce nine hundred million pairs a year. "This widespread human want in the midst of plenty," he declared, "is America's paramount problem. . . . Men without jobs cannot buy. I am not willing to sit silent and permit the capitalistic system to destroy itself by reason of blind adherence to old forms."[4]

The thirty-hour bill contained no minimum-wage provision, probably in the realistic assumption that the Supreme Court would find this a basis for declaring the whole plan unconstitutional. Black hoped the justices would not repeat the Court's 1918 majority reasoning of *Hammer* v. *Dagenhart*, that Congress could not prohibit shipment of products of child labor in interstate commerce because it thus regulated local labor conditions rather than commerce. His bill, he insisted, would not forbid labor to work longer than thirty hours, but simply prohibit the movement in interstate commerce of products manufactured by those who worked a longer week.[5]

Echoing Justice Oliver Wendell Holmes, Jr., Black argued that the commerce power included the power to prohibit, and that interpretation of the Constitution should allow for new situations which its authors could not have foreseen. Constitutional interpretation, he declared, had made it possible "to adjust laws written under its terms to fit alike the oxcart and the airplane, the handloom and the swift spinning of modern factories."[6]

William Green, president of the American Federation of Labor, hurried to Capitol Hill to testify in favor of the Black bill. At hearings before a subcommittee of George Norris' judiciary com-

[4] *Congressional Record*, 72nd Cong., 2nd Sess., 1443–44; 1876.
[5] New York *Times*, March 31, 1933.
[6] *Ibid.*

mittee, Green threatened that labor would engage in a general strike, if necessary, to compel industry to accept a thirty-hour week. Norris and other senators appeared startled. Black asked Green if a universal strike would mean "class war," to which the AFL leader replied: "It would be that." Noting that American unemployment had reached an all-time peak of 12,000,000, Green estimated that the thirty-hour bill would put 6,600,000 of these wage earners back to work.[7]

Only two witnesses opposed the bill. Black told the Senate witheringly that one was a Communist "who wished to destroy the capitalistic system"; and the other was a representative of the National Association of Manufacturers, "which wants to dominate the working man." But in the dying days of the Hoover administration, Black's proposal did not reach the Senate floor. Less than a week after the inauguration of Franklin Roosevelt, the Alabama senator notified the new President that he intended to resubmit his bill to a Democratic-led Congress. He urged Roosevelt to include "this imperatively necessary legislation" in his relief message to Congress. On March 30 a surprising 11–3 vote of the Judiciary Committee sent Black's novel proposal to the full Senate without the aid of the administration.[8]

The Senate spent only a week debating this new approach. Steel, textile, and paper manufacturers, milk producers, canners of salmon and other perishable foods protested frantically to their senators that the Black bill would ruin their businesses. Amendments were added to exempt workers in the milk and newspaper industries, and those in certain phases of agricultural processing. Hinting that the administration was not wholeheartedly behind Black's idea, majority leader Joe Robinson tried unsuccessfully to amend the bill to provide for a thirty-six-hour week. But on April 6, acting with surprising alacrity, the Senate brought the Black bill, its effectiveness limited to two years, to a vote. A

[7] *Ibid.*, January 6, 19, February 13, 1933; *Hearings* on S. 5167, January 5–9, 24–31, February 1–11, 1933, Judiciary Committee, George W. Norris, chairman, Group No. 46, Legislative Records, National Archives, Washington, D.C.

[8] New York *Times*, January 29, March 31, 1933; Hugo L. Black to Franklin D. Roosevelt, March 10, 1933, in Roosevelt Papers.

coalition of fifty-three liberal and prolabor senators put it across.[9]

National reaction to the Senate vote ranged from surprise to dismay. The New York *Herald-Tribune* feared "socialist regimentation in the Moscow manner," and the New York *Times* spoke disdainfully of the "curious, sentimental and superconstitutional theories and antics of the Senate majority." Tardily leaders of the United States Chamber of Commerce and National Association of Manufacturers mobilized to fight the bill. William Green hailed it as "the first practical step on the part of the government to deal constructively with the problem of unemployment." Under the heading, "Thirty Hour Bill Startles Nation," *Newsweek* reported that the country, in its jubilation over legal beer, had paid little attention to the rapid progress of "this revolutionary piece of labor legislation."[10]

The most powerful opponent of the Black bill proved to be neither the United States Chamber nor the NAM, but Roosevelt himself. Secretary of Labor Frances Perkins wrote later that the President regarded the bill as "cold and inhuman," a mass approach to the problem of unemployment and one tied to a static economy. Although sympathetic to Black's objective, Roosevelt was committed to a dynamic, expanding economic future rather than one predicated on curtailed production. Nor did he feel a thirty-hour week was essential to the health of workers. "Is there any harm," he asked Frances Perkins, "in people working an eight-hour day and forty-eight hours a week?" Roosevelt considered adding a minimum wage provision and a government agency empowered to grant flexible work hours, but every lawyer consulted by the administration warned that such a bill would be held unconstitutional. Asked about the Black bill in press conferences and cabinet meetings, the President hit upon a pet phrase, "the rhythm of the cow," to describe its need for flexibility.[11]

---

[9] New York *Times*, April 6, 7, 1933.

[10] "Thirty-Hour Week Startles Nation," *Newsweek*, I (April 15, 1933), 5–6.

[11] Frances Perkins, *The Roosevelt I Knew* (New York, 1946), 192–96. Roosevelt's reaction to the Black bill is described in less detail in James McGregor Burns, *Roosevelt, the Lion and the Fox* (New York, 1956); and Arthur M.

Unwilling to affront Senate liberals, Roosevelt was forced to evolve his own approach to unemployment. Feeling his way, he had dispatched Secretary Perkins to advise the Judiciary Committee of the administration's doubts. Before her appearance, Roosevelt telephoned several times to coach Miss Perkins, even asking if she would object if the hearing were attended by Mrs. Roosevelt and a guest, Miss Ishbel MacDonald, daughter of British Prime Minister Ramsay MacDonald. For Miss Perkins, testifying before klieg lights, photographers, reporters, and over the radio was a "trying experience." She recalled, "It was a full-dress affair. Senator Black apparently wanted it that way." She told the committee that the bill, in its original form, was unworkable, but might be made into workable law if modified with minimum wage provisions and flexibility for certain industries.[12]

Shortly after its Senate passage, the thirty-hour plan was the topic of a Cabinet meeting. Black was invited to the White House to discuss it with Miss Perkins and Secretary of Commerce Daniel C. Roper. Roosevelt's mind, Miss Perkins said, was "as innocent as a child's of any such program as NRA" before the Black bill passed. But now the President quietly requested several advisors to work up the administration's own industrial recovery plan. Rexford G. Tugwell, Hugh S. Johnson, Donald R. Richberg, Senator Robert F. Wagner, Miss Perkins, and other administration theorists began to draft the National Industrial Recovery Act. By mid-May, it was ready to be presented to Congress. Its framers said the new bill was broad enough to take care of maximum work hours. Joe Robinson commented that the Black bill, on which a House committee was holding hearings, was "not now in the picture."[13]

Schlesinger, Jr., *The Coming of the New Deal*, 91. Joseph Alsop and Robert Kintner, in *Men Around the President* (New York, 1939), 36, said, "The threat of the Black bill terrified the White House." Raymond Moley, in *After Seven Years* (New York, 1939), said (p. 186) the bill was "born of the old labor tactics of driving for concessions when the 'enemy' was weakest."

[12] Perkins, *The Roosevelt I Knew*, 192–96.

[13] *Ibid.*, 197–200; Schlesinger, *The Coming of the New Deal*, 98; New York *Times*, May 2, 12, 1933.

With administration support thus publicly withdrawn, Black's "ninety-day wonder" was shunted aside. Large employers in Alabama were relieved. The Birmingham *News*, so enthusiastic about Black a few months earlier, doubted both the desirability and constitutionality of his program. The Birmingham *Age-Herald* warned that the American industrial structure "resists overnight transformation." Donald Comer, leading Bourbon of Alabama's textile industry, wrote Black that his mills could not pay the same wage for six hours as for ten. Comer said he feared competition from imported goods. He predicted that farms would be left untended as boys and girls abandoned "sun-up to sun-down" in favor of industry's thirty-hour week. The Birmingham *Post*, frequently critical of Black, was surprised that the senator pushed his bill "despite protests from industrial interests back home." [14]

His own plan spurned, Black argued against NRA. He espoused the view of many liberals that its industry-wide codes violated the Sherman antitrust law. Congress should either uphold its antitrust legislation, he declared, or remove it from the books. At a press conference, Roosevelt described NRA as an elastic plan, not a "fiat," like the Black bill, laying down hard and fast terms. After NRA was approved, the tactful Miss Perkins suggested that Roosevelt try to soothe any ruffled feelings which Senator Black might harbor. Dutifully the President wrote to thank Hugo for his work in preparing public opinion to accept the idea of a limit on work hours, as specified in many NRA codes. But the letter failed to reconcile Black to the defeat by his own party's leadership of his proposal for alleviating economic depression. [15]

Black withdrew temporarily from the fray, but organized labor was soon restive over the Blue Eagle. As early as September, 1933, William Green expressed dissatisfaction with work hours provided

[14] Birmingham *News*, April 7, 1933; Birmingham *Age-Herald*, April 7, 1933; Birmingham *Post*, May 3, 1933; Donald Comer to Hugo Black, April 15, 1933, Hugo L. Black Papers.
[15] Franklin D. Roosevelt to Hugo L. Black, June 24, 1933, in Roosevelt Papers; New York *Times*, June 14, 1933; text of Roosevelt's press conference of July 5, 1933, in Roosevelt Papers.

in the codes. Unless the work week were reduced to thirty hours, he threatened that labor would go to Congress again and support a thirty-hour bill. A year later, at their annual convention in San Francisco, members of the AFL, cheering and whistling, adopted the thirty-hour week as one of the major planks in their program for economic recovery.

His thirty-hour fight lost, Black turned his attention to a favorite target, the subsidy program for private shipping lines. He warned Roosevelt against appointing anyone connected with subsidized companies to an important position in his administration. During Hoover's last days in office, Senator Black had received a tip that the Post Office Department was hurrying to sign one final mail contract before Democrats took over.[16]

Postmaster General Walter F. Brown was about to award the Philadelphia Mail Steamship Company a ten-year contract to carry the mail between Philadelphia-Baltimore and Liverpool-Manchester for one million dollars a year. It was to go into effect on March 1, three days before the change in administrations. Hastily Black proposed a resolution ordering that the matter be postponed until Democrats were in office. The contract, he told the Senate angrily, was "a raid on the public treasury . . . gross, outrageous, and corrupt fraud." He demanded to know, "Why the haste to award this contract in the closing hours of this session of Congress?"[17]

To halt passage of the Black resolution, Pennsylvania's David Reed filibustered until forty minutes past the hour when the contract was to have been signed. Frustrated, Black threatened to withhold the necessary appropriation. He told the Senate that the Chase National Bank and the House of Morgan controlled the Philadelphia firm and sought "one more little bite out of the Treasury before the Democratic administration gets in." But

[16] Hugo L. Black to Franklin D. Roosevelt, February 28, 1933, in Roosevelt Papers.
[17] *Congressional Record*, 72nd Cong., 2nd Sess., 5114–30; New York *Times*, March 1, 1933.

Postmaster General Brown, in a sudden reversal, notified his Senate adversary that he had decided to leave the matter to his successor. It was later revealed that the Philadelphia firm declined the contract because it had no ships. The United States Shipping Board, with Senator Black as watchdog, had refused to make a last-minute sale.[18]

When Democrats took control of Congress, Black was named chairman of a special Senate subcommittee to investigate the ocean mail subsidy program. The subcommittee, created at his suggestion, was to determine what the government received in return for an expenditure of $25,000,000 a year for overseas mail delivery. On May 1, Black began work, pursuing the inquiry single-handedly much of the time.[19]

Testifying before Chairman Black, shipping officials admitted frankly that government mail contracts were meant, not as payment for mail delivery, but as subsidies to equalize the difference in operating costs between American and foreign vessels. If fat contracts were withdrawn, shippers protested, it would mean the destruction of American lines in foreign trade. But some ship operators who drew large subsidies, Hugo retorted, employed few Americans and wanted to revise the laws so they could hire more foreign seamen at low wages. Their subsidies, he charged, were frittered away on fat salaries, expense accounts, dividends, and highly paid lobbyists.[20]

Summoned before the Senate subcommittee, shippers faced an unnerving prospect. Black's reputation as a rigorous cross-examiner so alarmed the president of one line that he brought his personal physician to the witness stand with him to check his pulse. Although Black warned them not to collaborate on testimony, several shipping officials got together for a clandestine

[18] *Congressional Record*, 72nd Cong., 2nd Sess., 5310; New York *Times*, March 2, 3, 1933, January 24, 1934.

[19] *Congressional Record*, 73d Cong., 1st Sess., 177; New York *Times*, May 2, September 30, 1933.

[20] New York *Times*, September 30, 1933; *Congressional Record*, 73d Cong., 2nd Sess., 3178–79.

meeting in the Mayflower Hotel. The following day the chairman knew all about the meeting and even corrected one witness on the time he had departed from the supposedly secret conference. *Newsweek* called Black a "useful Torquemada." [21]

By insistent questioning Black built his case against shippers. One of his first targets was the Export Steamship Corporation of Washington, D.C., whose sole owner, Black brought out, lived in the same hotel as the chairman of the United States Shipping Board. The two men were friends and frequent poker companions. Needled by Black, the company treasurer admitted that his corporation, whose liabilities outweighed its assets by three to one, had obtained mail contracts despite a law that required companies with such contracts to be in a liquid condition. Since 1929 the company had collected more in subsidy payments than it had paid for eighteen surplus vessels it bought at bargain prices from the Shipping Board. In the year of the great crash, the Export Steamship Corporation had received an average of $66,000 a pound for the mail it had carried. [22] "It's obvious the government will never get anything back," Black commented drily, "but it is worth while to show how it lost all this money." [23]

Under Chairman Black's grilling, J. E. Dockendorff, president of the subsidized Black Diamond Steamship Corporation, conceded that he had received salary and other benefits totaling more than $1,000,000 between 1919 and 1932. A witness for Lykes Brothers Steamship Company admitted to Black that it was a problem to get any mail for its ships to carry from New Orleans to other Gulf ports and the West Indies. Nonetheless, Lykes had collected $1,587,000 in subsidies in less than five years. If the mail which it delivered had been paid for on a poundage basis,

[21] "Senator Black Uncovers Shipping Board Extravagance," *Newsweek*, II (October 7, 1933), 7–8; "Alabama Senator is Keen-Witted Investigator," *Newsweek*, II (November 11, 1933), 17; New York *Times*, October 6, 1933.

[22] United States Congress, Senate, Special Committee on Investigation of Air Mail and Ocean Mail Contracts, *Hearings*, 73d Cong., 2nd Sess., 1933, Parts 1, 2, 3. New York *Times*, September 28, 30, 1933.

[23] "Senator Black Uncovers Shipping Board Extravagance," 7–8.

Black calculated it would have cost the government only $1,903. He drew from the Lykes spokesman an admission that one of his ships had delivered a single mail pouch to Santo Domingo but had failed to show the weight of the pouch in its report to the government. Probably, Black suggested, because the pouch was empty.[24]

Off and on for almost six months, Black pursued the ocean mail hearings. His revelations of favoritism and loose control of government pursestrings attracted some allies, but neither sensational publicity nor widespread public indignation. Then Fulton Lewis, Jr., a writer for Hearst newspapers, proposed that Senator Black turn the spotlight on airmail contracts. Lewis himself had probed this issue. When the Hearst papers refused to publish his findings, he turned his files over to Black. Announcing this new phase of his investigation, the senator promised disclosures even more startling than those concerning the shipping industry. In the airmail probe, as *Time* put it, he was to "hit pay dirt . . . and hot water." [25]

Within a few days, as Chairman Black promised, the airmail probe made front pages over the nation and stayed there. Its first embarrassed victim was former Postmaster General Brown. Black produced a Post Office Department clerk who testified that, on orders from Brown, he had burned papers relating to airmail contracts. Brown first insisted that he had merely disposed of personal letters so he would not leave the office "all cluttered up with immaterial files" for his successor, James A. Farley. But upon second thought, Brown appeared in Farley's office to deliver two packets which he said contained official records of air and ocean mail contracts made in his administration. He explained he had found the papers "unexpectedly" among some personal letters. Perhaps, he told Farley, they had been placed there by someone "engaged in character assassination." But Senator Black charged that important papers were still missing.[26]

24 New York *Times*, October 2, 4, 6, 25, December 6, 1933.
25 "Investigation by Headlines," *Time*, XXVI (August 26, 1935), 14–17.
26 New York *Times*, January 10, 11, 20, 1934.

The episode of the missing papers added a spice of drama to the message Black was attempting to impart to Roosevelt and the nation. He charged that the Hoover administration, in awarding airmail contracts, had favored large aviation holding companies and ignored the competitive bids of small, independent operators. At a secret meeting in the Post Office Department in 1930, airline executives and post-office officials had divided twenty-four of the twenty-seven airmail contracts between three giant holding companies, Aviation Corporation of Delaware, United Aircraft and Transport Corporation, and North American Aviation, Incorporated. In a nationwide radio address, Black reported that these companies and Northwest Airways, Incorporated, received 97 percent of airmail subsidy funds in 1932. Government subsidies, he declared, were being used to support stock pyramiding, corporate empire building, and such financial and political juggling as to enable one insider to realize more than $9,000,000 from an initial investment of $253 in aviation stocks and another to run a $40 investment to a paper profit of more than $5,000,000. Recalling his ocean mail revelations, Black urged that the government either abandon shipping subsidies, operate its own shipping lines, or completely revise the system of federal aid.[27]

After two weeks of highly publicized hearings, Senator Black went to lunch at the White House to describe his findings to Roosevelt, who urged him to press his inquiry to the limit. Black reminded Roosevelt that the President had the authority, under a rider to the Independent Offices Supply Bill of 1934, to cancel mail contracts. At his press conference that afternoon, Roosevelt told newspapermen this was the first he had known that he had such authority. "Are you glad you have it?" asked one reporter. "Yes," Roosevelt replied firmly. Farley warned the President that the Black committee had stumbled on some facts which might come out and prove embarrassing. One of Roosevelt's fishing companions had received twenty-five thousand shares in a shipping

[27] *Ibid.*, January 17, 18, 25, 1934; Paul D. Tillett, *The Army Flies the Mails* (Indianapolis, Inter-University Case Program #24), 11–17.

company for helping secure a favorable contract. Another man interested in shipping contracts had contributed fifty thousand dollars to Roosevelt's presidential campaign. The President, about to take a short voyage on his yacht, was undismayed. "Jim," said Roosevelt gaily, "so long as it doesn't happen until after my boat trip, it's all right." [28]

Armed with presidential blessing, Black produced another sensation. Papers dealing with the airmail contract negotiations of 1932 had also disappeared from the files of William MacCracken, who had been assistant secretary of commerce in the Hoover administration and presided over the secret "spoils conference" of 1932. MacCracken, a Washington representative for airlines in 1934, claimed a lawyer's privilege of refusing to divulge papers regarding his clients. In an atmosphere charged with excitement, the Senate passed Black's motion ordering its sergeant-at-arms to arrest MacCracken, two airline executives, and a clerical employee for attempting to destroy evidence sought by a Senate committee. [29]

During the next few days, the Senate indulged in what one member described as an *"opéra bouffe."* Its sergeant-at-arms, Chesley W. Jurney, set out on his unusual mission, adorned in black morning coat, gray striped trousers, a Western sheriff's ten-gallon hat, a silver-headed cane, and a red carnation. Upon his arrest MacCracken was released in the custody of his lawyer Frank Hogan, the defender of Edward L. Doheny and Albert B. Fall in Teapot Dome days. MacCracken later disappeared, protesting that he was a private citizen and could not be compelled to show cause why he had committed a past act. While MacCracken's letter was read in the chamber, a grim-faced Senator Black hurriedly prepared a resolution directing his quarry's re-arrest. Sergeant-at-arms Jurney set out once again. [30]

In a rare procedure, the three remaining defendants were

[28] New York *Times*, January 27, 1934; Transcript of Roosevelt's press conference of January 26, 1934, Roosevelt Papers; James A. Farley, *Jim Farley's Story* (New York, 1948), 41–42.
[29] New York *Times*, February 3, 1934.
[30] *Ibid.*, February 3, 6, 10, 1934.

brought to trial before the bar of the Senate, with Black acting as prosecutor. Triumphantly he confronted them with the missing letters, pieced together from scraps of paper retrieved by post-office clerks who searched three hundred bags of trash from Mac-Cracken's office building. After five hours of deliberation, the Senate freed two of the defendants but sentenced MacCracken and a fourth to ten-day jail terms for contempt of the Senate. MacCracken later gave himself up in order to institute a court test of the Senate's right to arrest him. It was now Sergeant-at-Arms Jurney's turn to flee from a United States marshal seeking to serve him with a writ of *habeas corpus* for detaining MacCracken.[31]

While Washington chuckled over these comic opera chases, Roosevelt pondered his move. Democrats had pledged to reform procedures under which government contracts were granted, and to fight corruption, favoritism, and personal influence. Farley urged that commercial lines continue to carry the mail until new contracts could be negotiated, but the President thought this course lacked the dramatic impact to inspire legislative reforms. Why should beneficiaries of the old system continue to profit from contracts obtained by collusion and without competitive bidding? Too, the President was not unaware of the role Black's revelations might play in the 1934 elections. It was suggested that the Army Air Corps, which pioneered air mail service, could take over temporarily. On February 9 Roosevelt, his mind made up, instructed a reluctant Farley to cancel all existing airmail contracts as of February 19. The Air Corps was given ten days' notice of its new duty.[32]

The administration's dramatic move aroused a storm. Colonel Charles A. Lindbergh, American folk hero and technical advisor

[31] *Ibid.*, February 11, 12, 13, 1934. One man promptly served his ten-day sentence, but MacCracken appealed to federal courts and eventually to the Supreme Court. In February, 1935, the Court upheld the power of a House of Congress to punish a private citizen for obstructing the performance of its legislative duties, even though he had ceased to obstruct. Thereupon MacCracken served his sentence. (*Jurney* v. *McCracken*, 294 U.S., 125.)

[32] Tillett, *The Army Flies the Mails*, 25–28; New York *Times*, February 10, 1934.

to Transcontinental Air Transport, chided Roosevelt for condemning commercial aviation without a trial. Before Lindbergh's
wire reached the White House, its text appeared in morning newspapers of February 12. Roosevelt frostily refused to answer. White
House Press Secretary Stephen Early informed the press that it
was customary to allow the President the courtesy of reading a
message addressed to him before releasing it to the press. Obviously, Early said, Lindbergh's message was intended for publicity
purposes. In the House, Representative Hamilton Fish of New
York created an uproar when his effort to read Lindbergh's telegram into the *Congressional Record* was blocked. Roosevelt's
"summary" action, Fish declared heatedly, was "worthy of Fas-
cism, Hitlerism, or Sovietism at their best." Will Rogers commented: "It's like finding a crooked railroad president and stopping
all the trains." As the San Francisco *Chronicle* noted, a battle royal
for public sympathy was shaping up.[33]

While debate raged in the press, the Air Corps feverishly
stripped its warplanes of gunnery and installed what equipment
for blind flying it could find. Relentlessly Black pushed on with
his inquiry. Brown returned to the stand to defend himself from
charges of granting contracts by collusion and without competitive bidding. His aim, he explained, was to develop an efficient,
modern aviation system. "There was no sense," he testified, "in
taking this government's money and dishing it out . . . to every
little fellow that was flying around the map and was not going to
do anything to develop aviation in the broad sense." By using subsidy money strategically, Brown said he hoped to create a strong,
integrated airline network which would carry mail, passengers,
and express. He compared the growth of airlines to that of railroads in the previous century, contending that economic forces
would inevitably bring about the absorption of small, uneconomi-
cal lines by larger carriers.[34]

[33] New York *Times*, February 12, 14, 1934; Tillett, *The Army Flies the
Mails*, 33–34.
[34] Tillett, *The Army Flies the Mail*, 8–10.

Committee sessions were not without comic overtones. At one point Brown testified that Farley had made a "personal remark" about the airmail investigation. "Repeat it! Repeat!" shouted Chairman Black. The former post office official refused to do so without Farley's consent. "Then we'll get him in here," Hugo declared, biting on his cigar.[35]

During the week that elapsed before the two men were brought face to face, speculation mounted as to the nature of the "personal remark." Finally Brown revealed his secret: Farley had told him that he had "no sympathy for these political investigations" and that Chairman Black was "just a publicity hound, but don't tell anybody I told you, for I have to get along with him." Black was the first to laugh. As the tension broke, his laughter could be heard above that of the spectators. Senators and secretaries from nearby offices hurried to the committee room to find the cause of the commotion. "Is that all of it?" asked Black, dropping back in his chair in another fit of laughter. Farley tactfully denied making any such remark.[36]

Witnesses before the Black committee justifiably feared interrogation by its formidable chairman. In punishing MacCracken and others for contempt of the Senate, Black had bested Frank Hogan, a leading figure of the Washington bar. Raymond Clapper, a longtime observer of Capitol Hill, contrasted Black's technique with that of "patient, plodding Tom Walsh," who had exposed Teapot Dome. Black, Clapper wrote, wrung testimony from witnesses by convincing them that he already had the facts and only wished to have them confirmed for the record. At one session the chairman frequently referred to a paper in his hand, giving the impression that it had the facts written on it. After the witness broke down and told his story, reporters found that the paper dealt with another matter altogether. A "hunch player," Hugo occasionally fired a question on mere chance. "Once in a while,"

[35] Special Senate Committee on Air Mail and Ocean Mail Contracts, *Hearings*, 2627.
[36] *Ibid.*, 2742; New York *Times*, February 24, 25, 1934.

Clapper said, "he hooks a fish." The chairman, Clapper wrote, "sits back easily in his chair, puffs slowly on his cigar, rolls his large, open eyes quite innocently, and with a wise smile, undertakes to refresh the memory of a squirming witness."[37]

Black was reputed to be a "walking dictionary" of the relationships between airlines, shippers, and the government. He was supplied with a steady flow of documentary material by an old Alabama friend, Andrew G. Patterson, who served as the committee's chief investigator. Patterson, a former probate judge, had been head of Alabama's Public Service Commission and had run unsuccessfully for governor in 1926. Black brought him to Washington in May, 1933, as a trusted right-hand man.[38]

Anti-New Deal newspapers like the Chicago Tribune and the Cincinnati Times-Star condemned Black and his hearings. "The object of his [Black's] questioning is less to discover the facts about air mail contracts than to bully and abuse men whom he doesn't like, personally or politically," declared the Tribune. Black told the New York Times that he considered himself a lawyer seeking facts, not a public prosecutor. Washington correspondents found the hearings good copy and their chairman lively and cooperative. Many speculated that Black would rank with the Senate's great inquisitors, Walsh, Wheeler, and Missouri's Jim Reed.[39]

In February and March, 1934, with the nation experiencing one of its stormiest winters in many a year, it became tragically apparent that army pilots, in open-cockpit planes without proper instruments for blind flying, could not cope with their sudden assignment. Practicing for mail runs, two pilots died on the snowy slopes of a western mountain range, and a third was killed when his ship stalled, went into a spin, and crashed near the little town of Jerome, Idaho. Meanwhile Captain Eddie Rickenbacker, famed World War ace and vice-president of Eastern Air Transport, and

[37] Raymond Clapper, "Hugo Black, Nemesis of Subsidy Spoilsmen," Review of Reviews, LXXXIX (April, 1934), 18–20.

[38] Ibid.

[39] "Air Mail Subsidies Under Fire," Literary Digest, CXVII (February 17, 1934), 9; New York Times, February 6, 1934.

two pilots delivered the last commercial cargo of air mail from Los Angeles to Newark in a record time of 13 hours, 4 minutes, and 20 seconds. After only four fueling stops, their new Douglas transport arrived just two hours ahead of a heavy snowstorm. Newspapers hailed Rickenbacker's flight as a "triumphant finale" to commercial operations and noted that bad weather forced the army to abandon eastern flights on the initial day of its assignment.[40]

In its first week of operations, the Air Corps lost three more pilots. Mystified citizens poured angry protests on Congress, precipitating a rare Saturday afternoon floor debate in the House which lasted six hours. In California a woman telephoned Air Corps Captain Ira C. Baker: "You bloody butcher, you are killing these young boys!" Rickenbacker harshly accused the administration of "legalized murder," a phrase quickly taken up by Hamilton Fish. Most blame fell on the hapless Farley, who all along had cautioned the administration to proceed slowly. Hailed before the Senate investigating committee, Farley was excoriated by Vermont's Warren Austin as the man responsible for the "lives of those young men who have been killed." Chairman Black, attempting to recoup for the administration, displayed a newspaper headline announcing the crash of a commercial airliner with a loss of eight lives. At the White House, Roosevelt refused to comment on the airmail situation, leaving Farley to take the lightning. The loyal Democratic chairman recalled later that he was accustomed to abuse and criticism, but when he was called a "murderer," he had looked to Roosevelt for help. "No help came," Farley said sadly.[41]

On the night of March 9, four more pilots died when their planes plummeted to earth in Ohio, Florida, and Wyoming. Early the next morning, Major General Benjamin D. "Benny" Foulois, Chief of the Army Air Corps, and General Douglas MacArthur,

---

[40] Tillett, *The Army Flies the Mails*, 43; Norman E. Borden, Jr., *Air Mail Emergency, 1934* (Freeport, Maine, 1968), 53–80.
[41] Borden, *Air Mail Emergency*, 52–80; Farley, *Jim Farley's Story*, 41–42.

Army Chief of Staff, were ushered into a large bedroom on the
second floor of the White House. Their commander-in-chief was
ensconced in the majestic Lincoln bed. Foulois, who had never
met Roosevelt before, was vaguely surprised that there was no
sign of the famous grin he had seen so often in the newsreels.
Without a word of greeting, the President, scowling fiercely
through his pince-nez, barked at his Air Corps chief: "General,
when are these air-mail killings going to stop?"[42]

Roosevelt was furious that he and his administration had been
placed in this embarrassing position by his own impulsiveness.
As Arthur Krock wrote in the New York *Times*, the administration
was on the defensive for the first time since it had taken office.
The American people, which at first thought there had been "dirty
work at the crossroads," now believed that Roosevelt had acted
too hastily in canceling the contracts and thrusting this chore upon
an obviously unprepared Air Corps. The President demanded that
Foulois either give him a personal guarantee that fatalities would
end or cease flying the mails. Foulois, unable to meet the guarantee, ordered all airmail flights suspended while he made a personal inspection of the corps. Brigadier General William "Billy"
Mitchell, ardent exponent of a separate air force, wrote Roosevelt
that the crashes were the result of inadequate equipment and lack
of training for bad-weather flying. He said "merchants" in the
Hoover and Coolidge administrations had plundered army air
appropriations, reducing the Air Corps to a "pitiful condition."[43]

In the face of mounting public hostility, the administration began to back down. Roosevelt proposed that plans be made to return
the air mail to private carriers under conditions "barring evils of
the past." Black set to work on a bill to extricate the administration from its predicament. But it soon became apparent that the
administration could not await passage of a measure to establish

[42] Benjamin D. Foulois, *From the Wright Brothers to the Astronauts, The
Memoirs of Major General Benjamin D. Foulois* (New York, 1968), 254.

[43] New York *Times*, February 25, 1934; Foulois, *From the Wright Brothers
to the Astronauts*, 256–57; Brigadier General William Mitchell to Franklin D.
Roosevelt, Roosevelt Papers.

a permanent basis for delivering the air mail. On the day General Foulois ordered operations resumed, an eleventh pilot was killed in a training flight.[44]

Farley and Roosevelt agreed to use the postmaster general's power to issue temporary contracts, specifying that no company whose contract had been annulled for fraud and collusion might bid. But in the end, the former contractors, purged of individuals who had been present at the "spoils conference," and with their corporate names changed, were allowed to bid. They held a virtual monopoly on the multiengined aircraft which postal authorities considered essential for carrying passengers.[45]

As the Air Corps began to phase out its disastrous operation, the twelfth pilot died in an accident attributed to bad weather and flying without proper instruments. On June 1, to the general relief of the Roosevelt administration, the army carried its last load of air mail. Two weeks later, Hugo Black was one of a small group invited to the President's office to witness the signing of the Air Mail Act of 1934, based largely on proposals submitted by him and by Senator Kenneth McKellar. The act forbade interlocking directorships, set a $17,500 ceiling on salaries in subsidized firms, limited each company to three routes, and specified that any persons convicted of collusion to prevent competitive bidding would face a ten-thousand-dollar fine or five years in the Atlanta penitentiary. The temporary contracts were extended for one year. If performance were judged satisfactory, they could be extended indefinitely.[46]

The brouhaha over airmail contracts, touched off by Black, had given the Democratic administration its first sour taste of public disfavor. Roosevelt and Black hurried on to other matters, leaving Farley and Foulois to deal as best they could with their roles of scapegoats. Although tainted by twelve deaths, the episode had

[44] New York *Times*, March 8, 28, 1934; Foulois, *From the Wright Brothers to the Astronauts*, 257.
[45] Tillett, *The Army Flies the Mails*, 60–61.
[46] *Ibid.*, 62.

its constructive results. Bids for the temporary contracts ran as low as 17.5 cents a pound, roughly a third of the average during Brown's last year in office. The cost of airmail subsidies fell from $19.4 million in 1933 to less than $8 million in 1934. Although the "Big Three" regained most of their contracts, several independents obtained government subsidies. Under the 1934 Air Mail Act, Roosevelt was empowered to appoint a Federal Aviation Commission to develop broad policy on all phases of aviation. Its report resulted eventually in the Civil Aeronautics Act of 1938, creating the Civil Aeronautics Authority. But as former Postmaster General Brown had foreseen, independent lines gradually became fewer, and large companies bigger.[47]

Despite its humiliation, the Air Corps, too, reaped eventual benefit from the focusing of public attention upon its inadequate equipment and meager appropriations. The experience renewed the controversy over a separate air force. Twenty years and two wars later, General Foulois expressed the opinion that the twelve airmail pilots had not died in vain. Their sacrifice, he said, started a chain of developments which led to a national air defense system and an independent air force.[48]

For Black the experience had important personal consequences. Many of his recommendations had been translated into law. For months the subject of airmail contracts had been in the public press, studded with the names of such notables as Lindbergh, Rickenbacker, Orville Wright, "Billy" Mitchell, and Amelia Earhart. Now the American public was almost equally familiar with the name of a hitherto obscure Alabama senator.

[47] Schlesinger, *The Coming of the New Deal*, 454; Tillett, *The Army Flies the Mails*, 62–63.
[48] Tillett, *The Army Flies the Mails*, 68–69.

XI

⊓⊓⊓⊓⊓⊓⊓⊓⊓⊓⊓⊓⊓⊓⊓⊓⊓⊓⊓⊓⊓⊓⊓⊓⊓⊓

Chairman Black's
Three-Ring
Circus

Disturbing news from Alabama shared the nation's front pages with Black's hearings. The notorious Scottsboro case, steeped with sex and racism, was retried in the spring of 1933 before rapt spectators in a fetid Decatur courtroom. Seven defendants, hurriedly condemned to death two years before, had been given new hope when the Supreme Court, in *Powell* v. *Alabama*, reversed their convictions on grounds of inadequate counsel.

Samuel S. Leibowitz, one of the country's leading criminal lawyers, was brought from New York by the International Labor Defense to represent Haywood Patterson, the first to face retrial. Decatur was tense with the clash of reason and prejudice. After an all-white jury declared Patterson guilty, Judge James Edwin Horton, Jr., set aside the verdict and ordered a new trial, thereby ending his career as an elected judge on the Alabama bench. Years later he explained to an interviewer that his family motto was *fiat justitia ruat coelum*—let justice be done though the heavens may fall.[1]

As if to illustrate another face of southern justice, lynch parties executed their own verdicts late that summer. Three Negroes, awaiting trial in Tuscaloosa for the rape-murder of a young white woman, were offered legal counsel by the ILD. Fearful that Tuscaloosa might succeed Scottsboro in worldwide notoriety, a mob

[1] Carter, *Scottsboro*, 273.

drove the "Commie lawyers" out of town. As the defendants were being moved to Birmingham for safety, they were seized from sheriff's deputies, taken into the woods, and shot. One lived to tell the story. Fear of rape had become almost an obsession. When a mentally retarded white woman in Tuscaloosa accused a crippled, elderly Negro of raping her, seven white men riddled his body with bullets. This was too much for some Alabama newspapers. The Birmingham *News* and the *Age-Herald* could not condone such mob violence, but the Tuscaloosa *News* contended that trouble had been ignited by the intrusion of ILD lawyers into Alabama's legal affairs.[2]

In the hope of following the scent of racial hostility back into statewide power, the Klan stirred. Sensing a fresh devil to pursue, it invited all Americans, "Jews and Catholics included," to join its fight against Communism. In 1934 Bibb Graves returned to the governor's chair with ardent support from the White Legion, an organization dedicated to execution of the Scottsboro defendants and expulsion of "red lawyers" from Alabama. Like Senator Black, Graves found the path to reelection tougher than in the days of minority primaries. He was forced into a runoff to win the Democratic nomination over Major Frank Dixon, a representative of Birmingham's power structure and a severe critic of the first Graves administration.[3]

Drys, too, took new heart. In a statewide referendum on retaining Alabama's prohibition laws, they won fifty-two of sixty-seven counties in February, 1935, and even defeated a drive by moderates for legal beer and wine. Rural counties, with many a still hidden in their woods and fields, delivered the votes to overcome big-city wets. On the sidelines Klansmen piously distributed handbills opposing any change in the state's twenty-year record of legal prohibition. "Impoverished farmers, voting dry but living wet, peddle 'shine for 75 cents a gallon—bring your own jug,"

---

[2] *Ibid.*, 276–77; "What Alabama Thinks of Its Lynching," *Literary Digest*, CXVI (September 2, 1933), 8.

[3] "Primaries Fights Begin," *Newsweek*, III (May 12, 1934), 8–9; "The Klan Revives," *Nation*, CXXIX (July 2, 1934), 20; Birmingham *Post*, October 16, 1934.

Newsweek observed. Within a year liquor flowed freely in Mobile's bars and Birmingham's "blind tigers." As wets pointed out to Governor Graves, such sales produced no tax revenue for his state's depleted treasury, rewarding only bootleggers and 'shiners. In the meantime county relief directors reported to the governor that Alabama's relief rolls were getting more crowded every month.[4]

In Birmingham that same February, Federal Judge W. I. Grubb ruled that sale of electric energy by the Tennessee Valley Authority, in competition with such private utilities as Alabama Power, was illegal. The New York *Times* sought comment from Senator Black, who promptly predicted that the Supreme Court would reverse the decision. Black and Judge Grubb had been on opposite sides before. As attorney for the obscure Negro convict who had been kept at work in the steel mills twenty-two days after his sentence had expired, Black had won his first law case in Birmingham against Grubb, representing the steel company. In the TVA case, the Supreme Court would also uphold Black's view. But it was a source of considerable embarrassment to Alabama's senators and other state supporters of TVA that the authority's headquarters had been located in Tennessee. Black protested to Roosevelt that it was hard enough to defend the New Deal in Alabama without "this real stumbling block."[5]

By mid-1935, with business hardening its attitude toward the New Deal and the plain folk of Alabama alarmed over race and reds, Black kept a wary eye on his political home base. It was no time to favor the antilynching bill, introduced by Edward P. Costigan of Colorado and Robert Wagner of New York on behalf of the National Association for the Advancement of Colored People. While the administration kept prudent silence, southern Democrats rallied to filibuster against the measure.[6]

---

[4] Sellers, *The Prohibition Movement in Alabama*, 242; "Farmers and 'Shiners Outvote City Folks," *Newsweek*, V (March 9, 1935), 11; "Clamorous Wets in Dry Alabama," *Literary Digest*, CXXI (March 28, 1936), 7.

[5] Hugo L. Black to Franklin D. Roosevelt, August 13, 1934, in Roosevelt Papers; New York *Times*, February 23, 1935.

[6] "Congress Considers the Costigan-Wagner Anti-Lynching Bill," *Congressional Digest*, XIV (June, 1935), 185–86.

The bill's sponsors argued that a federal anti-lynching law was imperative because state laws and police had failed to protect citizens in the matter of due process of law. The Costigan-Wagner proposal called for federal prosecution of state or community law officials when prisoners within their custody were killed by a mob of three or more. If found guilty of neglect of duty, a local or state officer could be fined or imprisoned.[7]

Although joining the filibuster, Black tried to appease his friends in organized labor who supported the proposed law. He warned that the Costigan-Wagner bill, like the Fourteenth Amendment, would "curse the very people it was intended to benefit." He suggested that law officials would be forced to prosecute strikers if rioting and deaths occurred during strikes. The plan, he predicted ominously, would make every sheriff a strikebreaker for fear he would be prosecuted for failing to protect company property. Black had read in Macaulay's *History of England*, he told the Senate, that the idea of penalizing someone other than the person who committed the crime had been tried in England after the Norman conquest and judged a failure.[8]

His role in the filibuster won Black criticism from some who were ignorant of the realities of southern politics. Had he favored an antilynching law, he would have dissipated his influence toward assuring that Alabama would send a pro-Roosevelt delegation to the 1936 Democratic convention. Black and Bankhead needed all their ingenuity and political strength. After the death of W. I. Grubb in late 1935, Bankhead declined the proffer of a federal judgeship. But in seeking his second Senate term in 1936, Bankhead faced opposition from many who had supported him in the 1930 fight against Heflin. Alabama industrialists objected to his New Deal activities, especially his support of the Agricultural Adjustment Act and Cotton Control Act.[9]

Visiting Alabama, Turner Catledge of the New York *Times* reported that the New Deal was being vehemently attacked by

[7] *Ibid.*   [8] *Ibid.*
[9] New York *Times*, December 15, 1935.

many financial and industrial leaders "whose economic lives and spheres of influence have been disturbed by Roosevelt's policies." Unlike her sister states in the Southeast, Alabama had not benefited so bountifully from the New Deal, he observed, because her steel, iron, and coal industries had not experienced the same upturn as had manufacturing enterprises in other sections. Small farmers and sharecroppers suffered from adverse crop conditions and the production cutbacks of the Bankhead Cotton Control Act. Catledge concluded that New Deal agricultural policies had brought considerable benefits to larger farmers, but that Alabama needed long-term industrial activity in order to prosper.[10]

In the Birmingham area, about twenty thousand families depended on some form of federal assistance. Black found Birmingham's unemployment problem so distressing that in November, 1935, he made a personal appeal to Roosevelt for help. Marvin McIntyre, the President's secretary, wrote Commerce Secretary Harold Ickes: "The senator [Black] feels it is imperative that additional steps be taken to relieve the unemployment situation in Birmingham." As a measure of his standing with the administration, Black secured a number of grants and loans for relief of his suffering city.[11]

Although Alabama had enthusiastically elected a slate of Roosevelt delegates in 1932, the task was more difficult four years later. Graves and the two senators moved to head off any possibility of rebellion by disgruntled business leaders, many of whom were clustered around Birmingham, where anti-Roosevelt feelings were strong and the Liberty League popular. At a meeting of the Democratic State Executive Committee in Montgomery, the governor, both senators, and the chairman, John D. McQueen of Tuscaloosa, were named delegates-at-large to the Democratic convention. A resolution extolling Roosevelt achievements was passed. Wiring the news to McIntyre, Graves said he was sure the President

[10] *Ibid.*
[11] Hugo L. Black to Franklin D. Roosevelt, November 12, 1935; Marvin McIntyre to Harold L. Ickes, November 13, 1935, in Roosevelt Papers.

would be pleased. But this zeal provoked some Alabama Democrats, who charged that the committee had executed a "coup" with a bare quorum present.[12]

In January, 1936, the executive committee voted to appoint the entire Alabama delegation for the first time since 1924, rather than elect its members in the primary. The committee named thirty-six delegates, each with a half vote, and upheld its previous action in naming Graves, Black, Bankhead, and McQueen as delegates-at-large, with a whole vote apiece. Reading in the newspapers that Alabama had already selected its delegation, Jim Farley hurriedly telephoned Graves and Black. The governor assured Farley that he controlled the delegation and that it would cast Alabama's twenty-two votes at Philadelphia under the unit rule. Black, too, reassured Farley that Alabama was safe for Roosevelt.[13]

Judge Leon McCord, Democratic national committeeman for Alabama and a political rival of Governor Graves, challenged the committee's action in the courts. But when Alabama's supreme court decided that it had no right to interfere in party politics, McCord said he would press the fight no further. "That," Graves declared with satisfaction, "definitely and finally pledges the Alabama delegation to unanimous support of the renomination of President Roosevelt."[14]

Black, having tasted national attention, had no intention of allowing Alabama's political squabbles to engage all his talents. Early in 1935, as Roosevelt's advisors shaped the second New Deal, a strange chorus of dissent was heard in the land. The ranting of Father Charles Coughlin against Roosevelt, labor unions, Com-

[12] Bibb Graves to Marvin McIntyre, November 13, 1936, in Roosevelt Papers; New York *Times*, December 15, 1935; Birmingham *News*, March 1, 1936.
[13] Birmingham *News*, January 19, 1936; Birmingham *Post*, January 18, 1936; Memorandum from James A. Farley to Franklin D. Roosevelt, January 21, 1936, in Roosevelt Papers.
[14] New York *Times*, March 1, 1936; Birmingham *News*, March 28, 1936.

munists, and international bankers frightened thousands of radio listeners. In California Dr. Francis E. Townsend aroused visions of two hundred dollars a month in the heads of destitute oldsters. Louisiana's Huey Long, with his orchid shirts and his enticing slogan, "Every man a king," had succeeded Tom Heflin as an attraction for tourists in the Senate galleries. The Reverend Gerald L. K. Smith echoed Long's demand that the government "share the wealth" by guaranteeing every family a minimum annual income of five thousand dollars.

To offset these siren calls, Roosevelt asked Congress to enact a national works program for the jobless, social security, slum clearance, and housing programs. Black, still smarting from the administration's disdain for his thirty-hour bill, announced that he planned to reintroduce it. Trying to arouse grass-roots support for a shorter work week, he joined the chorus of radio prophets. In their living rooms, thousands heard the soft southern accent and spellbinding cadences that had made Hugo famous as a stump speaker in Alabama. "This government must decide," he told them, "between a permanent governmental dole and a shorter work week and work day." [15]

Appearing before the American Association for Social Security in New York City, Black attacked the "wildly extravagant proposals" and "impossible schemes" of Townsend and Long. It was not a question of whether the United States should enact a system of social security, he said; merely a matter of what form it would take. During hearings on the administration proposal, Black and Frances Perkins expressed opposition to the idea that employees should bear part of the proposed 3 percent payroll tax to finance unemployment compensation. Black said the plan should be financed through state taxation of excess profits, rather than by curtailing the buying power of the people. Miss Perkins credited Black with pointing out to her the importance of immediate government contributions to social security so that the wealthy, who

[15] "The Thirty-Hour Week," a radio address by Hugo Black, delivered February 5, 1935, *Vital Speeches*, III (September 1, 1937), 681–84.

derived their income from investments, would pay their share through taxation.[16]

During the Senate fight over Roosevelt's proposed work relief program, Black aligned himself with Wagner, Huey Long, Nebraska's Pat McCarran, and AFL leaders to demand that reliefers be paid the "prevailing wage scale" in their areas. The President had advocated pay of about fifty dollars a month, almost twice what a man would receive from the dole. Black's vote for the McCarran "prevailing wage" amendment aroused the ire of a warm supporter back home, Judge Joseph J. Willett of Anniston. Defending his stand Black wrote the judge that his vote was in line with principles he had advocated "since long before I came to the Senate." While he believed that men employed on government projects should be paid the prevailing hourly rate, Black assured Judge Willett: "I strongly favor the idea of making the aggregate amount received for relief wages smaller than the aggregate amount received in private industry. I fully agree with the idea that this is essential in order to create the proper inducement for public workers to seek private employment when it can be obtained."[17]

The thirty-hour bill, cosponsored by Representative William P. Connery, Jr., of New York was rejected by the Senate in April, 1935. A month later the Supreme Court declared NRA unconstitutional. Loyal administration man though he was, Black could not resist lecturing the Senate on the "utter impossibility of setting up standards by which business groups, acting as code authorities, might legislate for industry." He insisted that his thirty-hour bill was based on "well-recognized powers of Congress" and certainly

[16] New York *Times*, January 26, 1935; "Social Security," an address by Senator Hugo L. Black, December 15, 1934, reprinted in *Vital Speeches*, III (September 1, 1937), 689–90. Miss Perkins, in *The Roosevelt I Knew*, recalled: "Senator Hugo Black once pointed out to me that the burden on small employers and the poorer paid workers would be too great to allow for the gradual expansion of the coverage and benefits unless the tax resources of the whole United States were involved from the beginning."

[17] Hugo L. Black to Judge Joseph J. Willett, Sr., March 4, 1935, Willett Papers; William E. Leuchtenberg, *Franklin Roosevelt and the New Deal* (New York, 1963), 124–25.

did not confer upon business "the right to legislate for itself." Privately Black urged Roosevelt to support the thirty-hour plan, but the President replied that he still hoped to work out something like NRA.[18]

In August, David Walsh of Massachusetts proposed that, in work done under government contracts, child and convict labor be banned and the forty-hour week observed. An effort was made in the Senate to substitute the thirty-hour bill for Walsh's proposal. Speaking for Black's plan, Huey Long shouted: "If you put the administration's feet to the fire, they won't dare defeat this bill!" But Black, evidently resigned to defeat, spoke only briefly in behalf of the bill he had sponsored since 1932. The Senate voted 61–23 against substituting a thirty-hour plan for the Walsh bill, but the Black-Connery bill would appear again on the calendars of Congress.[19]

Although embroiled in controversies over the economy, Black had not forgotten his old adversaries, merchant shippers and the United States Shipping Board. Urging Commerce Secretary Roper to formulate a new plan, he expressed his opposition to subsidies but said that, if they were essential to the existence of an American merchant marine, they should be properly safeguarded. Shippers should be required to build good ships, pay decent wages, submit to a uniform accounting system, and observe a limit on their executive salaries. Roper wrote Roosevelt that congressional investigations had convinced him that direct subsidies should be substituted for mail contracts. He recommended that the new system be administered by a maritime commission. Roosevelt, in his March, 1935, message to Congress, indicated he favored such a plan.[20]

---

[18] Hugo L. Black to Franklin D. Roosevelt, May 27, 1935, in Roosevelt Papers; New York *Times*, May 28, 29, 1935.

[19] New York *Times*, August 13, 1935.

[20] South Trimble, Jr., solicitor, Department of Commerce, to Commerce Secretary Daniel C. Roper, January 28, 1935; Daniel C. Roper to Franklin D. Roosevelt, January 28, 1935, in Roosevelt Papers; New York *Times*, June 2, 1935.

After lunching with the President one April day, Treasury Secretary Henry Morgenthau noted peevishly in his diary that the occasion had been "spoiled" by Senator Black, who had insisted on talking about ocean mail contracts. In June, Black sent the President the final report of his investigating committee. He concluded that the United States had little to show but a fleet of antiquated ships for the $800,000,000 it had spent on the merchant marine since the end of the World War. He hammered away at his constant theme that much of the government's mail contract money had been diverted into salaries, commissions, bonuses, excess operating costs, and other ventures, rather than used to develop a merchant fleet.[21]

On one hot afternoon, Black was conducting a hearing on efforts by shipping lobbyists to defeat the direct subsidy plan. A message arrived that the Senate, by voice vote, had just passed a resolution in favor of ocean mail contracts. Leaving his witness in mid-sentence, Black rushed to the floor. He proposed a substitute to cancel all ocean mail contracts as of April 30, 1936. The Senate refused to retract its approval of the original resolution, offered by New York's Royal Copeland. But Secretary Roper warned shippers at their annual conference in November to be prepared to compromise with the government or see shipping contracts transferred to government-owned lines.[22]

In the closing hours before adjournment in June, 1936, Congress approved the Merchant Marine Act of 1936, a system of aiding private shippers through direct subsidies. Funds were to be administered by a new agency, the United States Maritime Commission, that would replace the old shipping board. Henceforth government aid would come in the form of direct payments of up to 50 percent of the cost of ship construction. Operators were to put up 25 percent of the remainder in cash, and the government

[21] Diary of Henry Morgenthau, Jr., IX, 208, Roosevelt Library, Hyde Park, New York; Hugo L. Black to Franklin D. Roosevelt, June 18, 1935, in Roosevelt Papers; New York *Times*, June 28, 1935.
[22] New York *Times*, August 24, November 19, 1935.

was to lend the final 25 percent at 3.5 percent interest over a twenty-year period. All ocean mail contracts made under the post-master general were to be canceled after June 30, 1937. For Black, the victory was sweet. He took greatest satisfaction in a provision forbidding any subsidized company to pay an annual salary of more than $25,000.[23]

Capitol Hill's hidden persuaders had exasperated Black since his first days as a senator. During the Hoover administration, he had seen how effectively they pressured Congress to raise American tariff barriers. But in the spring of 1935, public utilities and their lobbyists, in a fury against the administration-sponsored "death sentence" provision of the Wheeler-Rayburn bill, put on the big-gest show of public outrage that oldtimers on the Hill could re-member. Mailmen and Western Union messengers were burdened by a blizzard of letters and telegrams, supposedly from angry con-stituents protesting Roosevelt's proposal to break up huge holding companies which could not justify their existence.[24]

Such unusual public interest in a complex economic matter aroused Senate suspicions. In May the Senate passed the Black bill, a plan Hugo had originally urged in 1929 to require lobbyists to register their names, objectives, salaries, and monthly expenses with the secretary of the Senate and clerk of the House. Roosevelt himself gave the bill a nudge in the House. "Senator Black is most anxious that you get the lobby bill out and passed," he wrote Hatton Sumners, chairman of the House judiciary committee. "He says it is pretty weak but much better than nothing. Can you do this? FDR." Sumners could. Both houses promptly authorized in-vestigations of lobbying activities.[25]

In June the Senate approved the death sentence by a single vote. But in the House, many Democrats broke ranks to join Republicans in substituting a milder version for the controversial

[23] *Ibid.*, June 21, 22, 28, 1936.   [24] *Ibid.*, July 17, 1935.
[25] Franklin D. Roosevelt to Hatton Sumners, June 28, 1935, in Roosevelt Papers.

provision. Instead of requiring holding companies to justify their existence to the SEC, the House required the commission to defend any dissolution order. While conferees argued over their differences, two lobbying investigations got under way. Black headed the Senate committee, whose membership included two of his closest Democratic colleagues, Sherman Minton of Indiana and Lewis B. Schwellenbach of Washington, as well as Republicans Lynn Frazier of North Dakota and Ernest Gibson of Vermont. In the House the investigation was handled by New York's Representative John J. O'Connor, who conducted it in the rules committee, of which he was chairman.

Black's hearings grabbed the headlines instantly. Philip W. Gadsden, chairman of the Committee of Public Utility Executives, was hauled before the Black committee early one July morning to testify, without preparation, about lobbying activities. He had been subpoenaed at his Washington hotel and brought immediately by taxi to the Hill. Next the committee turned its inquiry on 816 telegrams which Representative S. J. Driscoll of Pennsylvania had received from people in Warren whose names began with "B." A Western Union official testified that most of them were dictated by a representative of Associated Gas and Electric Company, one of the nation's largest holding companies. A messenger boy told the committee that he was paid three cents apiece to get signatures on telegrams opposing the Wheeler-Rayburn bill. Although Western Union usually kept copies of its messages for a year, the files of these telegrams had already been destroyed in its Warren office.[26]

Arthur Krock, prestigious Washington bureau chief for the New York *Times*, commented caustically that Black had embarked on "another headline hunt." Washington's weather was hot, Krock wrote, and "legislation is getting largely emotional." But Turner Catledge, Senate reporter for the *Times*, said the Black com-

[26] United States Congress, Senate, Special Committee to Investigate Lobbying Activities, *Hearings*, 74th Cong., 1st Sess., Part I, National Archives, Washington, D.C.; New York *Times*, July 14, 17, 18, 1935.

mittee's disclosures of faked telegrams indicated that many members of Congress had been duped into voting against the President's proposal. Catledge believed Black's revelations would help Roosevelt win eventual passage of the death sentence.[27]

Administration forces stalled while the Black committee did its utmost to stir up public outrage against utility lobbyists. Morgenthau noted in his diary that Senator Black was "in an awful hurry" to get a blanket order allowing his committee to examine income tax returns. The press was delighted to have such diversion during the torpid Washington summer. Reporters dubbed the hearings "Chairman Black's three-ring circus," and described Hugo as throwing open the doors of his committee room to announce that "the show" was about to start. The chairman's alert countenance, labeled "the inquisitor," frequently appeared in news photographs. It was rumored that Black had the help of Scripps-Howard's Ruth Finney and of Paul Y. Anderson of the St. Louis *Post-Dispatch*, who had been associated with Tom Walsh in the Teapot Dome probe. "Hugo Black is no Tom Walsh, but with the silent partner of Tom Walsh leaning over his shoulder, a Senate investigation is still no place for a man with something to hide," commented *Time*.[28]

In a one-day sensation, the Black committee aroused an advertising man from his bed in Plainfield, New Jersey at 1:00 A.M. and brought him immediately to Washington to testify. The rumpled, weary witness admitted suggesting to utility interests that they instigate a whispering campaign that Roosevelt and his advisors were either incompetent or insane. "Do you claim you had any basis on earth to try to circulate a report to the people of the United States that the President was insane?" Black demanded. "If so, give it now." The shamed witness replied: "No. None whatever."[29]

[27] New York *Times*, July 17, 28, 1935.
[28] Morgenthau Diary, July 24, 1935, Roosevelt Library; "Investigation by Headlines," *Time*, XXVI (August 26, 1935), 14–17.
[29] Special Senate Committee to Investigate Lobbying Activities, *Hearings*, 236; New York *Times*, August 4, 1935.

As the hot August days dragged on, there were more disclosures. Patrick J. Hurley, Secretary of War in the Hoover administration, and Joseph P. Tumulty, Woodrow Wilson's secretary, admitted having received $100,000 apiece from utility clients for propaganda activities. Hurley, a recalcitrant witness, protested that the committee was concentrating on Republicans. Ordering Hurley to sit down, Black announced sharply: "We are not going to countenance any efforts to drag politics into these hearings." [30]

Again, Black took to the radio. He told an NBC audience that Americans had a constitutional right to petition, but that no "sordid or powerful group" had a right to present its views "behind a mask concealing the identity of that group." Reviewing his committee's findings, he said that holding companies had paid for some 250,000 telegrams of protest. Records from telegraph offices, Black told his listeners, showed that, of 14,782 telegrams of protest sent from eleven different locations, only 3 had been paid for by private citizens. In their effort to create the impression of a "perfect storm of public indignation," utilities had instructed stenographers to type 5,000,000 letters to be sent to members of Congress. Such acts, Black declared, were "deliberate deception," conducted by a "high-powered, deceptive, telegram-fixing, letter-framing, Washington-visiting, $5,000,000 lobby." He predicted that Americans would soon be paying in utility bills for these millions of dollars spent in lobbying. "Just contemplate," he told his listeners, "what a good time people are having on your money in Washington!" [31]

As House and Senate investigators competed for headlines, friction between them flared into the open. Asked if he were going to investigate faked telegrams, Chairman O'Connor said his committee had no intention of taking up a line of inquiry from which the Black committee had reaped so much notice. Beneath this clash lay the issue of the death sentence itself. The Black com-

[30] New York *Times*, August 8, 1935.
[31] "Lobby Investigation," a speech by Hugo L. Black, delivered over the National Broadcasting Corporation network, August 8, 1935, *Vital Speeches*, I (August 26, 1935), 762–65.

mittee, *Time* magazine speculated, was being conducted in behalf of passage of the provision, while the House committee opposed it.[32]

Both committees sought a prime witness, Howard C. Hopson, president of Associated Gas and Electric Company, a large holding company. For weeks Hopson ignored or evaded subpoena by the Senate committee. Rather than face Black, the utility executive chose to appear in secret before a closed meeting of the O'Connor committee. Discovering that his elusive witness was near at hand, the senator persuaded his colleagues to cite Hopson for contempt of the Senate. The citation, served upon Hopson as he left the House committee room, directed him to appear the next day before Chairman Black. His quarry finally cornered, Black conducted a scorching examination, which reminded a *Times* reporter of the "stormy days of Teapot Dome." He warned the utility president against philosophizing or expressing opinions. "We intend for you to state the facts," Black told Hopson sternly, "and you are going to do so." When Hopson remarked that the administration had lobbied in behalf of the Wheeler-Rayburn bill, the chairman cut him off sharply: "That's enough. We don't care for your opinion of the administration's acts." [33]

Under questioning Hopson admitted that he had succeeded in influencing editorial policy, particularly in the Hearst and Gannett newspaper chains, by threats to remove utility advertising. He conceded that his company had spent almost a million dollars in its campaign against the Wheeler-Rayburn bill. When Black confronted him with a foot-high stack of telegrams opposing the bill, Hopson protested: "You have me on the hip, because you have copies of these things and I have not." At the close of the long day, Hopson was described as "gasping and indignant." His attorney protested that the witness was tired and in no condition to undergo a "third degree." Black, his face flushed with anger, retorted that a Senate inquiry was not a third-degree.[34]

[32] New York *Times*, August 4, 1935; "Investigation by Headlines," 14–17.
[33] New York *Times*, August 16, 1935.
[34] *Ibid.*

Hopson's appearance climaxed a lengthy and spirited investigation. Despite Black's findings, the House again decisively defeated the death-sentence provision, and Roosevelt was forced to compromise in his fight against the holding companies. Although the mandatory death sentence was eliminated from the Public Utilities Holding Company Act, all holding companies more than twice removed from operating companies were to be wiped out, and the Securities and Exchange Commission was empowered to eliminate those beyond the first degree adjudged not in the public interest. Most of the large utility empires would be broken up within three years.[35]

In exposing to millions of Americans the lobbying methods of utilities, Hugo Black had made an invaluable contribution to the administration's case. The liberal *Nation* cited his campaigns against shippers and lobbyists in listing Black as one of twenty-seven Americans who deserved the praise of fellow countrymen. Even schoolchildren read how the "quick-witted" senator had trapped "the master mind" of the utility corporation. In a remote corner of the Appalachian foothills, the Ashland *Progress* rejoiced over the "courageous and splendid work" of Clay County's native son in exposing the "low and contemptible methods" of utility lobbyists.[36]

As election year opened, Roosevelt seemed willing to rest on his record, confident of November's verdict. In an inflammatory message to Congress, he taunted his business opponents. "They engage in vast propaganda to spread fear and discord among the people," Roosevelt thundered. "They would 'gang up' against the people's liberties." Such rhetoric pleased Black, and he praised the message extravagantly: "Had he [Roosevelt] not already been the outstanding leader of progressive and liberal thought in the world, this would have made him so." His enthusiasm did not

---

[35] Leuchtenburg, *Roosevelt and the New Deal*, 156.
[36] "Cross-Questioner," *Scholastic*, XXVII (September 21, 1935), 25. The *Nation's* tribute was quoted in the Birmingham *Post*, December 26, 1935, and the Ashland *Progress* editorial was reprinted by the *Post*, September 3, 1935.

prevent Black from helping to override the President's veto of the Adjusted Compensation Act for immediate payment of the veterans' bonus. However, he and Robert La Follette, Jr., led the Senate fight to penalize corporations which failed to distribute their profits as dividends in order that their wealthy stockholders could avoid payment of surtaxes. After a stormy Senate floor fight, the administration won a graduated tax on undistributed profits.[37]

In March *aficionados* of congressional hearings were pleased by the return of what *Newsweek* called "their favorite players." After six months away from the headlines, Black reconvened his committee for a rousing preview of election year politics. During its recess the Black committee had used a subpoena *duces tecum*, the so-called "dragnet" subpoena, to secure from Western Union and Postal Telegraph copies of thousands of telegrams sent by firms, organizations, and individuals in behalf of various causes. Most were messages of protest from utility companies, but the committee also possessed telegrams from a variety of anti-New Deal organizations, among them the Liberty League, Crusaders, Sentinels of the Republic, National Economy League, and the Women's National Republican Club. Clerks of the Federal Communications Commission performed the tremendous job of examining these messages for evidence of lobbying irregularities.[38]

Investigation by subpoena *duces tecum* aroused outcries in the anti-Roosevelt press that the committee had violated the Fourth Amendment's prohibition against general warrants and its guarantee of the "right of the people to be secure in their . . . papers against unreasonable search and seizures." Personal correspondence was being read, they protested, "on mere supposition that lobbying might be revealed." The Baltimore *Sun* said "resistance to New Deal policies" was grounds for investigation by the Black committee, which ignored such effective lobbies as the American Legion and American Federation of Labor. The Chicago *Tribune*

[37] New York *Times*, January 4, 28; June 2–7, 1936; Basil Rauch, *The History of the New Deal, 1933–38* (New York, 1944), 228–29.
[38] "Black Booty," *Time*, XXVII (March 16, 1936), 17–18.

cartooned Hugo, in Klan regalia, riding over a countryside marked "intimidation of all who oppose Roosevelt." The New York *Times* compared the senator's eyes to those of Rhadamanthus, mythological judge of the underworld. "As Mr. Black's virtue gets austerer," said the *Times*, "the Senate chamber has a small, lingering and humorous odor of boiling oil and melted lead." Raymond Clapper, of Scripps-Howard, castigated such "Nazi methods"; and Walter Lippmann said the Black committee acted as both prosecutor and judge, with newspaper readers as the jury.[39]

Fellow legislators, too, had their reservations. William E. Borah, who had often sided with Black, asked the Federal Communications Commission to explain to the Senate why it had assisted the Black committee. He sought information, Borah explained; later he might find himself in favor of the committee's methods. But Oregon's Frederick Steiwer charged "Ogpu methods," and in the House, James W. Wadsworth of New York spoke of "terrorism" and "pillage." The American Civil Liberties Union warned that the Black committee's tactics could be used against minority political parties, progressive groups, and religious organizations. Even though it found itself on the same side of this issue as the Liberty League, the Civil Liberties Union said its duty was to defend civil rights, not to examine the philosophies of those whose rights were violated.[40]

As the furor mounted, Silas Hardy Strawn, a prominent Republican critic of the New Deal and former president of both the United States Chamber of Commerce and the American Bar Association, decided to contest the Black committee. His Chicago law firm, Winston, Strawn, and Shaw, employed Frank J. Hogan to seek a court injunction restraining Western Union from turning over to the Black committee copies of confidential telegrams to its clients. Such correspondence, Hogan contended, was private and privileged, not subject to a "general inquisitorial fishing expedition."[41]

[39] *Ibid.*, New York *Times*, March 10, 11, 22, 24, 1936.
[40] New York *Times*, March 10, 24, 1936.
[41] *Ibid.*, March 3, 1936.

Bristling under attack Black defended his committee in a speech to the Senate. He denied that a lawyer's privilege to client relations extended to lobbying activities. He said his committee, in subpoenaing the telegrams of Winston, Strawn, and Shaw, sought to prove that the Liberty League had paid for messages opposing the holding company bill. Since utility companies had destroyed their own files, he roared, "the only place on earth where the committee can get this information is from the telegraph companies." But the Liberty League, he told the Senate, objected to "having these telegrams raised from the ashes of flaming incinerators" so the Senate and the public might know what "secret and deceptive measures were taken to defeat wholesome legislation for the people." The speech ended on a note of threat. If the court granted the injunction sought by Winston, Strawn, and Shaw, Black declared he would ask for immediate legislation to deprive courts of the power to enjoin the securing of evidence sought by congressional committees.[42]

Undeterred, Chief Justice Alfred A. Wheat, of the District of Columbia Supreme Court, issued a temporary injunction restraining the committee from seizing the telegraphic correspondence of Winston, Strawn, and Shaw. At this critical moment, Black attracted a new and powerful enemy who unwittingly was to prove a boon to the committee. William Randolph Hearst applied for an injunction to restrain the committee from securing a specific telegram. Denying Hearst's request, Chief Justice Wheat explained that it involved a particular piece of evidence, not a general search.[43]

Next day Representative John J. McSwain, chairman of the House military affairs committee, triumphantly read to the House the Hearst telegram, which had been given to him by Chairman Black. It proved to be a suggestion from Hearst to one of his editorial writers for a series of editorials urging impeachment of McSwain, whom Hearst called "a Communist in spirit and a traitor

---

[42] *Ibid.*, March 10, 1936.
[43] *Ibid.*, March 12, 1936. The temporary injunction won by Winston, Strawn, and Shaw was later made permanent, New York *Times*, June 26, 1936.

in fact." House members laughed loudly at the Communist charge and cheered McSwain as he denounced Hearst. After the telegram was read to the House, Black withdrew his subpoena directing Western Union to produce the message, leaving Hearst with no legal recourse. Provoked by Hearst's attack on the popular McSwain, the House passed the Black bill, which had already cleared the Senate, calling for registration of congressional lobbyists. But the House bill required only representatives of organizations engaged "principally" in lobbying to register. Black announced he would push for a bill "with some teeth in it." Biting an unlighted cigar, he declared, "Lobbying is lobbying."[44]

But Hearst was not so easily put down. Invoking the First Amendment's guarantee of freedom of the press, he made a second request for an injunction against seizure by the Black committee of a number of telegrams exchanged between Hearst and his editorial employees. Black told the Senate he needed legal aid to fight his battles. He insisted that blanket subpoenas had been issued during other Senate investigations, including Teapot Dome. Protests had been just as loud in the past, he claimed, but now they came from those who wanted to "combine burning with injunction" to prevent Congress from obtaining evidence. His Democratic colleagues, Lewis Schwellenbach and Sherman Minton, rallied to their chairman's aid. Minton said freedom of the press, to Hearst, meant "license to traduce and vilify public officers as swine and traitors to their country." Schwellenbach said Hearst feared that the committee would find out that H. C. Hopson, by his advertising money, had controlled the editorial policy of the Hearst chain. When Vice-President John Nance Garner put the question on passage of a resolution to give the Black committee a ten-thousand-dollar appropriation for legal aid, there was not a single "no" vote. Black brought his old partner Crampton Harris up from Birmingham to handle the fight against Hearst.[45]

The House, which had not forgotten the feud over Hopson, was

44 New York *Times*, March 18, 27, 1936.
45 *Ibid.*, March 21, 31; April 2, 1936.

in no mood to support Black's investigative techniques. In an election year, controversial votes would have to be explained at home. The Black committee, furthermore, had revealed connections between certain House members and lobbyists for railroad and utility interests. In an effort to win approval, Black appeared before the House rules committee. "My judgment is that the citizen has no right to seek to arrest the exercise of the legislative functions, and subordinate the Congress to the courts," he testified. But all the persuasiveness of his powerful Alabama colleague Majority Leader Will Bankhead could not win over the House. Despite Bankhead's pleas, the House voted 153 to 137 against the resolution. Representative Emmanuel Celler of New York commented that "a certain senator needed a rap across the knuckles." Finally the Senate acted alone to approve the employment of Harris by passing a resolution authorizing its audit and control committee to pay the ten-thousand-dollar fee.[46]

While the two houses engaged in these disharmonious exchanges, Chief Justice Wheat denied the second Hearst request for an injunction, declaring that the guarantee of press freedom in the First Amendment applied only to the right of the press to criticize public officials. Hearst appealed to the United States Circuit Court of Appeals. In its defense the Black committee, perhaps in the words of its chairman, paraphrased John Marshall: "The power to enjoin the Senate is the power to destroy the Senate." The fight with Hearst ended in November, 1936, when the Court of Appeals denied the appeal. Blanket seizure of telegrams might be illegal, the appeal court said, but it was powerless to act against a legislative body.[47]

Arthur Krock, a relentless critic of Black's tactics, said the Hearst affair came like "manna from Heaven" to the beleaguered Black committee in the midst of charges that it had violated the Fourth Amendment. With a well-known and generally unpopular

[46] S. Res. 286, 74th Cong., 2nd Sess., Group 46, Legislative Records, National Archives; New York *Times*, April 5, 9, 16, 21, 1936.
[47] New York *Times*, May 10, November 10, 1936.

opponent entering the lists against him, Black was able to turn public attention away from his committee and onto the publisher. Noting that Hearst's legal maneuvers had met with no success, Krock concluded: "As an expert in rough tactics, Mr. Hearst might have felt grudging admiration for such an adversary."[48]

Although the controversy with Hearst overshadowed its other activities, the Black committee, that election year spring, investigated a variety of organizations which its chairman said had vague names but specific interests. In a radio speech, Black reminded listeners that the Liberty League had paid for telegrams to fight the Wheeler-Rayburn bill and the Crusaders had sponsored a series of radio talks to oppose the Tennessee Valley Authority. The Farmers' Independence Council of America had as one of its goals "elimination" of the New Deal; and the Southern Committee to Uphold the Constitution, which had inspired an anti-New Deal convention in Macon, Georgia, had been financed by DuPont interests and John J. Raskob, former chairman of the Democratic National Committee. Even Arthur Krock admitted that the Black committee produced much interesting material "when it was not ignoring the Fourth Amendment."[49]

In summary Black reported that organizations which his committee scrutinized were almost exclusively financed by wealthy individuals, banks, and utility companies. Over an eighteen-month period, more than a million dollars had been given to the Liberty League, American Federation of Utility Investors, American Taxpayers League, Crusaders, and Southern Committee to Uphold the Constitution. Ninety percent of this sum, Black said, had come from representatives of the DuPont, J. P. Morgan, Andrew Mellon, and John D. Rockefeller, Jr., investments, as well as from banks, brokers, utility companies, and oil companies.[50]

"Congress," wrote Arthur Krock in April, 1936, "is always

---

[48] *Ibid.*, April 6, 1936.
[49] *Ibid.*, March 6, 20; April 9, 17, 21, 1936.
[50] A summary of the committee report was published by the New York *Times*, June 21, 1936.

afraid of its inquisitors." Therefore, the *Times'* lofty columnist theorized, Black and his committee at first met little opposition from their colleagues, who feared that criticism might be interpreted back home as friendship for those under investigation. But by adopting the tactic of wholesale subpoenaing of telegrams, the Black committee laid itself open to valid criticism and narrowly escaped a public debacle. Antiadministration newspapers were delighted to find a cudgel to discredit the hearings which so enthralled their readers. Even many liberals thought Black had gone too far. As one student of his career put it, he had invaded the "privacy which his liberal friends held more sacred than the legislation he was trying to help." Raymond Moley, drifting away from the New Deal, thought that Black, in his "frenzy," had "struck at the innocent as well as the guilty." George Creel, the over-zealous propagandist of World War days, described the Alabama senator as having the industry of a beaver and the pertinacity of a woodpecker. Black, Creel said, would be one of the Senate's foremost members "were it not for the fact that he still thinks in terms of the time when he was prosecuting attorney. . . . Almost everybody, to Hugo's gimlet eye, is a potential defendant."[51]

Presenting his side in an article for *Harper's* magazine, Black recalled how he had opposed power lobbyists in 1928 when they wanted to transfer a utilities investigation from Congress to the Federal Trade Commission. He reminded his readers that letters regarding air mail contracts had been destroyed. Quoting the evasive answers given to the FTC by an electric company official, Black wrote: "This sort of thing severely taxes the patience of an investigator. It accounts for what newspaper editorial enemies of investigations often refer to as the bullying and badgering of witnesses." Despite the barriers encountered by congressional investigators, Black believed their work had been the basis of important legislation and had saved taxpayers "countless millions"

[51] Wesley McCune, *The Nine Young Men* (New York, 1947), 29; Raymond Moley, *After Seven Years* (New York, 1939), 315; George Creel, "Goose-Killers," *Colliers,* XCIX (January 9, 1937), 26–50.

through exposures like Teapot Dome. "Special privilege," he wrote, "thrives in secrecy and darkness and is destroyed by the rays of pitiless publicity."[52]

Although Black had loyal support from Minton and Schwellenbach, the investigations had been mostly a one-man show. Mindful of his friends in the press, Black produced two sensations a day, one timed for morning papers and the other for afternoon dailies. His hearings attracted reporters from major wire services and scores of newspapers, members of the House and Senate, and important Washington personages. As a cross-examiner the chairman was reputed to be tough but fair, employing patient plodding or sharp sarcasm, but often bidding his witness good-day with a friendly handshake. Black's fabled memory stood him in good stead. When one witness, whose salary was sixty thousand dollars a year, asked for his daily witness fee of three dollars on the ground that he had been "forced" to testify, the chairman quickly flipped back through pages of testimony to reply: "Forced? Why this transcript shows you testified: 'I want everybody to know I came here of my own volition and I've been trying to come before this committee for a week!'"[53]

Black had conducted three major investigations in four years and had concrete results to show for his labors. Methods of subsidizing the merchant marine and airlines had been revised. For the first time in its history, Congress was exercising some check upon lobbyists. The drama of the hearings, with their exposures of faked telegrams, burned papers, hidden control of newspaper editorial policy, and expenditures of vast sums of money, was to no small degree responsible for the partial victory won by the administration in the Public Utility Holding Company Act. Democrats reaped political hay when the Black committee turned "the rays of pitiless publicity" on subsidy programs of Republican ad-

[52] Hugo L. Black, "Inside a Senate Investigation," *Harper's*, CLXXII (February, 1936), 275–86.
[53] "Black: A Man of Parts: Senator, Investigator, and Individual, *Newsweek*, VII (March 14, 1936), 21.

ministrations and on big business interests fighting the New Deal. The power of Congress to investigate, Black wrote in *Harper's*, was "one of the most powerful weapons in the hands of the people." His aggressive use of this weapon in the service of the New Deal won Black the President's gratitude and favor, and entrée to the administration's high councils.

XII

⊓⊔⊓⊔⊓⊔⊓⊔⊓⊔⊓⊔⊓⊔⊓⊔⊓⊔⊓⊔⊓⊔⊓⊔⊓⊔⊓⊔⊓⊔

I Nominate
Hugo L.
Black

There was a premonition of fall in the chilly air rising off the Hudson and in the library of Hyde Park a fire burned cheerily. Franklin Roosevelt, bobbing back and forth in a high-backed, spring rocker, and twenty-eight of his trusted advisors discussed with relish the campaign ahead. Hugo Black, with his almost unalloyed record of loyalty to New Deal policies and with a militancy against "malefactors of great wealth" which matched Roosevelt's own, found himself in 1936 a member of this inner circle.[1]

That fall, with La Follette, Schwellenbach, New York's Mayor Fiorello La Guardia, and other liberal leaders, Black helped organize the National Progressive Conference, made up of those from various political parties who favored Roosevelt's reelection. He served on the Democratic platform committee. Stumping the Midwest, Black made enthusiastic speeches for the President. "Roosevelt himself couldn't have done better," a high school history teacher commented. Reporting to the President from Indianapolis, Black urged him to allay midwestern fears of involvement in another European war by declaring firmly that he would keep America at peace.[2]

Republicans also took note of Hugo Black. Presented by Re-

[1] New York *Times*, September 25, 1936.
[2] *Ibid.*, September 12, 1936; Hugo L. Black to Franklin D. Roosevelt, October 18, 1936, in Roosevelt Papers; Davis, *Uncle Hugo*, 28.

publican National Committeeman Earl Warren to a crowd of more than fifty thousand in the Los Angeles Coliseum, Alfred M. Landon spiritedly attacked the Alabama senator's investigatory tactics, perhaps, as the New York *Times* suspected, as a gesture to Hearst. "One Congressional investigation characterized as a 'fishing expedition,' openly and flagrantly violated the constitutional restrictions against unreasonable search and seizure," Landon declared.[3]

Following Roosevelt's overwhelming triumph at the polls, loyal New Dealers basked in reflected glory. But already looking to 1940, the *Weekly Call*, a labor newspaper published in Birmingham, reported that Alabama's senior senator was being seriously considered for the national ticket. In the *Weekly Call's* opinion, Black's yeoman services to labor would make him the logical successor to Roosevelt. As if in response to this tantalizing thought, Black stubbornly proferred the thirty-hour bill to the new Congress, lopsided with Democrats. But the President had more pressing matters on his mind. Buoyed by fresh evidence of his popularity, Roosevelt turned upon the recalcitrant Supreme Court.[4]

New Deal thinkers, Black among them, had long been searching for ways to make the Court more amenable to Roosevelt's programs. In 1935 Black and Hatton Sumners had sponsored a bill to speed up procedures for testing federal laws before the High Court. The Black-Sumners bill would have permitted a direct appeal to the Supreme Court from any injunction granted by a lower court against a federal agency. Once notice of appeal was given, such cases were to receive preferential consideration. The prospect of passage of such a bill had the unusual effect of bringing Chief Justice Hughes and Associate Justices Brandeis and Van Devanter to testify against it at closed hearings of the Senate judiciary

---

[3] New York *Times*, October 21, 1936.
[4] The *Weekly Call's* endorsement was reprinted in a new magazine, heavily subsidized by business and industry, entitled *Alabama*, I (December 14, 1936), 10. New York *Times*, January 6, 1937.

committee. The measure was unnecessary, the justices contended; injunction cases were being handled efficiently by customary methods. Black retorted that federal courts were under attack for "tedious and unnecessary delay." He told the judges, "I think it is a just criticism."[5]

In January, 1937, as Washington buzzed with rumors of a forthcoming attack on the Court, Black reintroduced this proposal. He also suggested to Roosevelt that, except on constitutional matters, the high court be separated into two divisions to decide cases, with the chief justice sitting on each. Two more justices might be added to the Supreme Court, he proposed, because nine men made a "wholly inadequate number" to deal with the growing burden of cases. Roosevelt waited to reply until after he had sprung on a startled Congress a carefully guarded secret. "We seem to have been thinking along the same or else parallel lines," he wrote Black.[6]

But Black's plan paled beside the boldness of the President's own scheme to enlarge—the anti-New Deal press said "pack"— the court by adding a new federal judge or a Supreme Court justice to match every incumbent over seventy years of age who had not resigned or retired. The size of the high court, under this plan, could reach fifteen. Conceiving his idea without advice from congressional leaders, Roosevelt counted on the American people to pressure Congress for its approval. But Vice-President Garner gave the plan a thumbs-down sign; Hatton Sumners, chairman of the House judiciary committee, remarked cheerfully: "Boys, here's where I cash in my chips." Many another southern Democrat, already disaffected with New Deal economic policies, seized this unexpected opportunity to split openly with the President. On the

[5] United States Congress, Senate, Committee on the Judiciary, *Hearings on S.2176, Federal Court Procedures*, 74th Cong., 1st Sess., March 25, 1935, 12–13, Legislative Records, National Archives, Washington, D.C.; New York *Times,* March 26, 1935.

[6] Hugo L. Black to Franklin D. Roosevelt, January 28, 1937; Franklin D. Roosevelt to Hugo L. Black, February 6, 1937, in Roosevelt Papers; New York *Times,* January 16, 1937.

day of its proposal, Black told reporters firmly: "I favor the plan." [7]

While a national hue and cry over the plan raged throughout the spring of 1937, Black remained one of the President's most vocal supporters. He told listeners over the Mutual Broadcasting System that the Constitution had left to Congress the right to increase or decrease the number of justices in order to guard the people's liberties against lifetime judges wholly free from their control. "A majority of our judges," he scolded, "should not amend the Constitution according to their economic predilections every time they decide a case." Appearing with La Follette and Assistant Attorney General Robert H. Jackson at an American Labor Party rally in Carnegie Hall, he reminded the audience that Thomas Jefferson and Andrew Jackson had also been accused of unconstitutional actions toward the Supreme Court. At a Town Hall debate in Washington, Black said the argument was not really over the President's right to increase the Court, but over such issues as minimum wages, maximum hours, child labor, and farm relief. He chided Yale students when a satirical "Roosevelt for King" movement on their campus coincided with the Supreme Court controversy. Nobody knew who started these "supposedly funny" collegiate movements, Black told the press. "It is no joke," he said sternly, "to ridicule the President of the United States." [8]

In the Senate West Virginia's Rush D. Holt, a rebellious Democrat, told his colleagues he had never been consulted by the administration "on the appointment of a janitor," but that he had been promised a voice in naming a West Virginia federal judge if he would go along with the Court plan. Jumping up, Black shot back scornfully: "I would hate to admit my reputation was such that people would offer me things like that and get away with it." [9]

With many onetime supporters defecting over the Court plan,

[7] Burns, *Roosevelt, the Lion and the Fox*, 294–95; New York *Times*, February 6, 1937.

[8] Hugo L. Black, "Reorganization of the Federal Judiciary," a radio address delivered February 23, 1937, *Vital Speeches*, III (September 1, 1937), 674–77; New York *Times*, March 15, 25, 1937.

[9] New York *Times*, March 30, 1937.

Roosevelt could not fail to appreciate such a zealous defender. Black and Farley lunched with the President early in April to talk about strategy for getting the bill through the Senate. "All I have to do," said Roosevelt cockily, "is deliver a better speech, and the opposition will be beating a path to the White House door." Black warned that the bill's opponents were delaying until they could arouse more public anger. "We'll smoke 'em out," the President insisted. "If delay helps them, we must press for an early vote."[10]

But unexpected events in the Court itself changed the course and strategy of the battle. With Justice Owen Roberts switching from his previous position, the Court voted 5–4 to validate the National Labor Relations Act, uphold a minimum wage law in the state of Washington, and approve the principles of old-age pensions and unemployment insurance. Chief Justice Hughes, in a letter to Burton K. Wheeler, made a highly successful defense of his court against Roosevelt's charges of inefficiency. Finally, while he was reading the morning newspapers in bed on May 18, the President received a message that Justice Van Devanter planned to retire. Roosevelt was to have an opportunity to name a justice. The first vacancy on the high court had long been promised to the loyal but conservative Robinson, a prospect highly acceptable to many senators, who publicly urged the President to name their Arkansas colleague.[11]

The Court was not the only issue to rankle feelings between White House and Capitol Hill. Business leaders and manufacturers, especially those from the South, prodded senators and representatives to fight the administration's latest proposal on regulation of hours, wages, and working conditions. Roosevelt had persuaded Black to abandon the thirty-hour proposal in favor of the Fair Labor Standards bill, an administration plan drafted after months of work by Thomas G. Corcoran and Benjamin V. Cohen. In

[10] Farley, *Jim Farley's Story*, 78–79.
[11] New York *Times*, May 19, 1937. The Supreme Court Retirement Act, signed by Roosevelt on March 1, 1937, permitted justices to retire at seventy. By retiring rather than resigning, they would continue to receive their full salaries.

tribute to their long sponsorship of the regulatory principle, Black's and William Connery's names were affixed to it. Anxious for a united front on labor legislation, the President instructed his son James to line up Charlton Ogburn, general counsel of the AFL, behind the new plan. "We have promised it. We cannot stand still," Roosevelt told Robinson and Black.[12]

The new Black-Connery bill differed from both the thirty-hour plan and from NRA. The provision for code-making had been eliminated in favor of a five-member Fair Labor Standards Board to act as a regulatory agency. The measure relied for authority, not upon the "general welfare" clause of the Constitution, as had the recovery measure, but upon the power to regulate interstate commerce. It would ban the movement in commerce of "unfair goods," produced under substandard labor conditions, including the labor of children under the age of sixteen. It did not encompass the regulation of "fair trade practices" and marketing methods, as had NRA, nor specify a definite limit on work hours or a fixed minimum wage. Such figures, Roosevelt feared, would merely provide targets for his opponents. Congress was asked to give the proposed board the authority to fix a basic work week of not less than thirty and not more than forty hours, and to set minimum wages.[13]

During that torrid Washington summer, Black bore the burden of guiding the Black-Connery bill to passage by the Senate. As chairman of the Senate's education and labor committee, he presided over a month of hearings held jointly by Senate and House committees, a tactic suggested by the President as a means of speeding action on the bill. The cosponsor, Representative Connery, died in midsummer, leaving Black as the bill's most vocal proponent in Congress. During the hearings, divisions appeared within ranks of both business and labor. Although spokesmen for

[12] Franklin D. Roosevelt to James Roosevelt, May 24, 1937, in Roosevelt Papers; New York *Times*, May 24, 1937; Burns, *Roosevelt, the Lion and the Fox*, 311.

[13] S. 2475, 75th Cong., 1st Sess., May 24, 1937, Legislative Records, National Archives; New York *Times*, May 24, 1937; "Wages," *Newsweek*, IX (June 5, 1937), 9–10.

the United States Chamber of Commerce, National Association of Manufacturers, and other business organizations testified against the bill, some northern businessmen appeared before Chairman Black to testify in favor of the proposal as a means of offsetting competition from southern firms with lower-paid workers. Most southern manufacturers either opposed the bill or demanded regional differentials, declaring their firms would be forced out of business if they were compelled to pay the same wage as the rest of the country. Labor leaders expressed varied reservations about the provision on wages.[14]

The Senate education and labor committee made some major changes of its own, drastically curbing the powers of the proposed board. Minimum wages of more than forty cents an hour were forbidden, as well as a standard work week of less than forty hours. Many industries, including farming, dairying, forestry, fishing, and local retailing, were exempt. Child labor standards were lowered to permit children under sixteen to work in jobs which would not injure their health nor interfere with their education. Then the revised bill, approved unanimously, was reported to the Senate on July 8, 1937.[15]

Opening the debate Black declared the bill's main objectives were to raise wages, shorten hours, and abolish child labor. In answer to dire predictions that it would bring about the closing of factories, he quoted extracts from Dickens and Macaulay, reporting similar apprehensions a century before in England over the question of whether women and children should work a fifteen-hour day in factories.[16]

As the administration's major spokesman, Black confronted an angry pack of fellow Southerners. Prodded by industrial leaders back home, members of the southern bloc, one after another, un-

---

[14] James McGregor Burns, *Congress on Trial: The Legislative Process and the Administrative State* (New York, 1949), 70; John S. Forsythe, "Legislative History of the Fair Labor Standards Act," *Law and Contemporary Problems*, VI (Summer, 1939), 467–68.

[15] *Congressional Record*, 75th Cong., 1st Sess., 6894.

[16] *Ibid.*, 7650–7946.

furled the old bloody shirt. Northerners, they thundered, wanted to "crucify" southern industry in order to stifle its competition and halt its rise from the ashes of Civil War. Behind this rhetoric lay a determination to maintain the old southern lures of lower wages and a tractable labor force. It thinly concealed the traditional southern fear of a federal regulatory board which might intrude upon state police powers. Ellison D. "Cotton Ed" Smith of South Carolina pictured for the Senate living conditions in the South "so kindly that it takes only fifty cents a day for one to live comfortably and reasonably."[17]

Black's reply to his colleague was as dramatic a performance as any he gave during ten years in the Senate. He waved mill vouchers, showing payment of $2.68 for four days' work and $4.48 for four and a half days' work. "That figures up to about eight cents an hour," he told the Senate angrily. "I subscribe to the gospel that a man who is born in Alabama and who can do as much work as a man born in any state in New England is entitled to the same pay if he does the same work." When Mississippi's Pat Harrison remarked scornfully that the bill had "a lot of lovely poetry in it," Black cried: "Thank God it has! All through the ages, poets have raised their voices in behalf of the weak."[18]

On July 31, after five days of sharp, often bitter debate and the longest series of votes taken on any measure since the Smoot-Hawley tariff, the Senate approved, 56–28, a wages and hours bill, modified even more by amendments. In the House the plan received a favorable report from the labor committee, but the rules committee, dominated by a coalition of Republicans and southern Democrats, refused to allow the House to consider it. Few in Washington were optimistic enough that summer to foresee that it would finally emerge as the Fair Labor Standards Act of 1938.[19]

[17] *Ibid.*, 7650–7946; "Wage-Hour Bill Survives Southern Oratory on Uses of Poverty," *Newsweek*, X (August 7, 1937), 13.

[18] *Congressional Record*, 75th Cong., 1st Sess., 7949–51.

[19] *Ibid.*, 7957; Paul Douglas and Joseph Hackman, "The Fair Labor Standards Act of 1938," *Political Science Quarterly*, LIII (December, 1938), 491–515.

At the height of these twin battles over the Court plan and the wages and hours law, the Senate received an unexpected shock. Joe Robinson, worn out by the struggle to hold fractious Democratic ranks together, died July 14. The Court plan died with Robinson, whose influence had been the main hope of a favorable compromise. On July 22 the Senate voted to recommit the original reorganization bill. The proposal for appointing new judges and justices was, in effect, defeated. In an effort to mend party strife, Democrats in early August held what the press described as a "harmony dinner" in honor of their new leader, Alben Barkley of Kentucky. But the very next day, a new dispute broke out over the Wagner-Van Nuys antilynching bill. Black, with most of the dissident Southerners, voted for a motion to end discussion of the antilynching issue without action and to take up a new topic. In a vote which split Democratic ranks almost in half, the motion failed. Barkley, already finding his new post difficult, was overheard to murmur to a fellow senator: "That was a hell of a harmony dinner we had last night." [20]

As the President later described the court fight, he had lost a battle but won the war. Now he was free to appoint an ardent New Dealer who would assure the administration of a safe majority in favor of its programs. Preferably the new justice should come from the South or West, regions underrepresented on the Court. Roosevelt toyed briefly with the notion of delaying the nomination until Congress recessed, then making an interim nomination. But realizing this would only prolong the angry dispute, he ordered the Justice Department to speed up its search for an acceptable name. Newspapermen familiar with Roosevelt's moods described him in those August dog days as "sore and vengeful." He wanted to surprise the Senate and, in particular, to give its rebellious Southerners a bitter pill they would have to swallow. If his nominee pleased the administration's powerful new allies in

[20] New York *Times*, August 12, 1937; Leuchtenberg, *Franklin Roosevelt and the New Deal*, 236–38. On August 26, Roosevelt signed the Judicial Procedure Reform Act, which provided for reforms in lower court procedures but omitted any provision for the appointment of new justices and judges.

organized labor, so much the better. The Justice Department compiled a list of possible nominees which eventually contained the names of sixty men.[21]

When he noticed years before that Alabama voters criticized Oscar Underwood for becoming "too national," Hugo Black resolved to avoid this political pitfall. Between sessions, he came home to Birmingham and took to the hustings. In the summer of 1936, he toured sixty-one of Alabama's sixty-seven counties. Despite his busy schedule, he made himself constantly available to constituents visiting Washington. Those who came after office hours found these instructions on his door: "To Alabamians who cannot wait until tomorrow—go to elevators, ask boy to show you phone where you can call, ask for extension 17 and state your business."[22]

But ten years had passed since Black had been an intimate of the Klan-dry coalition through whose political machinery average Alabamians had voiced their aspirations. Quick tours of Alabama's rural areas could never give him the same feel for the prejudices of his followers as he had gotten when he rubbed elbows, day after day, with working class clients and jurors. The glare of klieg lights in Senate committee rooms where he presided, the dazzle of frequent visits to the White House, the sight of his name mentioned for national office, were bound to dim somewhat his view of those Alabamians who had twice elected him as their senator. In midsummer, 1937, a political writer for the Birmingham *News* expressed his opinion that Black was becoming a national figure with a national viewpoint, while his Alabama constituents, 72 percent of them living in rural areas, remained fundamentally conservative. Even the senator's best friends admitted that Hugo was "failing in his usual political sagacity," the *News* reported.[23]

[21] Harold Ickes, *The Secret Diary of Harold Ickes,* II (New York, 1953), 182–83; "Nominee No. 93," *Time,* XXX (August 23, 1937), 13.

[22] "Black: A Man of Parts: Senator, Investigator, and Individual," *Newsweek,* VII (March 14, 1936), 21.

[23] Birmingham *News,* July 18, 1937.

Ardent Jeffersonian though he was, Black realized that omnivorous reading, a decade in Washington, and the impact of the depression had nationalized his views. Because trade, economics, and tariffs were national concerns, "all that is wrong here in Alabama can never be righted if we try to right it in Alabama alone," he told a Birmingham *News* columnist. In a speech to Alabama's county commissioners, he tried to drive home the point that states and counties could no longer handle by themselves the immense problems of education, road building, and public works. "It is the purpose of all governments," he told them, "that all the people move forward in unison." In a philosophic mood, he wrote his friend, Judge Joseph Willett: "I can understand and appreciate the note of sadness running through your realistic discussion of a changing Governmental philosophy, brought about by a changed economic order. National business control, as distinguished from local business control, has made it necessary that many of us reshape and maybe remould traditional concepts that we really love."[24]

During the hectic spring and summer of 1937, Black peppered the Seventy-fifth Congress with proposals growing out of this philosophy. He urged that the Civilian Conservation Corps be made a permanent agency to help young men find employment. He sponsored a bill calling for a $300,000,000 annual program of federal grants in states for school improvement. He sought a study of the feasibility of federal health insurance, and was one of those who urged creation of a national housing authority to assist states and communities in developing slum-clearance and low-rent housing projects. To raise cotton prices before the fall harvest, he introduced a Senate resolution directing the Commodity Credit Corporation to make mandatory loans of twelve cents a pound on cotton. Even Roosevelt, with economy on his mind, opposed Black's education subsidy plan, and insisted that there be no more

[24] Childers, "Hugo Black, Always an Alabamian;" Birmingham *News*, August 23, 1936; Hugo L. Black to Joseph J. Willett, Sr., February 1, 1936, in Willett Papers.

federal agricultural loans until further production controls were approved.[25]

Proposals such as these may have sounded quixotic to Alabama industrial leaders, but the sight of their senator leading the fight for a federal wages and hours law struck them as virtually treasonous. Reflecting their fury, the Montgomery *Journal*, Selma *Times-Journal*, Dothan *Eagle*, and Gadsden *Times* fulminated against the Black-Connery bill; the Mobile *Register* commended its "humane objectives" but doubted that a five-man board could decide on proper wages and work hours for the whole nation. The Tallassee *Tribune* declared: "Senator Black should be retired . . . he is not representing the majority sentiment of the people of Alabama." The Headland *Wiregrass Farmer* said Black enjoyed holding up to disgrace "men who have had the temerity to question the wisdom of some of the aspects of the revolution." *Alabama* magazine, organ of the state's business establishment, said that Black, in supporting the Court plan and a wages and hours law, "has long since forgotten that he is commissioned and paid to represent, primarily, the people of Alabama."[26]

Lumber interests fought the bill bitterly. "The worst offenders of all against industrial decency in this state—the lumbermen—are the ones who are doing most of the agitating," a friend advised Black. But a few sawmill operators in Alabama and Mississippi were brave enough to write Senator Black that "chiseling operators" who paid "starvation wages" could be controlled only by a government scale.[27]

Even farmers were wheedled into joining the public outcry. The powerful Montgomery County Farm Bureau passed a resolution opposing a wages and hours law on the ground that it would result in higher prices for goods farmers bought. Black had long

[25] *Congressional Record*, 75 Cong., 1st Sess., 593, 5517; New York *Times*, May 20, 21, August 4, 1937.

[26] Mobile *Register*, August 3, 1937; "Buffeted Black," *Alabama*, II (July 12, 1937), 3; "Black Blasts," *Alabama*, II (August 2, 1937), 5–6.

[27] Tindall, *The Emergence of the New South*, 533–54; New York *Times*, July 28, 1937.

sought to convince farmers they would be more prosperous if the paychecks of their customers were larger. "Do not listen," he warned them, "to the shrewdly spoken and written words of those whose interest leads them to try to divide the farmers and the workers in business and industry." Replying to the Montgomery resolution, he charged that the Liberty League, Republicans, and other powerful interests were waging a campaign of "vilification and abuse" against him in order to replace him with a senator who would acquiesce in their views.[28]

State Democratic Chairman John McQueen wrote Farley that he firmly believed the great majority of Alabama Democrats to be "unalterably opposed" to passage of the Black-Connery bill. Many conservative Southerners, not aligned with any special interests, felt Black had encouraged a climate in which sit-down strikes and radical movements flourished. Names of potential senatorial candidates for 1938, including those of Representatives Lister Hill and Henry B. Steagall; Tom Heflin, and George H. Denny, chancellor of the University of Alabama, were talked of openly.[29]

Black still had friends and allies. Governor Graves, calling on Roosevelt at Warm Springs, assured the President that Alabama was "100 per cent behind" his Supreme Court plan because, Graves claimed, the state was enjoying prosperity after years of ten- and fourteen-cent cotton. "Every enemy of Roosevelt's," declared the governor, "is an enemy of mine." Organized labor around Birmingham continued to support Black enthusiastically. "When those who are opposed to President Roosevelt seek to supplant me in the Senate," Black wrote Judge Willett, "it is my intention to carry President Roosevelt's great Democratic platform directly to the people of Alabama." But the growing chorus of criticism worried him. In early August he sent out a circular letter defending the wages and hours bill and charging that "special interests" were trying to unseat him. With Josephine and

[28] Hugo L. Black, "The Farmer," radio address delivered March 9, 1935, *Vital Speeches*, III (September 1, 1937), 684–89; "Cocky," *Alabama*, II (July 26, 1937), 3.

[29] Tindall, *The Emergence of the New South*, 534; "Denny Chimes," *Alabama*, II (July 19, 1937), 3; Birmingham *News*, July 18, 1937.

the children, he took Sunday afternoon drives through the Virginia countryside to divert his mind from political problems.[30]

Interior Secretary Harold Ickes, among others, thought Hugo was "very discouraged and doesn't seem to have a great deal of fight left in him for next year." Ickes was one of the few to whom Roosevelt confided that he was considering the nomination of Senator Black. Roosevelt told Ickes he did not believe Black to be as able a lawyer as other prospects, but that the senator was altogether too liberal for his state. Ickes wrote in his diary that the President also sympathized with Black because his younger son, Sterling, was suffering from ear trouble and might need costly medical care. For this reason it was reported that Black might be considering retirement from the Senate to resume his lucrative law practice. "An appointment to the Supreme Court would take care of him financially for life," Ickes wrote in his journal, "and it is clear to see that the President's sympathies are very much aroused."[31]

Other candidates were urged upon Roosevelt. George Norris wanted the President to appoint a man who would construe the Constitution "in the light of present-day civilization." Norris suggested Wisconsin Governor Philip La Follette. Farley plugged for Owen D. Young or Judge Samuel G. Bratton of New Mexico. Roosevelt considered Lloyd Garrison, Dean of the University of Wisconsin Law School, but told Ickes the Senate might refuse to confirm Garrison. The Justice Department pared its list from sixty to twenty; then Roosevelt himself winnowed it to six, three federal circuit court judges and three New Dealers in Washington: Senator Sherman Minton of Indiana, Solicitor General Stanley Reed of Kentucky, and Hugo Black.[32]

The President himself struck off the judges as insufficiently lib-

[30] New York *Times*, March 21, 1937; Hugo L. Black to Judge James J. Willett, Sr., July 23, 1937, in Willett Papers; "Pro-Black, Anti-Black," *Literary Digest*, CXXIV (August 28, 1937), 6.

[31] Ickes, *The Secret Diary*, II, 182–83.

[32] George Norris to Franklin D. Roosevelt, July 28, 1937, in Roosevelt Papers; Farley, *Jim Farley's Story*, 97–98; Ickes, *The Secret Diary*, II, 182; "Nominee No. 93," *Time*, XXX (August 23, 1937), 13.

eral. Stanley Reed, also, was too mild for Roosevelt's taste of the moment. He had asked Attorney General Homer Cummings to suggest an evangelical New Deal liberal and a man whom the intractable Senate would have to confirm. This narrowed the field to Minton and Black. When Cummings broached the subject to Minton, the Indiana senator demurred. As a zealous defender of the President during Senate debates on the Court plan, Minton had spoken harshly and personally of the "nine, old men," accusing them of Toryism and insincerity. He thought they would take his own appointment as a personal insult. Minton further feared that he would be replaced in the Senate by the ambitious Paul V. McNutt. Because of these doubts, Minton's name was stricken. Cummings asked him to sound out his close friend Senator Black.[33]

Black reviewed for Minton the factors involved: the hard primary fight ahead, his son's illness, Josephine's wish that he return to private law practice in Birmingham. He told Minton that he had no desire to leave the Senate; that he preferred its political infighting to the seclusion of the bench. But he promised to talk it over with his wife. The next day he told Minton that he would accept a court nomination if it were offered.[34]

On the sultry night of August 11, Hugo Black was summoned to the cluttered upstairs study of the White House. After a few pleasantries, the President came directly to the point. Holding out a nomination form, Roosevelt said: "Hugo, I'd like to write your name here." Receiving the answer he expected, he inscribed the words, "Hugo L. Black, of Alabama," in his crisp handwriting and sealed the nomination in an envelope. Obsessed by his desire to bring the stubborn Senate to heel, Roosevelt gave no thought to his nominee's political past. Later he would tell the press that one didn't ask a man "questions of that sort."[35]

If he had sought advice from the politically astute Farley, Roosevelt might have been reminded that Black had entered the

[33] Joseph Alsop and Turner Catledge, *The 168 Days* (New York, 1938), 301–303.
[34] *Ibid.*, 305.
[35] Birmingham *News*, September 12, 1942.

Senate with the backing of the Klan. If he had talked it over with Charles Michelson, the Democratic ghost writer and former newspaperman, he might have learned of rumors that Black had actually been a Klan member. But neither these men nor any of his Senate leaders knew the President's intention. The identity of his final choice was known only to Roosevelt, Attorney General Cummings, the nominee, and his wife.[36]

Impatient as a small boy waiting for his surprise to be revealed, Roosevelt shared the news with Steve Early only moments before the presidential courier arrived at the Senate door. "Jesus Christ!" exclaimed Early and the President grinned. After the news broke, reporters asked Roosevelt how he had kept such a secret. "Very simple procedure," the President replied, "not telling anybody." Pleased with his ploy, he explained he had written the nomination in his own hand. "And they'll have to take him, too," Roosevelt remarked gleefully to Farley.[37]

Black, wearing a white linen suit, sat impassively at his desk in the Senate. An observant reporter noted that the senator held a sheaf of papers which he was methodically shredding into small bits. From the gallery Josephine Black, in dark suit and broad-brimmed hat, peered down anxiously. Henry Ashurst, chairman of the Judiciary Committee, asked unanimous consent to consider immediately a message from the President. Hiram Johnson, the old California Progressive who had supported Roosevelt in 1932 and 1936 but had fought the court plan, asked the nature of the message. Told it was a Supreme Court nomination, Johnson promptly objected to immediate consideration. Nevertheless, at the direction of Vice-President Garner, the Senate clerk opened the message and began to read: "I nominate Hugo L. Black . . . ."[38]

[36] Alsop and Catledge, *The 168 Days*, 303–305; Ickes, *The Secret Diary*, II, 191.

[37] "Roosevelt Takes Out Judicial Insurance, Enrages Foes and Upsets an Immemorial Usage," *Newsweek*, X (August 21, 1937), 7–9; text of Roosevelt press conference, August 13, 1937, in Roosevelt Papers; Farley, *Jim Farley's Story*, 98.

[38] *Congressional Record*, 75th Cong., 1st Sess., 8732–33; New York *Times*, August 13, 1937.

After a moment of stunned silence, Ashurst rose to ask again for immediate confirmation in accordance with the Senate's "immemorial usage." But Hiram Johnson was adamant. For the first time since 1888, an executive appointment of a senator or former senator was referred to a committee for investigation. The previous delay had occurred over President Cleveland's nomination of the former Senator Lucius Quintus Cincinnatus Lamar of Mississippi to become an associate justice of the Supreme Court.

A few of Black's colleagues gathered around to congratulate the nominee, but others allowed their displeasure to show on their faces. Turner Catledge wrote in the New York *Times* that the nomination "dropped like salt into political wounds already rubbed raw by the court issue." After ten years' dedication to his work, Black had not achieved the easy popularity accorded his onetime colleague Tom Heflin. Washington journalists described him as a "loner" and said he suffered from an "unpopularity complex." He was too ardent a partisan, too zealous an investigator to please the Senate's oligarchs. Many a colleague had felt the quick lash of Hugo's tongue. He even dared to taunt pompous Arthur Vandenberg. Once, after listening to the Michigan Republican deliver a three-hour speech, Black rose, complimented him gravely, and said he had only one question to ask: "Is the Senator for or against the bill?"[39]

Still spare at fifty-one, Black looked to be about forty; his blond hair was just beginning to recede from a high forehead. He usually appeared rumpled, his suit wrinkled from a characteristic habit of sprawling in his chair, tie askew, hair in need of trimming, an unlighted cigar stuck defiantly in one corner of his mouth. Although many senators never felt at ease with such a firebrand, reporters liked Black. He was "good copy," even if they often left an interview wondering how he had maneuvered them away from the thing they really wanted to know. He had never lost the Southerner's love for geniality, a good story, the savored recollection of southern cooking, but his passion for economic democracy left

[39] New York *Times*, August 13, 1937; Birmingham *Post*, August 18, 1937; Alsop and Catledge, *The 168 Days*, 301–302.

him little time to indulge in such pleasantries. One New York *Times* reporter, who admired Black, wrote that his face suggested two personalities—the "cool and philosophical student of motives" and the "crusading harrier of men." [40]

The nomination caught not only the Senate but the nation by surprise. In Alabama feelings were mixed. Black's opponents found themselves deprived of their favorite target and of the opportunity to defeat him. Now Black had been recommended for a powerful position beyond their reach. Mixed with hostility and frustration was state pride in a native son, the third Alabamian, and the first since the Civil War, to be nominated to the Supreme Court. Governor Graves was elated. "I'm proud for Alabama," he told reporters. Birmingham newspapers had their misgivings, but the Montgomery *Advertiser*, so long Hugo's foe, predicted magnanimously that he would become a justice of the Holmes-Brandeis tradition. [41]

The AFL was "immensely pleased," Charlton Ogburn assured the President. Philip La Follette wired Roosevelt: "Ten Strike!" William Allen White wrote approvingly in the Emporia, Kansas, *Gazette* that the President, by naming a liberal, a Southerner, and a man whom the Senate would have to confirm, had hit "a veritable three-bagger." But Columnist Dorothy Thompson called the nomination "cheap." She wrote angrily, "We have finally carried the spoils system to the Supreme Bench, openly and cynically." [42]

In a brief open hearing the day after Roosevelt announced his choice, a subcommittee of the Senate Judiciary Committee voted 5–1 to recommend the nomination favorably to the full committee. Warren Austin of Vermont, the lone dissenter, based his opposition on constitutional grounds. Others were soon to join Austin. According to the Constitution, a senator or representative was forbidden to take a civil office which had been created, or for

---

[40] Birmingham *Post*, August 18, 1937; New York *Times*, August 22, 1937.
[41] New York *Times*, August 13, 1937; Birmingham *Age-Herald*, Birmingham *News*, Montgomery *Advertiser*, August 13, 1937.
[42] Philip La Follette to Franklin D. Roosevelt, August 12, 1937; Charlton Ogburn to Franklin D. Roosevelt, August 12, 1937, in Roosevelt Papers; New York *Times*, August 15, 1937.

which the salary had been increased, while he served in Congress. Austin and others contended that Black would be filling a newly created office because Justice Van Devanter had not resigned but simply retired, and was still subject to call. They also raised the technicality that, while Black was a member, the Senate had passed the Sumners-McCarran Retirement Act, providing that justices might retire at full pay, thereby increasing their emoluments. Administration supporters replied pointedly that no such objections had been raised when the Senate had previously urged Roosevelt to name Senator Robinson to the Court.[43]

On Monday, August 16, the full judiciary committee held a closed hearing on the nomination. Reporters wrote afterwards that "tempers flared to white heat" and that Senators Edward Burke and William Dieterich had to be restrained from a fistfight. Burke wanted to question the nominee about his constitutional views and about his conduct of Senate investigations. Dieterich charged that the Nebraskan was trying to "besmirch" the nominee. But even if the committee had acceded to Burke's request, Black would not have been available that day. His office reported that the senator had taken his son Sterling to Johns Hopkins Hospital in Baltimore for an examination.[44]

The National Association for the Advancement of Colored People and the Public Affairs Committee of the Socialist Party sent telegrams suggesting that the Senate inquire into the nominee's relationship to the Klan. Norman Thomas, chairman of the Socialist group, also requested that the Senate question Black as to why he had made no public statement on the Scottsboro case, why he had fought against the Costigan-Wagner bill to provide equal relief funds for whites and Negroes, and why he opposed antilynching bills. But these matters did not arise in committee. After two hours the committee voted 13–4 to report the nomination favorably to the Senate.[45]

Floor debate opened that same day with Republican charges

[43] New York *Times*, August 14, 1937.
[44] *Ibid*., August 17, 1937.   [45] *Ibid*.

that the nomination was being "steamrollered" through the Senate. The ailing George Norris, away from Washington, received an urgent message. The White House wanted him to state publicly his support for the nominee. Norris complied. In a telegram to Henry Ashurst, he spoke of his "intimate association" with Black and his grief at the "bitter, unreasonable, and sometimes malicious attacks" made on him. "He is a worthy representative of the common people," Norris said. "He understands their hopes and ambitions, and their liberties in his hands will be safe." [46]

Meanwhile the ominous words "Ku Klux Klan" were being whispered around the Capitol's marble corridors. In Atlanta reporters sought out Imperial Wizard Hiram Evans. Were the rumors true, they asked. Faithful to his Klan oath, Evans replied that, so far as he knew, Senator Black was neither a Klansman nor a sympathizer. "I'm hoeing my own row," said the Wizard. Before the nomination was made, Duncan Aikman, of the New York *Times*, had once been bold enough to ask Black directly if he were a Klan member. "No comment," the senator replied. At some point during the debate, a few of Hugo's friends found the nominee awaiting the Senate's decision in the private office of Edwin A. Halsey, secretary of the Senate. They asked for a statement on the Klan matter. Black thought a few moments before answering. Perhaps he considered an open admission, but rejected the idea as presaging certain defeat for the nomination and for the President who had offered it. He would make no statement on the Klan question, he replied, except to say that he was not now a Klansman. But, he added slowly and deliberately, if any man were concerned lest he might have been a Klansman, he would ask that man to vote against his confirmation. [47]

Anticipating a floor fight, spectators packed Senate galleries the next day. It was Democratic Senator Royal S. Copeland who

[46] George L. Norris to Henry F. Ashurst, August 17, 1937, in Papers of George L. Norris.

[47] New York *Times*, August 18, 1937; "Klan Member on Supreme Court," *Newsweek*, X (September 20, 1937), 9–12; Alsop and Catledge, *The 168 Days*, 310–11.

brought the rumors into the open by demanding that Black's nomination be denied because he had been supported by the Klan during his 1926 campaign. Copeland read the Senate an account by the New York *Times* of how Black, to win votes in the closing days of his first Senate race, had attacked Al Smith because Smith, a Catholic, aspired to the presidency. Administration supporters quickly retorted that Copeland was now attacking Black in order to win the votes of New York's Catholics and Negroes for his candidacy for mayor of New York City.[48]

La Follette gave a tribute to the nominee, and Schwellenbach replied to Republican charges that Black had acted illegally in seizing wholesale batches of telegrams. Then Borah, the old Republican "irreconcilable," made the only statement in Black's behalf on the Klan question. "There has never been at any time," Borah said, "one iota of evidence that Senator Black was a member of the Klan. No one has suggested any source from which evidence could be gathered. . . . We know that Senator Black has said in private conversation, not since this matter came up, but at other times, that he was not a member of the Klan, and there is no evidence to the effect that he is. What is there to examine?" Borah added that he would "certainly" vote against a man "known to be a member of a secret organization organized to spread racial antipathies and religious intolerance through this country." These remarks would come back to plague Borah.[49]

Edward Burke offered to subpoena in Washington two witnesses who had been present when Black was initiated into the Klan. But no one moved to take up Burke's offer. After six hours of debate, administration lines held firm and Senate traditions carried the day. A motion to send the nomination back to committee was defeated, and the Senate faced the final roll call on confirmation. Borah startled his colleagues by voting against confirmation. He did so, he explained, because of his belief that the

[48] The debates on confirmation of Black are to be found in *Congressional Record*, 75th Cong., 1st Sess., 9097–9103.
[49] *Ibid.*, 9098.

Court still had nine justices because Van Devanter had retired, not resigned. Southern Democrats filed reluctantly into the administration's column. Ickes noted that even "Cotton Ed" Smith, who " 'God-damned' the nomination all over the place when it was first announced, didn't have the courage to stand up and vote against a fellow senator from the Deep South." Overhearing a bystander say Black's nomination was a great victory for the common people, Carter Glass roared: "They must be goddam common!" When all votes were in, Hugo Black had been confirmed, 63–16, as an associate justice of the Supreme Court.[50]

Administration supporters congratulated Roosevelt for prevailing, at last, over the stubborn Senate. "My cup runneth over," Minton wrote the President. Felix Frankfurter tried to hearten Roosevelt by reminding him of the "sewage" poured on Roger B. Taney when Andrew Jackson nominated him as chief justice. From all the Senate's talk about great legal experience and fine judicial qualities, Frankfurter wrote tartly, "one would suppose McReynolds, Sanford, Sutherland, Butler, Roberts were men of wide culture and juristic detachment when they got on the Court." The *Nation* called it the most courageous executive appointment since Wilson's nomination of Louis D. Brandeis, the first Jewish justice. Even *Business Week* commented: "Black will no longer have to demagogue to keep his head above water. No longer can the 'princes of privilege' down in Alabama threaten his political existence." But the disenchanted Raymond Moley wrote in *Newsweek*: "There have been worse appointments to high judicial offices; but . . . I can't remember where or when"; and Herbert Hoover commented dourly that the Court was "one-ninth packed."[51]

---

[50] *Ibid.*, 9103; Ickes, *The Secret Diary*, II, 196; "Roosevelt Takes Out Judicial Insurance," 7.

[51] Roosevelt Papers; Max Freedman (ed.), *Roosevelt and Frankfurter, Their Correspondence, 1928–1945* (Boston, 1967), 408; "Salute to Justice Black," *Nation*, CXLV (August 21, 1937), 183; "Life in Court May Tame Black," *Business Week*, LVI (August 21, 1937), 14–15; Raymond Moley, "An Inquisitor Comes to Glory," *Newsweek*, X (August 21, 1937), 40.

Summing up the long struggle of 1937 between Roosevelt and the Senate, Ickes wrote in his diary: "So Hugo Black becomes a member of the Supreme Court of the United States, while the economic royalists fume and squirm, and the President rolls his tongue around in his cheek." [52]

[52] Ickes, *The Secret Diary*, II, 196.

XIII

∏∏∏∏∏∏∏∏∏∏∏∏∏∏∏∏∏∏∏∏∏∏∏∏

I Did
Join
the Klan

Roosevelt and his nominee lost no time in making the appointment official. Two days after the Senate vote, the President summoned Black to his office and presented him with his commission. Ickes, sole witness to this ceremony, observed: "Black made no attempt to disguise the very genuine pleasure that this appointment gave him. He was delighted." Emerging from the oval office, his commission in a cardboard cylinder under one arm, the appointee told reporters: "I suppose I said 'thank you.'" In answer to a question, he replied that he did not know where or when he would take the oath of office.[1]

That same day he formally tendered his resignation as United States senator to Governor Graves, who responded with appropriate gallantry: "If our Senate is to lose in you its most potent champion of human welfare, it is pleasing to know that our other great forum will gain thereby." The governor promptly appointed his wife, Dixie, to fill out the remainder of Black's Senate term, which would end in January, 1939. Tom Heflin and Lister Hill began to tool up for Alabama's 1938 senatorial primary.[2]

About 6 P.M., with Washington suffused in the final glare of the August sun, Edwin Halsey, Senate secretary, received a telephone

[1] Ickes, *The Secret Diary*, II, 199–200; New York *Times*, August 20, 1937.
[2] A copy of Black's formal statement of resignation and of Graves's reply is in the Hugo L. Black Papers.

call from Black asking that arrangements be made for him to take the oath. Halsey inquired if other witnesses should be present. The appointee said he desired only Halsey and Charles F. Pace, financial clerk of the Senate, to act as notary. When Black arrived, Pace offered a typewritten paper containing the oath to support the Constitution, required of all public servants. Black, however, had brought with him printed forms prepared by the Department of Justice, which included not only the constitutional oath but a second "judicial oath," applying particularly to members of the Supreme Court. He took both oaths. Pace notarized the forms to be sent to the Justice Department and the Court itself. The ceremony was briefly reported in Washington newspapers the following day, but those who noticed it at all assumed that only the constitutional oath had been taken.[3]

Thus, on August 19, seven days after his nomination was sent to the Senate, Hugo Black became a full-fledged member of the Supreme Court, entitled under the Constitution to hold office "during good behavior" for his lifetime. In taking his oaths so promptly, he engaged in no illegal procedure but did depart from custom. By tradition the chief justice administered the constitutional oath in the robing room of the Court on the day a new member appeared to take office. The second oath was customarily administered by the Court clerk in the courtroom before the new justice ascended the bench. With the Court in recess until October, Justice Black evidently decided it was prudent, although unusual, to complete all the legal niceties. He ordered a ninety-dollar ebony silk judicial robe, received the initial installment of his twenty-thousand-dollar annual salary, and left with Mrs. Black for his first trip to Europe.[4]

Strangers, meanwhile, were probing into the new justice's political past. One was Ray Sprigle, a muckraking reporter for the Pittsburgh *Post-Gazette*, conspicuous in a western sombrero and

---

[3] The New York *Times*, September 16, 17, 1937, reported that it had gathered these details from an "authoritative source," probably Halsey or Pace.

[4] New York *Times*, September 16, 17, 1937.

swinging a silver-ringed cane. The other was Frank Prince, operator of a private detective agency in New York City and formerly a reporter for Hearst. Both men had unlimited expense accounts. Their inquiries led them to onetime Grand Dragon James Esdale, estranged from the Klan since 1928 and disbarred by the Alabama State Bar in 1937 on charges of having solicited professional employment and of having violated the rule against an attorney being bail for his client. Sprigle and Prince wangled the evidence they wanted from Esdale. Triumphantly they returned east with a stenographic transcript of Black's "thank you" speech to the Klan klorero after the Democratic primary of 1926 and, as evidence of his actual membership, a copy of his note of resignation from Robert E. Lee Klan No. 1.[5]

In a series of six articles syndicated by the North American Newspaper Alliance beginning September 13, Sprigle dramatically displayed his evidence for the nation to read. Newspapers over the country spread across their front pages Sprigle's sensational accusation that the new justice "is a member of the hooded brotherhood that for ten long, blood-drenched years ruled the Southland with lash and noose and torch." To justify this bold statement, Sprigle contended that the note of resignation was a deliberate ruse, designed to protect the Klan's political candidate from criticism by Catholic and Jewish voters and other anti-Klan forces. Sprigle further claimed that, by accepting the "grand passport," Black had, in effect, accepted life membership in the Klan.[6]

Facing his biggest press conference since announcing the Court plan, Roosevelt told reporters on September 14 to get out their pencils. He said he knew what was on their minds. He read them a brief prepared statement: he only knew what he had seen in the newspapers and he would have no comment until "Mr. Justice Black" returned from Europe. "May we ask, if it turns out that he

[5] "Black Scandal," *Time*, XXX (September 27, 1937), 10–11; Robert S. Allen, "Who Exposed Black?" *Nation*, CXLV (September 25, 1937), 308–12.
[6] The entire Sprigle series was published in the New York *Times*, September 13, 14, 15, 16, 17, 18, 1937.

is a member . . ," a reporter began, but the President cut him off sharply: "That is an 'if' question." Another asked whether Roosevelt, prior to nominating Black, had any information as to his Klan membership. The President's brief "No" was so emphatic that one reporter described it as a categorical denial and another as a "terse negative."[7]

"That the White House was stunned by the exposé," wrote one Washington observer, "is putting it mildly. From the President down, the inner circle was astounded and frightened." In the first panicky moments after the Sprigle series began, a cabinet member was reported to have urged Roosevelt to issue a statement saying that he would not have named Black had he known of his Klan connections. Rejecting this idea, Roosevelt said he would play for time and await public reaction. The New York *Times* revealed to a surprised capital that Black had already taken both oaths. "Regret and chagrin," the *Times* reported, was the mood of official Washington.[8]

Roosevelt confided to Ickes that it had never occurred to him to ask Black about his Klan connection. An embarrassed Attorney General Cummings, queried by the White House if he had investigated Black before placing his name on the Justice Department's list of possible nominees, replied weakly: "[Black's] record of public service and selection on two occasions by the state of Alabama as U. S. Senator made his suitability beyond question." In his diary Ickes recorded that Roosevelt, an open foe of the Klan since the Democratic convention of 1924, was now in the position of having either "deliberately or carelessly" named a Klan member to the Supreme Court. "There is no doubt that this incident is very bad for the President," Ickes wrote. "There has been nothing like it."[9]

With Burton K. Wheeler demanding a presidential investiga-

[7] Text of Roosevelt press conference, September 14, 1937, in Roosevelt Papers.

[8] Allen, "Who Exposed Black?" 312; New York *Times*, September 16, 1937.

[9] Ickes, *The Secret Diary*, II, 215; Memorandum from Attorney General Homer Cummings to Franklin D. Roosevelt, September 13, 1937, in Roosevelt Papers.

tion, Roosevelt reviewed his plight with Ickes and Borah. They agreed that onetime Klan membership was not grounds for impeachment and that the President had no more right to investigate a member of the Supreme Court than to investigate a member of the Senate. Roosevelt suggested that Black should make a statement when he returned from Europe; if he cleared himself in the minds of the public, he should remain on the Court.[10]

Belatedly reporters discovered that the two witnesses whom Senator Burke had offered to produce were both special assistants to Attorney General Cummings, probably at Black's recommendation. William E. Fort, once Black's law partner and the judge in the Stephenson case, refused to comment. Walter S. Brower, Black's assistant as Jefferson County solicitor, would only claim that he himself was not a Klansman.[11]

Bibb Graves admitted to a New York *Times* reporter that he had once been a Klan member but said he "could not recall" ever seeing Black at Klan meetings. He remembered receiving "some kind of badge" at the 1926 klorero but said it was "nonsense" to claim that this was a life membership. "I belonged to the Klan just as I belonged to every other Protestant organization," the governor said. "I was what was called 'a jiner' in those days." Many other Alabamians took the news with equanimity. Louis Pizitz, Jewish owner of a large Birmingham department store, commented that the dispute was "dirty politics." "Mr. Black is as much of a friend to Jews and Catholics as anybody," Pizitz said. Erskine Ramsay, the city's most prominent business leader and philanthropist, said he congratulated Black and hoped to congratulate him again when he became chief justice. A Birmingham barber, who said he had always been for Black, jibed: "A little political blast from New York won't convince me he isn't a mighty fine man." A locomotive engineer said, "I'm still for Black, Klan or no

[10] Ickes, *The Secret Diary*, II, 215.
[11] New York *Times*, September 22, 23, October 1, 2, 1937. Grand Dragon Esdale, in an interview with the author, said that Brower was one of the Klan's most active members.

Klan," and the operator of a fishing camp predicted: "Don't worry. Mr. Black will sit on the Supreme Court regardless of the political tricks of his enemies." Hiram Evans, interviewed in Atlanta, called those who criticized Black's Klan membership "un-American." [12]

Vacationing senators were tracked down and asked whether they would have voted for Black if they had known of his former membership. Some said they had been "misled;" others passed it off as a "tempest in a teapot." Hundreds of other Americans joined the furor. William Allen White now said Roosevelt had "dishonored" the High Court, but George Norris continued to insist that it was a "wonderfully good appointment." Ickes, confronted by the press, produced an embarrassed administration's most adroit counterthrust: "I really think the greatest expert on the Ku Klux Klan is [President] Hoover. I refer you to him. He accepted their support. Nobody criticized him." [13]

Administration supporters tried to hearten the President. "Well, what of it?" was the attitude of spokesmen for organized labor. The Order of Railway Conductors commented: "[Black's] being or not being a member of the Klan makes no difference to us." From Cleveland a man wrote Roosevelt: "Keep your usual calmness and jovial spirit . . . for the Tories are moving heaven and earth to try to get your goat." A Jew in Baltimore wrote: "I prayed to God that you would appoint more Klansmen of the type of Hugo Black." From St. Louis a former Klansman wrote: "Some say 'yes.' Some say 'no.' What the hell, you can't satisfy them all." Columnist Heywood Broun reminded his readers that "few justices of the Supreme Court swim up to the high bench as immaculate as Little Eva on the way to Heaven." Felix Frankfurter defended Black to his friend Franklin Roosevelt and helped prepare a draft of the President's radio speech for Constitution Day, September 17. "When people and lawyers have clashed," Frank-

[12] New York *Times*, September 14, 23, 1937; Birmingham *Post*. September 16, 1937.
[13] New York *Times*, September 23, October 1, 1937.

furter wrote, "ultimately people have had their way. When Congress and the Supreme Court have clashed . . . Congress has ultimately triumphed." After the speech, a pleased Frankfurter wired Roosevelt: "Grand and Grandly Delivered. As Holmes would say, there was the right poison in it." [14]

But critics of Roosevelt and the New Deal—cartoonists in particular—had a field day. The President was criticized for not having sought advice before the nomination, and Black was castigated for not revealing his Klan connection to Roosevelt or the Senate. *Newsweek* said the new justice must accept responsibility for his silence during the Senate debate "and for the private advice confidentially but freely passed around Senate cloakrooms that he had no actual Klan ties, however much he owed the Klan for his first nomination and election to the Senate." But the friendly *Nation*, admitting that Black had been a political opportunist when he joined the Klan, drew a distinction between opportunism and bigotry. Black, it said, had had to fight his way up from the "ignorance and bigotry of the Southern masses" to national prominence with only rudimentary schooling and without benefit of the Harvard education which produced New England Brahmins and Louis D. Brandeis. The exposé, the *Nation* concluded, was an effort by "powerful oligarchical minorities," led by William Randolph Hearst and Paul Block, publisher of the Pittsburgh *Post-Gazette*, to destroy Black's usefulness on the bench and force Roosevelt to abandon his fight to liberalize the judiciary. The *Christian Century* said those who raised the furor "do not fear Black the Klansman as much as they hate Black the Inquisitor." [15]

"Isn't it terrible about Black?" the President's secretary, Marguerite LeHand, remarked to Treasury Secretary Morgenthau. "What can the President do about it?" Morgenthau asked. "That's

[14] Excerpts from letters to the White House, Roosevelt Papers; Freedman (ed.), *Roosevelt and Frankfurter*, 409–17.

[15] "Senate is Sorry, President is Angry, and the Justice is Silent," *Newsweek*, X (September 27, 1937), 10–11; "The Education of Hugo Black," *Nation*, CXLV (October 2, 1937), 337–38; "Klansman Black Became Black the Inquisitor," *Christian Century*, LIV (September 29, 1937), 1189–90.

just the trouble," Miss LeHand replied. "He doesn't know what to do." At his Hyde Park press conference on September 21, Roosevelt was asked again if he had questioned Black before nominating him. This time the President made reporters laugh by replying that he wouldn't ask Ernest Lindley, a member of the press corps, how many illegitimate children he had before appointing him to a government post. "That is something you do not ask," Roosevelt said. He told reporters he had nothing to add to his statement of the previous week, leaving the New York *Times* to assume that he had had no word from Justice Black. Roosevelt was reported to have told friends that he felt Black owed it to him to make a public statement.[16]

Knowing Justice Black was en route home by ship, Roosevelt decided September 22 to begin a long-discussed tour of the West. Hamilton Fish claimed that the trip was a "studied attempt" to avoid meeting the justice before he took his seat on the court. Scolding the President for failing to defend his appointee, the liberal *New Republic* commented that there was a "generally recognized moral statute of limitations that runs against the errors of a man's early career." [17]

While his countrymen gossiped, speculated, and pointed the accusing finger, the central figure of the *cause célèbre* tried in vain to escape pursuing reporters. A representative of the New York *Times* telephoned his Paris hotel on September 10 to tell the justice that the newspaper planned to publish the Sprigle series. Mrs. Black answered that her husband was asleep, but she would give him the message. The following day the *Times* sent Black an outline of the main points of the articles. There was no reply. On September 12 the Blacks left Paris, reportedly for Italy, but reporters located them the next day in London. The justice told a New York *Times* representative that he did not intend to make

[16] Morgenthau *Diary*, September 20, 1937, Book 89, 52; Memorandum on presidential press conference of September 21, 1937, Roosevelt Papers; New York *Times*, September 22, 1937.
[17] "FDR Takes a Run-Out Powder on the Black Sheep," *New Republic*, XCII (September 29, 1937), 213; New York *Times*, September 22, 1937.

any statement. But London newspapers were filled with the Sprigle series, giving average Britishers their first knowledge of the Ku Klux Klan. There were many notable visitors in London that season after the coronation of King George VI, but most attention centered upon the Blacks. Reporters pursued them constantly. Toughened by years of experience in courtrooms, political campaigns, and Senate debates, Black was accustomed to the glare of the limelight—to pressure, harsh criticism, and a constant entourage of reporters. But his sensitive wife Josephine found it a searing experience. When the Blacks were unexpectedly accosted by a newspaperman in a dim hotel corridor, she was badly frightened. Trying to cheer her, her husband told her that, once they returned home, he would have the motto, "This, too, will pass," framed and hung over her bed.[18]

Sightseeing under these conditions was almost out of the question. The Blacks managed to escape their pursuers one day for a ride into the English countryside, but the justice reluctantly cancelled a trip to Ireland, homeland of his ancestors. In a London bookstore, Black searched for some volumes of Grote's *Aristotle* to complete his collection. Only a handful of Londoners glimpsed their embattled visitor. Even Sherman Minton, in the city at the same time, did not see his old Senate friend.[19]

The strain on Black was evident in his dealings with the press, whose good will and cooperation he had always cultivated. It was reported that he had snapped at a Hearst representative: "I don't see you. I don't know you. I don't answer you." According to the New York *Times*, when a reporter knocked on the Blacks' hotel door, the justice opened it a crack to tell him: "I've come here for a vacation and I don't wish to be bothered." In exasperation he complained to the hotel management about his lack of privacy and gave instructions that all visitors be told that he was "permanently out." Cornered by reporters, he snapped: "I've been

[18] New York *Times*, Sept. 14, 15, 16, 1937; interview with Justice Black, September, 1967.
[19] *Ibid.*; "The Education of Hugo Black," 338.

hounded by you fellows ever since I left home. I won't even listen to what you have to say because I know what you want. You simply want to ask me questions so you can write, 'Black refused to answer.' " [20]

On September 20 the justice and Mrs. Black eluded reporters long enough to board the mail steamer *City of Norfolk*, bound for that out-of-the-way Virginia port. Their names were not on the passenger list for they had originally planned to return to New York aboard the S. S. *Manhattan*, on which Minton, two other senators, and Justice James G. McReynolds would have been fellow passengers.[21]

The *City of Norfolk* made its way slowly through stormy seas, allowing Justice Black an eight-day respite to collect his thoughts and plan his next move. The Blacks sat at the captain's table, sometimes played shuffleboard, and made no reference to their troubles. There was no mention of the Sprigle stories in the ship's newspaper. Their eighty-three fellow passengers agreed that everyone liked Mrs. Black, but their opinions about the justice were divided. Sometime during the voyage, Hugo Black decided to plead his case directly to the jury of American public opinion. The National Broadcasting Company offered him its facilities for a nationwide radio address. Approaching Norfolk, Black cabled the network: "Thanks for offer. Will inform you if I desire to avail myself of it." His mind made up, some of the burden began to lift. The confident, fighting spirit, fused in the crucibles of Alabama courtrooms and Senate committee rooms, rose to this new challenge. As the *City of Norfolk* plowed westward, the Gallup Poll reported that 59 percent of the Americans whom it interviewed thought the Justice should resign if it were proved that he had been a Klan member.[22]

Ten years earlier another spectacular public figure, Charles A.

---

[20] New York *Times*, September 14, 15, 16, 1937; "Black Back," *Time*, XXX (October 11, 1937), 50.

[21] New York *Times*, September 22, 1937; "Black Back," 50.

[22] New York *Times*, September 30, 1937; *Christian Science Monitor*, September 29, 1937; Birmingham *News*, October 3, 1937.

Lindbergh, had come back from Europe to remote Chesapeake Bay in hope of a quiet homecoming. His attempt had been no more successful than Black's. At dawn on September 28, seventy-five newspapermen and photographers waited at Old Point Comfort. In case their quarry tried to elude them, a boatload of reporters had patrolled the docks all night. Among them was Ray Sprigle, cocky in his sombrero.[23]

During the ocean voyage, Justice Black had regained his public poise. He made no effort to evade waiting reporters but refused to speak until newsreel cameramen had disconnected their sound tracks. In contrast to his manner overseas, he was smiling and affable. Only occasionally did a question bring a cold, hard glint to his eyes. When a representative of the Pittsburgh *Post-Gazette* offered him copies of the Sprigle stories, he snapped: "You take that back to Mr. Block." He appreciated "this great reception," he told the press. "When I have any statement to make that's definite and final on any subject, I will make it in such a way that I cannot be misquoted and that the nation can hear me." Asked if he would get in touch with Roosevelt before making his statement, the justice evaded a direct reply, saying he had no plans to go out west to see the President. A guileful woman reporter wanted to know where the press could find him in Washington. "I'll probably go to my office in the Supreme Court," he replied firmly. Reporters inferred from this that he had no intention of resigning. Max Lerner, editor of the *Nation*, who was invited to breakfast in the Blacks' stateroom, was impressed that the justice made reporters feel that his quarrel was not with them but with their bosses.[24]

A small knot of friends and relatives stood by, including Mrs. Black's sister, Mrs. Clifford Durr, and her husband; her brother, Sterling Foster; Thomas Woodward, a member of the Maritime Commission who had aided Black in the shipping investigation;

---

[23] *Ibid.*
[24] Max Lerner, "Hugo Black—a Personal History," *Nation*, CLXV (October 9, 1937), 367–69; "Black Back," 50; New York *Times*, September 30, 1937; Diary of Henry Morgenthau, Jr., Diary, September 30, 1937, in Roosevelt Papers; *Christian Science Monitor*, September 29, 1937.

and Mrs. Woodward. They accompanied him on the drive back to Washington, stopping for two hours in Richmond for lunch and, so the New York *Times* speculated, in order that Justice Black could telephone the President.[25]

Black, Clifford Durr, and Claude E. Hamilton, Jr., a friend from Birmingham who owed his job as a Reconstruction Finance Corporation attorney to Black, worked all day September 30 preparing and revising the speech. Thomas Corcoran, the President's congressional liaison, saw the first draft in which Black admitted joining the Klan for political purposes. Corcoran protested that Black failed to denounce the Klan. To do so, the justice told Corcoran, would be "throwing down" friends in Alabama who had helped him over the years.[26]

Three nationwide networks, delighted to be chosen over the hostile newspapers to break this momentous news, cleared thirty minutes of time on the evening of Friday, October 1, for an unprecedented address by a Supreme Court justice on a controversial topic. The audience was estimated at thirty million, second only to that which had heard Edward VIII renounce the throne of Great Britain a year earlier. "Black radio parties" were held in many homes, and a spate of fiery crosses burned on northern hillsides, one briefly lighting the woods around Hyde Park. People in Birmingham wondered, "Will Hugo admit being a Klan member?"[27]

The justice spoke from Claude Hamilton's modest home in a neighborhood of Chevy Chase, Maryland, preferred by government employes of the five-thousand- to ten-thousand-dollar-income class. A cluster of neighbors and newsreel cameramen waited on the lawn, but the speaker, who had arrived by taxi and entered through a cellar door, was already inside. A thirteen-year-old boy picked up used flashbulbs, and told reporters it was the

[25] New York *Times*, September 30, 1937.

[26] Farley, *Jim Farley's Story*, 98–99.

[27] "Living Room Chat," *Time*, XXX (October 11, 1937), 16–17; Rice, *The Ku Klux Klan in American Politics*, 93; interview with George Bentley, October 1, 1969.

biggest event ever to occur in his neighborhood except for a brush fire and a suicide.[28]

Justice Black, in gray suit, maroon tie, and a yellow pencil stuck in his coat pocket, sat in an antique chair before a battery of microphones. He showed no trace of nervousness, although Jim Farley thought he was on "as tough a spot as any man in public life has ever faced." A handful of guests, the women in evening gowns, sat in the adjoining dining room. Two Negro maids and a chauffeur listened from a doorway. Josephine, outwardly calm, wore black velvet.[29]

The speech lasted only eleven minutes. In contrast to his vigorous Senate style, Justice Black spoke deliberately, as though measuring each word, strengthening a phrase here, a sentence there, soothing millions of curious listeners with his soft, Alabama drawl. All his practice at persuasive speaking, to Alabama juries and voters, to Senate colleagues, and by radio to the American people, culminated in this brief talk. Like Franklin Roosevelt, he could make an audience feel that he spoke directly to each person. It was a masterful summation of a difficult case, addressed to the only jurors who mattered.

Justice Black said he was breaking Supreme Court precedent because this was an "extraordinary occasion." He condemned what he called a "concerted campaign" to revive prejudice and religious bigotry by trying to convince Americans that he was intolerant of minority groups. He affirmed his belief in the religious guarantees of the Bill of Rights and insisted that his Senate record refuted every implication of intolerance.

Then came the admission his audience awaited. "I did join the Klan," said Justice Black. "I never rejoined. What appeared then, or what appears now on the records of that organization, I do not know." He said he had never considered the "unsolicited card" as a "membership of any kind" in the Klan. "I never used it. I did not even keep it." Black said he had dropped the Klan before be-

[28] "Living Room Chat," *Time*, 16.
[29] Farley, *Jim Farley's Story*, 98; New York *Times*, October 2, 1937.

coming a senator and had had nothing to do with it since. He told his audience he had many friends among Catholics, Jews, and Negroes. Concluding, he declared firmly: "my discussion of this question is closed."[30]

An NBC announcer thanked True Story's Court of Human Relations for relinquishing its time so the nation could hear Justice Black. In the Hamilton dining room, one of the guests applauded. The justice lighted a cigarette. Someone asked if he were glad to get it off his chest, and he replied that he was but that he was not worried and never had been. He was prepared to work hard on the Court and he didn't think the other justices would "haze" him.[31]

Almost universally the press denounced the speech. "The work of a brilliant prosecutor suddenly turned to the defense," commented Scripps-Howard's New York *World-Telegram*. "Too damned clever." Even the proadministration New York *Post*, commenting on Justice Black's claim to Catholic, Jewish, and Negro friends, remarked acidly: "We might reply in kind that one of our best liberal friends was a Klansman but we still don't think he ought to be on the Supreme Court." Analyzing the speech, *Newsweek* decided that it was "defensive offense," a tactic practiced by lawyers, politicians, and generals. Much adverse reaction centered upon the justice's failure to denounce the Klan, to explain his silence during Senate debates on his nomination, and to inform the President beforehand. The *Christian Century* called it "a poor defense against a serious charge." *Commonweal* remarked: "Mr. Black's long experience in trimming his political sails to fit the prevailing wind stood him in good stead."[32]

In Montgomery, Grover C. Hall, editor of the *Advertiser*, came to the defense of the man he had so often opposed. "Most of the

[30] The complete text of Black's radio address was published in the New York *Times*, October 2, 1937.

[31] New York *Times*, October 2, 1937.

[32] "I Did Join . . . Resigned . . . The Case is Closed," *Newsweek*, X (October 11, 1937), 12–13; "Mr. Black Comes First," *Christian Century*, XXVI (October 15, 1937), 559–60; "A Study in Black and White," *Christian Century*, LIV (October 13, 1937), 255–57. A sampling of press comments from around the nation appeared in the New York *Times*, October 2, 1937.

people who hate Black today," Hall wrote, "do not give a hoot whether he was a Klansman or a Hottentot in 1925. They hate him because of what he said as a Senator, when no longer a Klansman, about social and economic conditions. They hate him because he was a Rooseveltian. . . . William Randolph Hearst, the fascist, hates Hugo Black as he hates no other recent senator—but not because Hugo as a cub politician in a wayward state once put on a hood." Hall, who won a Pulitzer Prize for his editorial opposition to the Klan, said he was sorry that Black was once a Klansman but delighted that "he can now disavow every evil thought that the Klan ever entertained." In the justice's home city, the Birmingham *Age-Herald* remarked moderately that expediency, while never commendable, was not an unforgivable sin, forever barring one from qualification for high trust.[33]

John L. Lewis thought the speech was "powerful and straightforward," but Norman Thomas regretted that Justice Black had failed "openly and manfully" to repudiate the Klan, and that "we haven't heard a word from him on the Scottsboro case." Senator Borah struggled to reconcile Black's admission with his assurance to the Senate that the nominee was not a Klan member. "Justice Black," Borah said, "stated the matter of his relationship with the Klan as I understood it to be when I spoke on the subject to the Senate. I understood he had been a member of the Klan but had not been a member since about eleven years." But the New York *Herald-Tribune* thought Black had deliberately allowed Borah to place himself in a "painfully false position . . . because he was afraid to jeopardize his ambition by a simple act of common honesty."[34]

Typical Americans also had their say, pouring hundreds of letters into the White House. An Oklahoma City lawyer wrote: "The trouble with the Supreme Court is they have been wearing the

[33] Montgomery *Advertiser*, October 3, 1937; Birmingham *Age-Herald*, October 3, 1937.
[34] "Pro-Black, Anti-Black," *Literary Digest*, CXXIV (August 28, 1937), 7; New York *Times*, October 2, 1937; "Klansman Black," *Commonweal*, XXVI (September 24, 1937), 483–84.

hood since Abe Lincoln's day, especially when they were construing the Constitution." A South Carolinian consoled the President: "Let the heathen rage for . . . they are the same heathen who opposed you ever since you took the side of the people against greed and special privilege." A farmers' cooperative assured Roosevelt: "The American people are not deceived. They know that the charges against Justice Black are camouflage. He is being opposed because he is a progressive. The people understand this." [35]

Opponents spoke more virulently. A Jewish doctor in Denver thought the speech marked "an all-time low in the morals of American public life." A Brooklyn Catholic told the President "your Ku Klux Klan Black appointment stinks worse than a dozen Teapot Dome scandals." The Union League of Chicago resolved that "decency and political expediency dictate [Black's] removal." A Negro wired that members of his race had broken political ties of many generations to support Roosevelt. "Negroes will be satisfied," he said, "with nothing less than prompt and effective action designed to remove this blot from the escutcheon of the judiciary." A man in Port Huron, Michigan, informed the President that a motion picture audience there had hissed when his photograph appeared on the screen. After the mail was sorted, it appeared to be divided almost evenly.[36]

Justice Black's niece Hazel wrote worriedly from Chicago to assure her uncle that his speech was "perfect." The justice replied that it was a "plain political fight" being waged by those who hated him and Roosevelt. "There was nothing new in the articles . . ," he wrote Hazel.

Governor Kilby supplied the "gold card" memorandum from his campaign files. It was widely published in Alabama in 1932 and all the leading papers throughout the nation as well as the magazines have repeatedly published the fact that I was formerly a member of the Klan. Of course, these papers knew it and were aware that everybody

[35] Letters regarding the Black speech, Roosevelt Papers.
[36] Ibid.

else knew it who had kept up with politics in the country. [Black did not mention President Roosevelt.] Just do not let all this stuff worry you. I have never missed one single minute's sleep . . . I have followed my course, and my conscience approved it. This armor has protected me and will continue to guard me from their poison shafts.[37]

But there was no public comment from the man responsible for all the commotion. Franklin Roosevelt, in Fort Lewis, Washington, 2,440 miles away from the White House, told reporters he did not hear the speech because he was riding in an open car with no radio. Back at Hyde Park on October 6, the President told the press: "Well, there isn't any comment." Two days later Roosevelt asked Farley what he had thought of the speech. The Democratic chairman said the justice had done the best he could under the circumstance but Farley still thought he should have "hit" the Klan. "It was a grand job," Roosevelt declared enthusiastically. "It did the trick. You just wait and see." Late in October, a national poll reported that only 44 percent of Americans still thought Justice Black should resign.[38]

Three days after the radio talk, Justice Black made his first appearance on the Supreme Court. Chief Justice Charles Evans Hughes, whose own nomination this new member had once opposed, greeted Black cordially in the robing room. With Hughes sat other justices whose philosophies and decisions had been scathingly criticized by Senator Black. Before the Court were two petitions that Justice Black be barred on the constitutional grounds which had been raised in the Senate. Meanwhile the President was on his way to Chicago where he was to deliver that night his famous speech proposing that democratic nations "quarantine" dictatorial states which threatened the peace of mankind. By chance or design, the quarantine speech would provoke another furor, crowding Justice Black's debut off the front pages.[39]

---

[37] Davis, *Uncle Hugo*, 30–32.
[38] Text of Roosevelt press conference, October 6, 1937, in Roosevelt Papers; Farley, *Jim Farley's Story*, 100.
[39] Merlo Pusey, *Charles Evans Hughes* (New York, 1951), 773–74.

Perhaps to avoid the possibility of a sensational challenge in the open courtroom, Justice Black did not repeat the judicial oath publicly. Since the new member had been confirmed and had already taken both his oaths, Chief Justice Hughes considered the matter closed. He planned, tactfully but firmly, to cut off the protestors by taking their petitions under advisement.

In the view of some three hundred spectators who packed the chamber, Associate Justice Hugo La Fayette Black, his face inscrutable, ascended the steps and took his place on the high bench.[40]

[40] New York *Times*, October 5, 1937.

Epilogue

"Show me the kind of steps a man made in the sand
five years ago, and I will show you the kind of steps
he is likely to make in the same sand five years hence."

Hugo L. Black

Time probably softened Justice Black's recollection of his apprenticeship on the Court, but Felix Frankfurter recorded in May, 1938, that there was a period of awkward adjustment for Roosevelt's first appointee. In one of his "Dear Frank" letters to the President, Frankfurter described Black's touchiness: "Various experiences of his life have been calculated to make him a bit of an Ishmaelite—to expect every hand to be raised against him, and therefore at times to be unwarrantedly suspicious when nothing but friendliness is intended."

Justices Harlan F. Stone, Stanley Reed, and Louis D. Brandeis had "the friendliest disposition" toward Justice Black, Frankfurter wrote Roosevelt. But Max Freedman, annotating the Roosevelt-Frankfurter letters, commented that Frankfurter was not being wholly straightforward in reporting the initial reaction of "Isaiah" (Brandeis). An object of shrill controversy at the time of his own nomination, Brandeis had doubts as to Black's suitability and "chafed" at the appointment. Frankfurter pleaded with both Brandeis and Reed to put aside their misgivings and give the new justice a chance to show his mettle.[1]

That opportunity came in 1940 when the Court handed down, on the birthday of Abraham Lincoln, its opinion in the case of *Chambers* v. *Florida*. Four blacks, convicted of the robbery and

[1] Freedman (ed.), *Roosevelt and Frankfurter*, 457–59.

murder of a white man, had appealed on the ground that their
"confessions" had been extorted after six days of constant and
gruelling cross-examination by police. Speaking for a unanimous
Court, Justice Black eloquently asserted the right of the defendants to due process of law, as guaranteed by the Fourteenth
Amendment:

> Due process of law, preserved for all by our Constitution, com-
> mands that no such practice as that disclosed by this record shall send
> any accused to his death. No higher duty, no more solemn responsi-
> bility, rests upon this Court than that of translating into living law and
> maintaining this constitutional shield deliberately planned and inscribed
> for the benefit of every human being subject to our Constitution—of
> whatever race, creed, or persuasion.
>
> *Chambers* v. *Florida 309 U.S. 227 (1940)*

When he was solicitor of Jefferson County, Hugo Black led the
fight against brutal interrogation of blacks by Bessemer police.
When he expressed these same views in 1940 as a controversial
Supreme Court justice who had once joined the Ku Klux Klan, he
caused a stir. No one was more delighted than Roosevelt. At his
press conference the next day, the President was asked if he would
care to supplement the praise being heaped upon Justice Black by
newspapers, many of which had inveighed against his appointment. Roosevelt replied with a twinkle: "I would put in a general
dig that some of the Press should not only give a little praise but
also a modicum of apology for things they have said in the last
two years. Is that fair?"[2]

From his seat on the Court, Justice Black witnessed the waning
of the New Deal, the determined mobilization of Americans for a
second World War, the neurosis of McCarthyism, and the revolution of American blacks, demanding with fervor and tumult
their long-denied civil rights. Inevitably these sea changes of
mid-century pounded at the steps of the Court. In decisions and
dissents, Justice Black fashioned the core of his constitutional

[2] Text of Roosevelt press conference, February 13, 1940, in Roosevelt Papers.

philosophy: the guarantees of the First Amendment and of the following nine are *absolute*; the due process clause of the Fourteenth Amendment binds the states to guarantee to their citizens *all* provisions of the Bill of Rights. In clear, cogent phrases, he affirmed his convictions:

I fear to see the consequences of the Court's practice of substituting its own concepts of decency and fundamental justice for the language of the Bill of Rights as its point of departure in interpreting and enforcing that Bill of Rights.
> *Justice Black dissenting in*
> *Adamson v. California 332 U.S. 46 (1947)*

Answers to the questions asked by the grand jury would have furnished a link in the chain of evidence needed in a prosecution of petitioner for violation of . . . the Smith Act. Prior decisions of this Court have clearly established that under such circumstances, the Constitution gives a witness the privilege of remaining silent. The attempt by the courts below to compel prisoners to testify runs counter to the Fifth Amendment as it has been interpreted from the beginning.
> *Blau v. U.S., 340 U.S. 159 (1950)*

It is apparent that Jaybird activities follow a plan purposefully designed to exclude Negroes from voting and at the same time to escape the Fifteenth Amendment's command that the right of citizens to vote shall not be denied nor abridged on account of race . . . . We affirm the District Court's holding that the combined Jaybird-Democratic-general election machinery has deprived these petitioners of their right to vote on account of their race and color.
> *Terry v. Adams 345 U.S. 461 (1953)*

It is neither sacrilegious nor antireligious to say that each separate government in this country should stay out of the business of writing or sanctioning official prayers and leave that purely religious function to the people themselves and to those the people choose to look to for religious guidance.
> *Engel v. Vitale 370 U.S. 421 (1962)*

From the very beginning, our state and national constitutions and laws have laid great emphasis on procedural and substantive safeguards designed to assure fair trials before impartial tribunals in which every defendant stands equal before the law. This noble ideal cannot be realized if the poor man charged with the crime has to face his accusers without a lawyer to assist him.

> *Gideon* v. *Wainwright 372 U.S. 335 (1963)*

As nearly as practicable, one man's vote in a congressional election is to be worth as much as another's.

> *Wesberry* v. *Sanders 376 U.S. 1 (1964)*

The time for mere "deliberate speed" has run out, and that phrase can no longer justify denying these Prince Edward school children their constitutional rights to an education equal to that afforded by the public schools in the other parts of Virginia.

> *Griffin* v. *School Board of Prince Edward*
> *County, 377 U.S. 218 (1964)*

As the years piled up, Justice Black moved to the seat of senior associate justice. Legend began to attach to him. He was labelled absolutist, libertarian, judicial activist, and, in economic matters, states' righter. Many fellow Alabamians, observing how *Brown* v. *Board of Education of Topeka* toppled their segregated structure of public education, and *Engel* v. *Vitale* cast its shadow upon official prayer in public schools, angrily called him Judas.

Thirty-five years have passed since Justice Black joined the Court. During that time, five Presidents and four Chief Justices ended their tenures, but Hugo Black continued to be a force in the ceaseless process of shaping American law and society, often amid the maelstrom of controversy. In September, 1971, when he resigned because of ill health, he was within a few months of setting a new record for longevity of service on the High Court. His working years ended, Hugo Black died a few days after his resignation from the Court.

An evaluation of Justice Black's Court career is beyond the

purview of this study. But perhaps it is incumbent upon a longtime student of his early career to venture some interpretation of Hugo Black, the politician.

The paradox between Black, the Klansman, and Black, the humanitarian, on the surface a striking contradiction, is readily explainable. There is no evidence in Black's philosophy or actions to suggest that his affiliation with the Klan was other than an act of purest expediency. Unacceptable to Alabama's traditional political leaders because of his views and his association with the laboring class, Black's only hope of election to high office lay in his appeal to the aspirations and prejudices of those plain people from whom he had sprung. He caught the Klan at the crest of its postwar revival and rode its tide to the Senate. Certainly he was not the first nor last figure in American politics to make use of demagoguery for success and survival. In this regard many other names come rushing to mind. When fanaticism ebbed Black was gradually released from this political debt, but his initial compromise led inevitably to others. From 1928 to 1932, he was forced to walk a political tightrope. Maneuvering delicately to seek support for reelection, he made common cause, for a time, with the Alabama establishment when he argued the case for William B. Bankhead against the cries of electoral fraud raised by J. Thomas Heflin.

During the Hoover years, while bewildered Americans sought to identify the causes of their great depression, Hugo Black had insisted that the nation's economic catastrophe was due in large measure to a concentration of wealth in the hands of a few, while the majority lacked purchasing power. Without prosperous customers, he argued, the American economic machine was doomed. Like Herbert Hoover, who had also risen from humble origins by his own efforts, Black scorned the palliative of a dole. But whereas Hoover, through his Reconstruction Finance Corporation, supported the concept that prosperity would trickle down from ownership to workers, Black advocated the antithetical theory that prosperity would rise upward from a well-paid, regularly employed labor force.

When he entered upon his second term amid the innovative atmosphere of the Hundred Days, Black hoped that Franklin Roosevelt would be as hospitable to his theories as Hoover had been inhospitable. But when the senator insistently put forth his proposal for a thirty-hour work week, the new administration countered with the National Industrial Recovery Act. After NRA was declared unconstitutional, Black again proferred his thirty-hour proposal, only to be persuaded by Roosevelt to sponsor instead another plan which would finally emerge as the Fair Labor Standards Act of 1938. As one of those who instigated and insisted upon nationwide standards of minimum wages and maximum work hours, Black made his most substantive contribution to the legislative program of the Roosevelt administration. As a Senate investigator, he produced revelations which focused national attention upon the flaws of subsidy programs for airlines and merchant shippers and upon the behind-the-scenes maneuvering of utility lobbyists. Although representing a state still predominantly rural, he became absorbed with problems of urban workingmen and advocated not only shorter hours and minimum wages, but also social security, abolition of child labor, government health insurance, subsidized housing, and a permanent program, patterned after the Civilian Conservation Corps, to engage the energies of unemployed youth.

Such activities, capped by his espousal of the Roosevelt Court plan, were scarcely calculated to please Black's newly won allies back home. Rumors that he was in political disfavor with his constituency reached even the White House. As a fledgling senator, indebted to certain political forces, Black had been cautious and expedient. As his state's senior senator during the burgeoning New Deal, he appeared willing to risk his political career almost recklessly. What might account for this contrast? The Birmingham *News* speculated in 1937 that the senator was losing his political sagacity, an unlikely explanation. Could Black have deliberately jeopardized his political home base on the chance that he might move to higher political office? His alliance with organized labor, begun as a youthful lawyer and forged in the bitter fight for a shorter work week, was strong. A relentless scourge of misbehavior by business interests, Black had opposed RFC on the ground that it gave special favors to big business, and NRA because he believed that it violated the antitrust laws.

Was it conceivable in the 1930s that a senator from the Deep South might envision himself some day in the vice-presidency or the presidency? Oscar Underwood of Alabama and William Gibbs McAdoo, a native of Georgia, had put forth strong bids for the Democratic nomination, and Woodrow Wilson, born in Virginia, had occupied the White House for eight years. Problems of the depression decade, in many ways, overshadowed the old animosity between North and South. Also, as the Montgomery *Advertiser* once commented, Hugo Black "always seemed to arrive ahead of schedule." It is not beyond the realm of possibility (although Justice Black later denied having had any such aspirations) that the dark horse of the county solicitor's race and the 1926 Senate campaign might have entertained this lofty vision and begun to lay the groundwork of national appeal. It need not follow that Black was motivated solely by ambition. Even after the passage of more than forty years, his Senate speeches in the *Congressional Record* ring with a sense of sincere and passionate advocacy. Personal ambition and a genuine desire to advance the progress of humanity are oftentimes interwoven.

The Klan haunted Black's career to the very threshhold of the Court. When the Senate debated his suitability to become a justice, Black equivocated as to the nature of his original Klan relationship. When he admitted his membership to millions of enthralled Americans, he glossed over its implications.

If Hugo Black ever dreamed of the presidency, the revelations of Raymond Sprigle quenched that dream forever. Paradoxically the compromise that set Black upon the road which led to the Court also rendered him unacceptable for the nation's highest office. But on the bench, remote from the vagaries of politics, he served almost as long as nine presidential terms.

Many years ago, when Justice Black was beginning his tenure on the Court, a fellow Alabamian, with shrewd insight into the new justice and the political soil from which he had sprung, explained that Black was only one of thousands of the "ablest and best men in the South" who joined the Klan for political reasons. In 1938 Judge E. E. Callaway wrote prophetically:

I know Justice Black and I know he is neither a Klansman, Communist, or Radical at heart, and, if he lives, he will prove to be a rational, progressive, Constitutional American. . . . No Catholic, Negro, Jew or individualist . . . need have any fear of Justice Black. The American people have no conception of the vicissitudes of adversity Justice Black had to overcome in his early life. . . . He had to be a political genius to survive. This is what enabled him to navigate the destructive rapids of the political philosophy that has disgraced Alabama and the South since the Civil War, and to prove himself a great American.[3]

[3] E. E. Callaway, "Notes on a Kleagle," *American Mercury* (February, 1938), XLIII, 248–49.

Bibliographical Essay

ORAL HISTORY

Recollections of young Hugo Black are still vivid in the memories of many Alabamians. With one whom they know and who speaks in their accents, they are cooperative and communicative. When it became known that I was working on a study of Black, I was frequently offered bits of personal data about my subject, amid the hubbub of a cocktail party, as I shopped at the neighborhood grocery, or even by anonymous letter, an exceedingly questionable source. As I indicated in the preface, Justice Black himself was the first to welcome serious students of his career, delighting them by his accessibility. In Ashland, Thomas Toland, a cousin, provided family background, and C. M. Pruet remembered boyhood experiences. In Birmingham, James Esdale, once Grand Dragon of the Alabama Ku Klux Klan, gave me upon two occasions his version of Black's Klan affliation and of the 1926 Senate race. Ben Ray, W. Cooper Green, and Hugh Locke talked to me at length about Alabama politics, and Albert Lee Smith recalled episodes from his long friendship with Black. Charles Harrison contributed recollections of Black as a Sunday school teacher, and George Bentley recalled Birmingham's social life in the 1920s. Hugh Sparrow, J. F. Rothermel, and George A. Cornish, who were newspaper reporters in Birmingham during the 1920s and 1930s, were helpful. In Montgomery, Virginia Foster Durr, sister of Josephine Black, and her husband Clifford Durr were most hospitable.

I discussed Black's Senate years with former Senator Lister Hill, whose service in the House of Representatives paralleled Black's Senate career and who succeeded to his Senate seat; Representative and former Senator Claude Pepper, of Florida, born in Clay County, Alabama; James A. Farley, former postmaster general, who knew Black in Democratic Party circles and during the air mail episode of 1934; Turner Catledge, who covered Capitol Hill for the New York *Times* during part of Black's senatorial career; and, briefly, Arthur Krock, columnist and head of the *Times* Washington bureau in the 1930s.

Although this study is not primarily based upon oral history, these recollections and dozens of others added to my perception and understanding.

MANUSCRIPTS

Black's Senate papers were in his possession at the time that this study was being prepared. He gave me access to them, but my survey of them revealed only a senator's workaday contacts with his constituents. Several scrapbooks of miscellaneous clippings are part of this collection. Black's Senate papers, in their sparsity, contrast markedly with the collection of J. Thomas Heflin Papers at the University of Alabama in Tuscaloosa. Use of the Heflin Papers is restricted. I am grateful to Howell Heflin, chief justice of the Alabama Supreme Court, for access to this large and fascinating accumulation. A much smaller collection of Heflin Papers is at Samford University, Birmingham, which also possesses the papers of Joseph J. Willett, Sr., and Joseph J. Willett, Jr., both of Anniston. The Willett Papers contain exchanges of correspondence with Senator Black. There are papers relating to Alabama politics in the W. B. Bankhead and Oscar W. Underwood files at the Alabama Department of Archives and History in Montgomery, but these are not extensive. The Papers of George W. Norris in the

Division of Manuscripts, Library of Congress, proved interesting only in the fact that they contain so little mention of Black, who was Norris' close Senate colleague. The Franklin D. Roosevelt Papers and the diary of Henry Morgenthau at Hyde Park contain numerous useful references.

DOCUMENTS

The Alabama Department of Archives and History houses *Acts of the Alabama Legislature* for various sessions, as well as copies of the *Alabama Official and Statistical Register* which reports the returns of primaries and elections. The Library of the Birmingham Bar Association has copies of *Alabama Reports* and the *Southern Reporter*, containing rulings of the Alabama Supreme Court on a number of cases involving Black, as well as minutes of the Birmingham Bar Association in its early days.

The *Congressional Record* is the prime source of material on Black's Senate career. Copies of hearings on the thirty-hour bill, air mail and ocean mail contracts, lobbying activities, and Black's proposal for Court reform are in the Legislative Records Division, National Archives, Washington, D.C., as well as in some libraries which serve as government depositories. Hearings by a special Senate committee investigating the Heflin-Bankhead contest are included in the George W. Norris Papers in the Library of Congress. There is interesting background on the Klan in the Ku Klux Klan File of the Department of Justice, stored in the National Archives, as well as in the *Hearings* on the Klan conducted in 1921 by the House Rules Committee, which are available on microfilm in the Library of Congress.

NEWSPAPERS

The Birmingham *News*, Birmingham *Age-Herald*, Birmingham *Ledger*, Birmingham *Post*, and Montgomery *Advertiser* are valuable for coverage of Black's Alabama years, but only if the researcher is constantly alert to the fact that these newspapers opposed Black during most of his political career. Their opposition is frequently reflected in news coverage as well as in editorial comment. The *News* and *Age-Herald* supported him for reelection in 1932 under circumstances related in the text. The Mobile *Register* contains extensive coverage of the "rum trials" when Black served as special prosecutor.

Among other Alabama publications, the *T.W.K. Monthly*, a Klan publication in Birmingham; the *Weekly Call*, a Birmingham labor paper; the Birmingham *Alabama Baptist*, the Birmingham *Methodist Christian Advocate*, and the Birmingham *Alabama Citizen*, a publication of the Alabama Anti-Saloon League, commented on Senator Black from varied points of view. Other Alabama newspapers, including the Ashland *Progress*, have been occasionally cited.

The New York *Times* published frequent references to Black during his Senate years. Although Justice Black felt that the *Times*, too, was hostile to him in those days, its Washington correspondents, Turner Catledge and Duncan Aikman, referred to the senator fairly, even favorably, and *Times*'s news coverage appears unbiased. However, Columnist Arthur Krock frequently criticized Black. The series of articles by Raymond Sprigle of the Pittsburgh *Post-Gazette* exposing Black's Klan membership, was published in its entirety in the *Times* September 13–18, 1937.

Several newspaper feature stories on Black were revealing, among them: Victor Sholis, "One Young Man, Hugo Black—A Country Boy's Rise," Chicago *Daily Times*, August 18, 1937; James Saxon Childers, "Hugo Black, Always an Alabamian," Birmingham *News*, January 31, 1937; Dan O. Dowe, "Hugo Black's Childhood in Clay County," Montgomery *Alabama Journal*, July 4, 1960; Duncan Aikman, "Justice Black, A Man of Two Personalities," New York *Times* magazine, August 22, 1937, as well as a number of interviews with Justice Black written over a period of years by Grover C. Hall, Jr., formerly editor of the Montgomery *Advertiser*.

BOOKS

Only a few books deal with Hugo Black's personal or political career. A small and artless memoir by an adoring niece is by far the most revealing. See Hazel Black Davis, *Uncle Hugo: An Intimate Portrait of Mr. Justice Black* (Amarillo, 1965). John P. Frank, one of the justice's early law clerks, also approaches his subject with almost unalloyed admiration in *Mr. Justice Black: The Man and His Opinions* (New York, 1949). Charlotte Williams treats the Alabama years briefly in *Hugo L. Black: A Study in the Judicial Process* (Baltimore, 1950). The essay by Daniel Berman in Stephen Parks Strickland's collection, *Hugo Black and the Supreme Court: A Symposium* (Indianapolis, 1967), presents a version of the pre-Court period.

Mitchell B. Garrett, *Horse and Buggy Days on Hatchet Creek* (Tuscaloosa, 1957), and Joseph C. Manning, *From Five to Twenty-Five: His Earlier Life as Recalled by Joseph Columbus Manning* (New York, 1929) are rich sources of Clay County lore. For the flavor of early Birmingham, see John C. Henley, Jr., *This is Birmingham* (Birmingham, 1960); John R. Hornaday, *The Book of Birmingham* (New York, 1921); George M. Cruickshank, *A History of Birmingham and Its Environs* (2 vols.; Chicago, 1920). Among sources consulted on Alabama history were: Willis Brewer, *Alabama: Her History, Resources, War Record and Public Men from 1540 to 1872* (Tuscaloosa, 1872); Marie Bankhead Owen, *Alabama: A Social and Economic History of the State* (Montgomery, 1938); Joel C. DuBose (ed.,) *Notable Men of Alabama* (2 vols.; Atlanta, 1904); Thomas McAdory Owen, *History of Alabama and Dictionary of Alabama Biography* (4 vols.; Chicago, 1921); Thomas Chalmers McCorvey, *Alabama Historical Sketches* (Charlottesville, Va., 1960); A. B. Moore, *History of Alabama* (Tuscaloosa, 1951); and Malcolm C. McMillan, *The Land Called Alabama* (Austin, 1968). For political events and social problems in the state, these are valuable: Allen J. Going, *Bourbon Democracy in Alabama* (Tuscaloosa, 1951);

Francis Sheldon Hackney, *From Populism to Progressivism in Alabama, 1890–1910* (Princeton, 1969); John B. Clark, *Populism in Alabama* (Auburn, 1927); James Benson Sellers, *The Prohibition Movement in Alabama, 1902–1943* (Chapel Hill, 1943); Robert David Ward and William Warren Rogers, *Labor Revolt in Alabama: The Great Strike of 1894* (Tuscaloosa, 1965); and Dan T. Carter, *Scottsboro: A Tragedy of the American South* (Baton Rouge, 1969).

Indispensable to an understanding of southern politics are C. Vann Woodward, *Origins of the New South, 1877–1913* (Baton Rouge, 1951), and George B. Tindall, *The Emergence of the New South, 1913–1945* (Baton Rouge, 1967). More specialized works are Sterling D. Spero and Abram L. Harris, *The Black Worker. The Negro and the Labor Movement* (New York, 1931); Allen A. Michie and Frank Ryhlick, *Dixie Demagogues* (New York, 1939); Horace R. Cayton and George S. Mitchell, *Black Workers and the New Unions* (Chapel Hill, 1939). The phenomenon of the twentieth century Klan is dealt with by Arnold S. Rice, *The Ku Klux Klan in American Politics* (Washington, 1962); David M. Chalmers, *Hooded Americanism: The First Century of the Ku Klux Klan, 1865 to the Present* (Garden City, 1965), and Charles C. Alexander, *The Ku Klux Klan in the Southwest* (Lexington, Ky., 1965). The comprehensive work on the early days of the Tennessee Valley Authority is Preston J. Hubbard, *Origins of the TVA: The Muscle Shoals Controversy, 1920–1932* (Nashville, 1961).

For the era of 1920 to 1940 in national politics, the following were useful: Harris Gaylord Warren, *Herbert Hoover and the Great Depression* (New York, 1959); John D. Hicks, *Republican Ascendancy, 1921–1933* (New York, 1960); Arthur M. Schlesinger, Jr., *The Age of Roosevelt* (3 vols.; Cambridge, Mass., 1960); Frank Freidel, *Franklin D. Roosevelt*, (3 vols.; Boston, 1952–56); James McGregor Burns, *Roosevelt, the Lion and the Fox* (New York, 1956); and *Congress on Trial: the Legislative Process and the Administrative State* (New York, 1949); William E. Leuchtenberg, *Franklin D. Roosevelt and the New Deal,*

1932–1940 (New York, 1965); and Basil Rauch, *The History of the New Deal, 1933–38* (New York, 1944).

Memoirs of prominent figures in the New Deal era contain a number of interesting references to Black. Among those are: Frances Perkins, *The Roosevelt I Knew* (New York, 1946); Raymond Moley, *After Seven Years* (New York, 1939); James A. Farley, *Jim Farley's Story: The Roosevelt Years* (New York, 1948); Harold Ickes, *The Secret Diary of Harold Ickes*, (3 vols.; New York, 1953); Charles Michelson, *The Ghost Talks* (New York, 1944); George W. Norris, *Fighting Liberal: The Autobiography of George W. Norris* (New York, 1946).

The airmail episode of 1934 has been the subject of several studies, among them: Paul D. Tillett, *The Army Flies the Mails* (Indianapolis, Inter-University Case Program #24); Norman E. Borden, Jr., *Air Mail Emergency, 1934* (Freeport, Maine, 1968); Benjamin D. Foulois, *From the Wright Brothers to the Astronauts: The Memoirs of Major General Benjamin D. Foulois* (New York, 1968).

The most comprehensive book dealing with the fight over Roosevelt's plan to enlarge the Supreme Court and the circumstances leading to the nomination of Hugo Black is Joseph Alsop and Turner Catledge, *The 168 Days* (New York, 1938). There are sidelights on the Court of that era in Merlo Pusey, *Charles Evans Hughes* (New York, 1951); Wesley McCune, *The Nine Young Men* (New York, 1947); and Max Freedman (ed.) *Roosevelt and Frankfurter: Their Correspondence, 1928–1945* (Boston, 1967).

PERIODICALS

The *Alabama Historical Quarterly* and the *Alabama Review* contain a number of scholarly articles useful to the student of this period. Among these are: Jerrell H. Shofner and William Warren Rogers, "Joseph C. Manning, Militant Agrarian, Enduring Populist," *Alabama Historical Quarterly*, XXIX (Spring-Summer,

1967); Lee N. Allen, "The 1924 Underwood Campaign in Alabama," *Alabama Review*, IX (July, 1956); Martin Torodah, "Underwood and the Tariff," *Alabama Review*, XX (April, 1967); Evans C. Johnson, "Underwood and Harding: a Bipartisan Friendship," *Alabama Historical Quarterly*, XXX (Spring, 1968); Evans C. Johnson, "Oscar W. Underwood and the Senatorial Campaign of 1920," *Alabama Review*, XXI (January, 1968); Winfred B. Sandlin, "Lycurgus Breckenridge Musgrove," *Alabama Review*, XX (July, 1967); J. Mills Thornton, III, "Alabama Politics, J. Thomas Heflin, and the Expulsion Movement of 1929," *Alabama Review*, XXI (April, 1968); and Hugh Dorsey Reagan, "Race as A Factor in the Presidential Election of 1928 in Alabama," *Alabama Review*, XIX (January, 1966). Also useful is Lee N. Allen, "The McAdoo Campaign for the Presidential Nomination in 1924," *Journal of Southern History*, XXIX (1963).

A number of articles deal with the Klan, anti-Catholicism, and the influence of drys in Alabama politics, among them: Charles P. Sweeney, "Bigotry in the South," *Nation*, CXIII (November 24, 1920); Charles P. Sweeney, "Bigotry Turns to Murder," *Nation*, CXIII (August 31, 1921), a comment on the Stephenson case; William G. Shepherd, "The Whip Hand," *Collier's*, LXXXI (January 7, 1928); William G. Shepherd, "The Whip Wins," *Collier's*, LXXXI (January 14, 1928); "Alabama's Floggers," *Literary Digest*, XCV (October 29, 1927); "Moral Lashes for Alabama Floggers," *Literary Digest*, XCV (December 17, 1927); Charles N. Feidelson, "Alabama's Super Government," *Nation*, CXXV (September 27, 1927); "What Alabama Thinks of its Lynching," *Literary Digest*, CXVI (September 2, 1933); "The Klan Revives," *Nation*, CXXIX (July 2, 1934); "Farmers and 'Shiners Outvote City Folks," *Newsweek*, V (March 9, 1935); "Clamorous Wets in Dry Alabama," *Literary Digest*, CXXI (March 28, 1936).

Some of Black's own writings and radio speeches are available. These include: "Reminiscences," a description of his law school days, *Alabama Law Review*, XVIII (Fall, 1965); "Inside a Senate

Investigation," *Harper's*, CLXXII (February, 1936); "Lobby Investigation," a speech reprinted in *Vital Speeches*, I (August 26,
1935); "Should the Meat Packers be Permitted to Enter the Chain
Store Field?" *Congressional Digest*, IX (August-September, 1930);
"Reorganization of the Federal Judiciary," and several other
speeches reprinted in *Vital Speeches*, III (September 1, 1937).

Alabama Magazine, a subsidized organ of business and industrial interests, began publication in the 1930s. Its files at the Birmingham Public Library contain a number of references to Black,
uniformly hostile. Valuable for its frank descriptions of young
Birmingham is *Survey, A Journal of Constructive Philanthropy*,
XXVII (January 6, 1912).

The comments of such periodicals as *Time, Newsweek, Business
Week, New Republic, American Mercury, Christian Century,
Literary Digest*, and *Commonweal* concerning Black's nomination
to the Court are too numerous to list. A number of them are cited
in the footnotes of this book. For a general summary of events surrounding the nomination, see Virginia V. Hamilton, "Hugo Black
and the K.K.K.," *American Heritage*, XIX (April, 1968).

THESES AND DISSERTATIONS

I would like to express a special debt to William Robert Snell,
whose study, "The Ku Klux Klan in Jefferson County, Alabama,
1916–1930" (M.A. thesis, Samford University, Birmingham,
1967) provided invaluable background material on the Klan during the era covered by this book. Francis Sheldon Hackney, "From
Populism to Progressivism in Alabama, 1890–1910" (Ph.D. dissertation, Yale University, 1966), now in book form (Princeton,
1969), is excellent. Martha Carolyn Mitchell, "Birmingham: Biography of a City of the New South" (Ph.D. dissertation, University
of Chicago, 1946) is useful. For labor troubles in early Birmingham, see Nancy Ruth Elmore, "The Birmingham Coal Strike of
1908" (M.A. thesis, University of Alabama, 1966). For the political career of Oscar W. Underwood, I am indebted to the work

of Evans C. Johnson, "Oscar W. Underwood: The Development of a National Statesman, 1894–1915," (Ph.D. dissertation, University of North Carolina, 1953). Hugh Dorsey Reagan, "The Presidential Election of 1928 in Alabama" (Ph.D. dissertation, University of Texas, 1961), is a revealing study. For insight into J. Thomas Heflin, two works are valuable: Ralph Melvis Tanner, "James Thomas Heflin: United States Senator, 1920–1931" (Ph.D. dissertation, University of Alabama, 1967); and Vincent J. Dooley, "United States Senator J. Thomas Heflin and the Democratic Party Revolt in Alabama" (M.A. thesis, Auburn University, 1963). For the career of Thomas E. Kilby, see Emily Owen, "The Career of Thomas E. Kilby in Local and State Politics" (M.A. thesis, University of Alabama, 1942). Scholarly works on Black include Daniel M. Berman, "The Political Philosophy of Hugo L. Black" (Ph.D. dissertation, Rutgers University, 1957); Gene L. Mason, "Hugo Black and the United States Senate" (M.A. thesis, University of Kansas, 1964); and Virginia V. Hamilton, "The Senate Career of Hugo L. Black" (Ph.D. dissertation, University of Alabama, 1968).

Index